A Decade of Collecting

This exhibition has been generously supported by a grant from the Atlantic Richfield Foundation

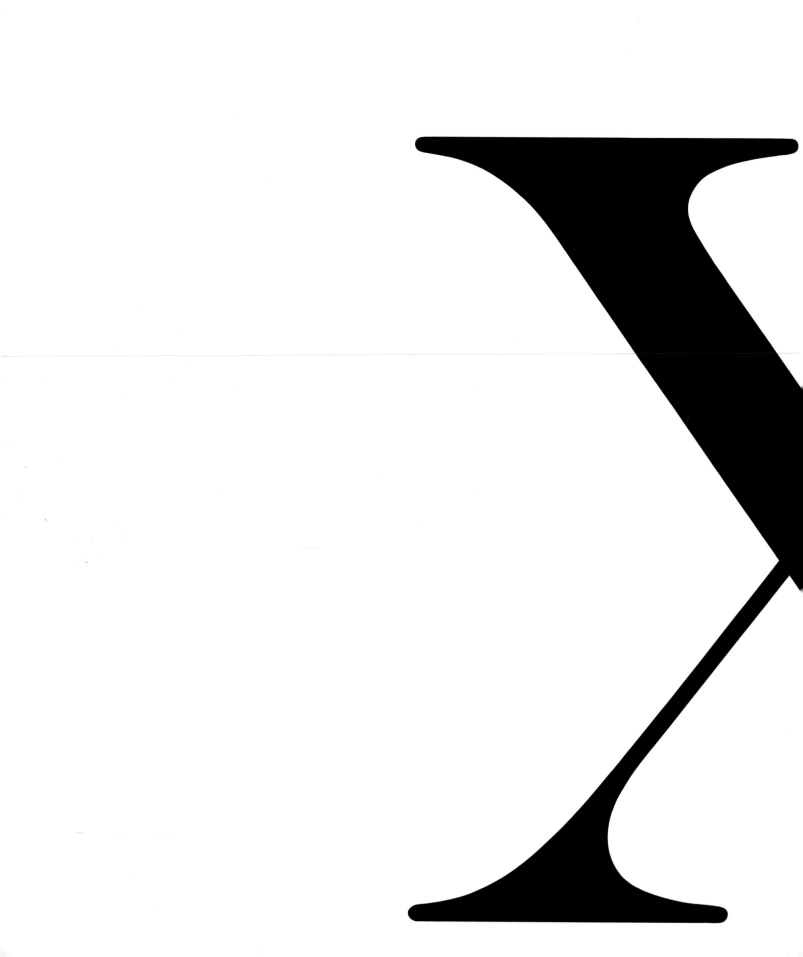

A Decade   of Collecting

1965-1975

Los Angeles County
Museum of Art

April 8 - June 29, 1975

ISBN 0-87587-064-3

Library of Congress
Catalog Card Number 74-25968

Published by the
Los Angeles County Museum of Art
5905 Wilshire Boulevard
Los Angeles, California 90036

Copyright ©1975 by
Museum Associates of the
Los Angeles County Museum of Art

Printed in the U.S.A.

Table of Contents

Preface

A little more than ten years ago, the Los Angeles County Museum of Art consisted of a contract between its private Board of Trustees and the County of Los Angeles, a modest collection of works of art scattered throughout a multi-purpose museum in Exposition Park, and the determination of a band of dedicated individuals to build an art museum in Southern California worthy of the community.

Under the energetic leadership of Edward W. Carter, Mrs. Freeman Gates, and Sidney F. Brody, and highlighted by major gifts from Mrs. Anna Bing Arnold and the late Howard F. Ahmanson, a small group of men and women raised from individuals, corporations, and foundations, named in Appendix I, more than $12,000,000 to construct a three-building complex on land in Hancock Park provided by the County of Los Angeles from an original gift by the late Captain G. Allan Hancock. On completion, the buildings were deeded to the Board of Supervisors as a gift to the people of Los Angeles County. The contract between the Trustees and the County provided that the Board of Supervisors would supply funds for the operation and main-tenance of the Museum and that the Trustees would bear the responsibility for developing policy and overseeing opera-tions. In addition the Trustees undertook to seek private funds and works of art to enrich the permanent collections.

The story of this first decade of the Museum is one of growth and achievement beyond even the most optimistic expectations. Both parties to this unique public-private undertaking have more than met their commitments to each other and to the people of Los Angeles County. The members of the Board of Supervisors, past and present, have provided the funds necessary for efficient museum operation and proper maintenance of buildings and grounds. The Museum, relying on the efforts of its Trustees, the energy and professionalism of its talented staff, and an ever-growing interest in the Museum by collectors in Southern California and elsewhere, has, since 1965, acquired works of art with a current value in excess of thirty million dollars—a quantum jump in the quality and breadth of the permanent collections. To the list of earlier major donors such as Balch, De Silva, Getty, Harrison, Hearst, and Mabury, have been added such names as Ahmanson, Arnold, Berg, Bright, Cantor, Hammer, Palevsky, and many others, as set forth in Appendix II.

In connection with the rapid growth in the permanent collections, the Trustees early recognized their obligation to protect and preserve the objects of art. Therefore a con-servation laboratory of the highest quality and greatest sophistication has been established, the principal such facility in the western United States. Though this laboratory primarily serves the Museum's collections, other museums and collectors now have available expert advice and specialized services.

The new Los Angeles County Museum of Art opened its doors in April 1965 with a major retrospective exhibition of the works of Pierre Bonnard. Since that time the Museum has mounted an unsurpassed series of exhibitions with associated scholarly publications, as listed in Appendix III.

We are proud that after only one decade, there are thirty thousand dues-paying members of the Museum whose enthusiasm and financial support have been essential to its success. The impact of the Museum on the community is also reflected by an average annual attendance of one and a half million, one of the highest in the nation.

Much of the activity within the Museum can be traced to the vigor of the nine volunteer councils whose members are drawn from the general membership of the Museum. The Art Museum Council, Costume Council, Graphic Arts Council, Modern and Contemporary Art Council, Far Eastern Art Council, American Art Council, and Decorative Arts Council sponsor innumerable activities in their special fields of interest and have assisted greatly in the acquisition of objects of art for the permanent collections.

The Docent Council and the Museum Service Council significantly expand the services available to the public from the Museum's relatively small professional staff. Docents, after a rigorous training program, provide guided tours through the permanent collections and special exhibitions for thousands of school children and adults each year. Museum Service Council members provide invaluable supplemental staffing in many areas of Museum operations.

The Museum early accepted the premise that the motion picture is a significant art form. This conviction has led to a lively film program—both historical and contemporary—in the Leo S. Bing Theater.

From the beginning the Trustees have wished to create an exciting total environment. Thus, in addition to ex-hibitions and scholarly lectures, there has been an ongoing music program featuring the Bing Concerts. On the occasion of certain exhibitions, presentations of character-istic dance and music have been organized to demonstrate the interrelationships of the several arts in particular cultures.

Finally, we acknowledge the key roles of Kenneth Donahue, the Museum's director for the past nine years; Richard F. Brown, its first director; the gifted group of curators and administrators; and the conscientious staff, all of whom have contributed immeasurably to the Museum's great achievements.

In summary, it can be said that the tenth anniversary of the Los Angeles County Museum of Art reflects a sense of commitment more than met, of creative fulfillment and vitality achieved. If the past is but prologue, the next decade in the life of the Museum should be remarkable indeed. To the many who have helped bring the Museum to its present happy state, we express jointly our deepest appreciation and congratulations.

Edward W. Carter	President 1962-1966
Sidney F. Brody	President 1966-1970
Franklin D. Murphy	President 1970-1974
Richard E. Sherwood	President 1974-

Introduction

For some decades and especially since the end of World War II, the civic and cultural leaders of Los Angeles have been impelled by an urgency to provide this community with the kind of cultural advantages enjoyed by the older metropolitan centers of the East and of Europe. Through their efforts, colleges and universities have flourished and the literary, performing, and visual arts have been liberally encouraged. A decade ago the new Music Center with its associated theaters and the new Art Museum complex were opened almost simultaneously. The same conviction, spirit, and energy which had brought the new Museum building into being, were thereupon redirected toward broadening and enriching the collection. As a result, the Los Angeles County Museum of Art now has, both in comprehensiveness and quality, one of the five major collections in the Western world of the art of India, the pre-eminent collection of Nepalese and Tibetan art, and distinguished specializations in Islamic art and Peruvian textiles. In other areas it has added exemplary works of such masters as Dürer, Fra Bartolommeo, Veronese, Hals, Rembrandt, Rubens, Ingres, Copley, Cole, Sargent, Rodin, Picasso, Matisse, Pollock, Rothko, Calder, and David Smith, and by the anonymous artists of the Assyrian reliefs, the T'ang horse, and the Benin plaque. In total the Museum has acquired during the past ten years almost three thousand works of art and has received promises of future gifts or bequests of more than three hundred additional works of extraordinary quality.

From this wealth of acquisitions, one hundred forty objects have been chosen for this exhibition to exemplify the character and scope of collecting in the decade, 1965-1975. The selection does not include, by any means, all the acquisitions of the highest quality. As many additional acquisitions as possible will be shown in the Ahmanson Gallery during this tenth anniversary year. This exhibition has been conceived as a tribute to the donors of works of art and acquisitions funds and to the many others who have given their physical and intellectual energy, their time, and their personal persuasiveness to make this ten years of collecting possible.

The collection transferred from Exposition Park was a comprehensive one representing the major areas of Western art and including a small Oriental collection, as well as departments of Prints and Drawings, Textiles and Costumes, and Decorative Arts. It had its origins in the collections of the Museum's first benefactors: Preston Harrison, Mr. and Mrs. Allan Balch, Paul Rodman Mabury and his sisters Bella and Carlotta. The Harrison Collection presented between 1918 and 1948 laid the foundation, with more than one hundred fifty American Realist, Impressionist, and Ash Can School paintings and drawings and another hundred modern French works. The Balch Collection bequeathed in 1939 added mid-nineteenth-century European paintings and nine old masters, among them Petrus

Christus, Pieter de Hooch, and Hans Holbein. The same year, the Mabury collection provided twenty-four additional paintings including works of Lotto, Delacroix, Corot, and a splendid Winslow Homer watercolor. The collection became a broadly historical one only through the contributions of William Randolph Hearst, the Hearst Foundation, and the Hearst Magazines, Inc. Shortly after Dr. William Valentiner became director-consultant in 1946 he established a close working relationship with Hearst and in the next six years received more than a million dollars from him for purchases of Egyptian, Greek, and Roman antiquities; medieval, Renaissance, and Baroque sculpture and decorative objects; and more than fifty old master paintings. Thousands of additional objects flowed from the Hearst warehouses until the donor's death in 1952. With funds provided by George Gard De Sylva in 1946, Valentiner bought paintings by Pissarro, Degas, Toulouse-Lautrec, Cézanne, and Picasso, bronzes by Degas, and two magnificent van Gogh drawings that form the nucleus of the Impressionist and Post-Impressionist collection. During this same period, Jean Paul Getty made a series of munificent donations: the Ardabil and Coronation carpets, two great Boucher tapestries, and the Rembrandt *Maarten Looten,* a masterpiece of the artist's early portraiture.

The collection now had reached the point at which an independent building with adequate gallery space had to assume first priority. During most of Dr. Richard Brown's incumbency as chief curator of art, 1956-1961, and as first director of the Los Angeles County Museum of Art, 1961-1966, the Trustees and staff were occupied with planning and building the new Museum and broadening the base of public support. Nevertheless, the modern collection grew abundantly during this time; with the addition of notable works by Cézanne, Monet, Mondrian, Schwitters, Stuart Davis, Guston, Nakian, and the German Expressionists it became the strongest area of the Museum. When installed in the new galleries in 1965, the collection could be seen for the first time as a unit to be analyzed, evaluated, and systematically embellished.

Two works given before 1965, precursors of this ten years of collecting, the Cézanne *Still Life with Cherries and Peaches* and the Monet *Beach at Honfleur,* are included in the exhibition since both were given specifically for the new Art Museum building.

The new building was a great stimulus to donors. Even while it was in construction, the Art Museum Council commissioned a Calder mobile for it. In the midst of the opening, negotiations were underway for the monumental Assyrian reliefs, eventually acquired by Anna Bing Arnold, which became the cornerstone of the acquisitions in the new Museum. Shortly after the opening, Trustee David

Bright died suddenly and bequeathed to the Museum, to which he had given so much of his energy as chairman of the Building Committee, a splendid collection of twenty-three modern paintings. Works by Picasso, Gris, Léger, Kupka, Modigliani, Miró, and Dubuffet added distinction to an existing area of strength, while paintings by Gottlieb, Rothko, Kline, and Pollock provided new and brilliant representation of the New York School.

For the first year and a half in the new building, the Board of Trustees and the professional staff were occupied with adapting the new facilities to the specialized functions of a museum, developing the staff which grew in a short period from sixty-five to two hundred fifty, and creating a local and international image of the Museum through an extraordinary program of exhibitions and publications. It was, therefore, not until January 1967 that the Trustees began a campaign to equal the twelve million dollars raised for the building with twelve million dollars for acquisitions. Justin Dart was chairman of the committee, Mrs. Freeman Gates and Edward W. Carter, vice chairmen. The goal was threefold: to fill lacunae in the collection, to develop areas of specialization in which the Museum could be internationally distinguished, and to increase the number of major masterpieces. The areas of greatest need were identified as early American painting, European old masters, Baroque to modern sculpture, and Asian art. It was with this in mind that the first acquisitions in the new program were made: paintings by Amberger, Copley, and Stuart, and eight modern sculptures. B. Gerald Cantor gave his first monumental Rodin, *Study for Balzac, Nude;* Mrs. Virginia Kingston presented a bronze Maillol *Flora;* Mrs. Anna Bing Arnold, the large Duchamp-Villon *Horse;* and the Art Museum Council, using the proceeds from years of fundraising activities, made its major purchase of the decade, the *Five Heads of Jeannette* by Matisse.

In mid-1969 the pace of acquisitions accelerated rapidly. In September Dr. Armand Hammer presented to the Museum a Renoir, a Modigliani, and a purchase fund from which the Rembrandt *Raman,* the Rubens *Israelites,* and the Sargent *Mrs. Livingston Davis* were acquired. Two years later he added a codicil to his will bequeathing to the Museum his entire painting collection, which will add enormous vitality to both the American and the nine-teenth- and early twentieth-century European galleries. Shortly thereafter, Phil Berg initiated the gift of his collection of more than 320 works of art, primarily archaeological and ethnic, which will provide examples of entire cultures not heretofore represented in the Museum. At the end of 1969, the Trustees made their most important purchase of the decade: the Indian, Nepalese, and Tibetan collection of Nasli and Alice Heeramaneck. It consisted of 345 superb sculptures, paintings, textiles, and objects of jade, crystal, and gold collected by the Heeramanecks over a period of forty years. It covers the history of Indian art from the Indus Valley civilization of the second millennium B.C. to the Mughal Courts of the eighteenth century, and includes an incredibly rich selection of patas, tankas, and bronzes from Nepal and Tibet, in Russell Lynes' words "a windfall of treasures." This gave the Museum collection its first area of specialization in depth. There were, however, some lacunae, especially in South Indian bronzes and Rajput paintings. A considerable part of the acquisitions effort over the next five years was concentrated on supplementing this collection. Anna Bing Arnold, the Michael J. Connell Foundation, Christian Humann, Mr. and Mrs. Harry Lenart, Paul Manheim, Mr. and Mrs. Hal Wallis, Paul Walter, and Mr. and Mrs. Jack Zimmerman all made major contributions.

Three more Heeramaneck collections came to the Museum in the spring of 1973. An Islamic collection of 650 paintings, ceramics, metalwork, and textiles contributed by Mrs. Joan Palevsky gave the Museum collection its second basis for national recognition. The Heeramanecks themselves presented a collection of small pre-Columbian ceramics and another of sixty-two superb Chinese and Korean ceramics.

The Museum was the recipient of two more private collections in 1973 and 1974. As a sequel to the De Sylva and Bright collections, the Kleiner Foundation donated nineteen works created by California artists between 1964 and 1971, along with the extraordinarily popular *Mirror Glass Labyrinth* by the New York artist, Lucas Samaras. When the sculpture garden was being planned in 1973, B. Gerald Cantor, the foremost living collector of Rodin, donated twenty-seven bronzes by that master, and has promised the *Monument to Balzac.* Taken together with the Rodin sculptures at Stanford and San Francisco, they make California one of the four world centers for Rodin studies.

In 1972 the Howard F. Ahmanson Company presented, in memory of Howard F. Ahmanson, the Rembrandt *Raising of Lazarus,* the first narrative painting by that master in the collection. Recognizing that the Museum had no great Florentine or Venetian Renaissance paintings and that the Dutch collection desperately needed a Hals to complement the four Rembrandts, the Ahmanson Foundation made three princely gifts in 1973 and 1974: Fra Bartolommeo's *Holy Family,* two monumental allegories by Paolo Veronese, and the distinguished *Portrait of Pieter Tjarck* by Frans Hals.

During the entire ten years, groups of anonymous donors who have banded together to form support councils for individual curatorial departments have been hard at work building those specialized collections. The major part of the acquisitions of the departments of Textiles and Costumes, Prints and Drawings, Modern Art, and Far Eastern Art were all made by such councils. Through the purchase of a few pieces each month, the Costume Council has enabled the Museum to assemble the most important collections of textiles and costumes west of Chicago and has recently undertaken the acquisition of the entire John Wise collection of Peruvian textiles. The Graphic Arts Council has acquired not only a broad spectrum of prints and drawings but a major group of Dürers and Rembrandts. In its twelve years of existence the Contemporary Art Council has provided more than seventy works by masters like Ruben Nakian, David Smith, Frank Stella, and Claes Oldenburg as well as works of talented young artists. The newly formed Far Eastern Art Council has already augmented the collection significantly by purchases and by the donations of its members, like Eric Lidow's recent gift of the Eastern Chou *Ting*. In addition to the specialized councils, the Art Museum Council for the past twenty years has been acquiring works of art for all departments, as exemplified by its recent collaboration with the Michael J. Connell Foundation to acquire the Museum's first Hudson River School landscape, the Thomas Cole *L'Allegro.*

The story of the collection in formation is interrupted at this point, but the promised gifts in the exhibition from Mr. and Mrs. Stanton Avery, Mr. and Mrs. Edward W. Carter, Mr. and Mrs. Arthur Gilbert, Dr. and Mrs. Armand Hammer, Mr. and Mrs. Taft Schreiber, Mr. and Mrs. William Sesnon, Jr., Mr. and Mrs. Ray Stark, and Mr. and Mrs. Hal Wallis, many of which represent large collections, are harbingers of the future giving us assurance that the collection will continue to grow in comprehensiveness and stature.

In expressing our gratitude to the donors who ultimately make acquisitions possible, I should like also to acknowledge the role of the Trustees who work indefatigably and without any personal recognition to make acquisition aspirations a reality and of the curators who ferret out works of art, evaluate them aesthetically and historically, analyze their importance to the collection, and recommend them to the Trustees and councils.

This catalog is the product of the entire professional staff. Since many works of art are being published here for the first time and since this catalog will serve as a source of information about the collection until more specialized ones are published over the next decades, considerable emphasis has been placed on the entries for each work of art. While the factual information at the beginning of each entry follows a standardized pattern, there is considerable variation in the text which follows. Each writer prepared his text on the basis of the special nature of his material and what he felt would be of the greatest value to the reader interested in his particular field. The authors are as follows: Rexford Stead, Ancient and Ethnic Arts; Pratapaditya Pal, Catherine Glynn, and Virginia Dofflemyer, Indian, Nepalese, Tibetan, and Islamic Art; George Kuwayama, Far Eastern

Art; Mary Kahlenberg and Susan Thomas with the research assistance of Leo Rosson, Textiles and Costumes; Ebria Feinblatt and Joseph Young, Prints and Drawings; William E. Jones, Decorative Arts; Alla T. Hall, Russian gates; Donelson Hoopes and Nancy Moure, American Art; Charles Millard and Julius Kaplan, Nineteenth-Century Art; Maurice Tuchman and Jane Livingston with the research assistance of Susan Hollis Clayson, Twentieth-Century Art. My task was the preparation of the entries for European Fifteenth- to Eighteenth-Century Painting and Sculpture.

I would like to record here my real and personal gratitude to the many who have made specific contributions to the exhibition catalog: first of all to the Atlantic Richfield Foundation for its support of the many aspects of this exhibition; to the writers of entries who have given substance to the publication; to the scholars Lorenz Eitner, Albert Elsen, Burton Fredericksen, Egbert Haverkamp-Begemann, Dieter Koepplin, Herbert Lank, Ulrich Middeldorf, Teresio Pignatti, Barbara Rumpf, Nicole Veronee-Verhaegen, and John Walsh, who have made their knowledge and connoisseurship freely available to us; to Helen Clay Frick and to Mildred Steinbach, Head Librarian of the Frick Art Reference Library, for their special courtesies; to Clarice Davis, Art Librarian at UCLA; and to Eleanor Hartman and her staff of the Museum Library. The listing of names is quite inadequate to express the depth of gratitude I have to Alla T. Hall for her assistance in preliminary preparations for the exhibition and in catalog research; to Jeanne Doyle for the judgment and infinite care she has given to editing the catalog and coordinating its design and production; to Nancy Grubb for her equally careful editorial work and Bernice Stein of the Museum Service Council for proofreading; to Ed Cornachio and his staff, John Gebhart, Joe Hazen, and Adam Avila who developed new color and black and white photographs of every object in the exhibition; to Patricia Needham and Emily Nilson for painstakingly verifying the lists of donors; and to Ken Parkhurst for applying the kind of creative energy to the design of this catalog that the artists used for the works it illustrates. There is in fact not a single member of the staff who has not in some way been involved in this tenth anniversary exhibition; while I cannot list all the names here, I do want to express appreciation for each one's particular contribution.

Kenneth Donahue   Director

Palace Reliefs of Ashurnasirpal II
Assyria (Kalah), 9th century B.C.
Gypseous alabaster
Tree of Life, Panels 1 and 2
92 x 33⅛ in. (233.7 x 84.1 cm.)
91 x 42½ in. (231.1 x 108.0 cm.)

The King and a Winged Genius,
Panel 3
90¾ x 83 in. (230.5 x 210.8 cm.)
Eagle-headed Daemon, Panel 4
88 x 70⅜ in. (223.5 x 178.8 cm.)

Winged Genius, Panel 5
93 x 77¼ in. (236.2 x 196.2 cm.)
Los Angeles County Funds
donated by Anna Bing Arnold, 1966

Worshiper Figure
Sumer (Mari?),
first half 3rd millennium B.C.
Alabaster
h: 11½ in. (30.1 cm.)
Gift of Phil Berg, 1971

3

Ceremonial Beaker
Northwest Iran, ca.1000-900 B.C.
Gold
h: 4¼ in. (10.8 cm.)
Gift of the Art Museum Council,1968

4

Whetstone Finial (?)
Iran, before 7th century B.C.
Gold
l: 2¾ in. (6.9 cm.)
Gift of Phil Berg,1971

5

Śālabhañjikā (Tree Dryads)
India (Madhya Pradesh, Sanchi),
A.D. 10-25
Sandstone
h: 25 in. (63.5 cm.)
The Nasli and Alice Heeramaneck
Collection, 1969

Head of a Bodhisattva
Pakistan (Jellalabad district),
4th-5th century
Stucco with polychrome
h: 10½ in. (26.7 cm.)
The Nasli and Alice Heeramaneck
Collection,1969

Buddha Śākyamuni
North India (Uttar Pradesh?),
6th century
Gilt bronze
15½ x 6¾ in. (39.4 x 17.1 cm.)
Gift of the Michael J. Connell
Foundation,1970

The River Goddesses
Gaṅgā and Yamunā
India (Madhya Pradesh), 8th century
Red sandstone
h: 27 in. (68.6 cm.)
The Nasli and Alice Heeramaneck
Collection, 1969

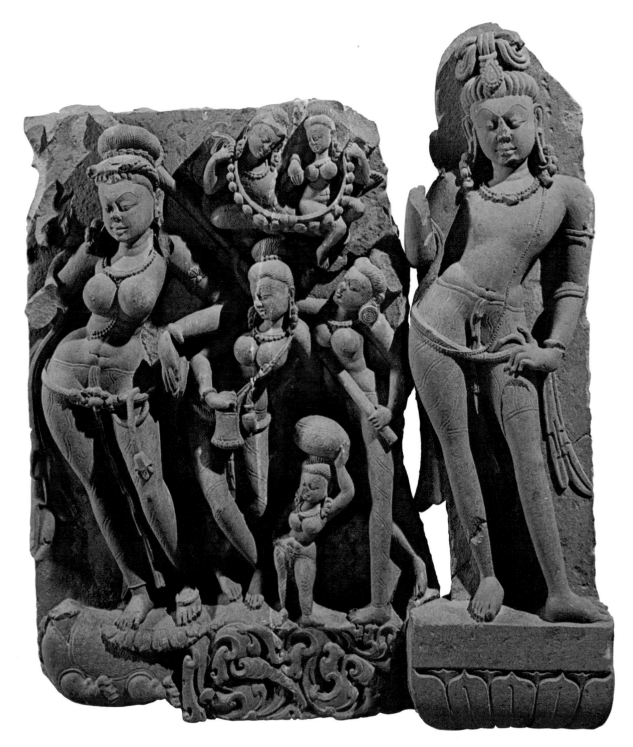

23

Buddhist Altar
India (Madhya Pradesh, Sirpur),
8th-9th century
Bronze with copper and silver inlay
h: 15 in. (38.1 cm.)
The Nasli and Alice Heeramaneck
Collection,1969

Dancing Gaṇeśa
India (Uttar Pradesh), 9th century
Red sandstone
h: 28½ in. (72.4 cm.)
Gift of Nasli M. Heeramaneck,1974

12

Śiva, the Lord of Dance (Naṭarāja)
India (Tamilnadu), ca.10th century
Bronze with green patina
h: 30 in. (76.2 cm.)
Anonymous gift,1974

13

The Bodhisattva Maitreya
India (Bihar),11th century
Gray sandstone
h: 33 in. (83.8 cm.)
Formerly the Nasli and
Alice Heeramaneck Collection
Museum Associates Purchase,1969

14

Krishṇa Rājamannār
South India (Tamilnadu),12th century
Bronze
Krishṇa—h: 34 in. (86.4 cm.)
Rukmiṇī—h: 27 in. (68.6 cm.)
Satyabhāmā—h: 28 in. (71.1 cm.)
Garuḍa—h: 19¼ in. (48.9 cm.)
Gift of Mr.and Mrs.Hal B.Wallis,1970

15

Bichitr (active early and
mid-17th century)
*Shah Shuja Enthroned with Gaj Singh
of Marwar,* Mughal style, ca.1633
Opaque watercolors and gold on paper
9⅞ x 7¼ in. (25.2 x 18.5 cm.)
The Nasli and Alice Heeramaneck
Collection,1969

29

Part of a Hanging or Curtain
India (Gujarat), early 17th century
Satin, with weft-patterned figures and
warp-patterned stripes, silk
67¾ x 43⅝ in. (172.1 x 110.8 cm.)
The Nasli and Alice Heeramaneck
Collection,1969

Fragment of a Dress or
Furnishing Fabric
India (Mughal), mid-17th century
Voided cut velvet, silk and gilt threads
72 x 21-23 in. (182.9 x 53.3-58.4 cm.)
Costume Council Fund,1971

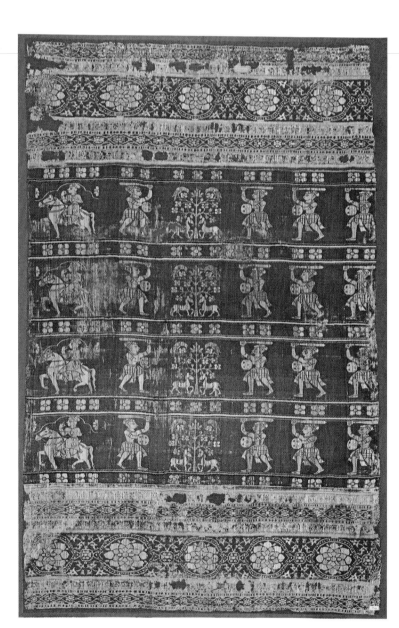

Kṛṣṇa and Rukmiṇī
Riding a Celestial Chariot
India (Rajput style, Bundi school),
ca.1675
Opaque watercolors on paper
11¼ x 9 in. (28.6 x 22.8 cm.)
Gift of Edwin Binney, 3rd,1974

Tathāgata Ratnasambhava and Acolytes
Nepal, 12th century
Opaque watercolors on cloth
16⅛ x 13 in. (41.0 x 33.0 cm.)
The Nasli and Alice Heeramaneck
Collection, 1969

Sambara and Vajravārāhī
Nepal, ca.1500
Opaque watercolors on cotton
54 x 45 in. (137.1 x 114.2 cm.)
Formerly the Nasli and
Alice Heeramaneck Collection
Museum Associates Purchase,1970

A Tathāgata
Surrounded by Bodhisattvas
Tibet,13th century
Opaque watercolors on linen
102 in. x 59 in. (245.1 x 149.8 cm.)
The Nasli and Alice Heeramaneck
Collection,1969

Arhat Vajrīputra in Landscape
Tibet,14th century
Opaque watercolors on cotton
25½ x 21¼ in. (64.8 x 54 cm.)
The Nasli and Alice Heeramaneck
Collection,1969

Portrait of an Abbot
Tibet,15th century
Gilt bronze
h: 11¼ in. (28.6 cm.)
Promised gift of Christian Humann

Bowl with Flaring Sides and Ring Foot
Persia (Nishapur),10th century
Ceramic
h: 3¼ in. (8.3 cm.); d: 9 in. (22.8 cm.)
The Nasli M. Heeramaneck Collection
Gift of Joan Palevsky,1973

Bracelet
Persia, 10th-11th century
Gold
h: 2 in. (5.1 cm.); d: 5 in. (12.7 cm.)
The Nasli M. Heeramaneck Collection
Gift of Joan Palevsky, 1973

Mihrab
Persia (Kashan), 1200-1225
Ceramic
40½ x 46⅞ in. (102.9 x 119.0 cm.)
The Nasli M. Heeramaneck Collection
Gift of Joan Palevsky, 1973

Folio from a Shah Nama Manuscript:
Isfandiyar Attacks the Simurgh
Persia (Shiraz), ca.1490
Opaque watercolors on paper
8⅞ x 6 in. (22.5 x 15.2 cm.)
The Nasli M. Heeramaneck Collection
Gift of Joan Palevsky,1973

Dish with Lobed Rim and Flaring Body
Turkey (Isnik),1550-1560
Ceramic
h: 2¾ in. (7.0 cm.),
d: 13⅜ in. (34.0 cm.)
The Nasli M. Heeramaneck Collection
Gift of Joan Palevsky,1973

Folio from a Shah Nama Manuscript:
Firdousi in a Bathhouse
Receiving Wages for Having Written
the Shah Nama
Persia (Shiraz),1550-1575
Opaque watercolors on paper
17¼ x 11¼ in. (43.7 x 28.5 cm.)
The Nasli M. Heeramaneck Collection
Gift of Joan Palevsky,1973

Horizontal Tile
Turkey (Isnik),1550-1600
Ceramic
29½ x 52¾ in. (75.0 x 134.0 cm.)
The Nasli M. Heeramaneck Collection
Gift of Joan Palevsky,1973

Flat-rimmed Dish with Narrow Foot
Persia (Kubachi?), ca.1600
Ceramic
h: 2½ in. (6.3 cm.);
d: 13⅜ in. (34.0 cm.)
The Nasli M. Heeramaneck Collection
Gift of Joan Palevsky,1973

Part of a Garment
Turkey (Bursa or Istanbul),
second half 16th-early 17th century
Compound satin with supplemental
twill weave, silk and gilt on a
yellow silk core
53 x 30¾ in. (134.7 x 78.0 cm.),
seamed in center
Gift of Edwin Binney, 3rd,1974

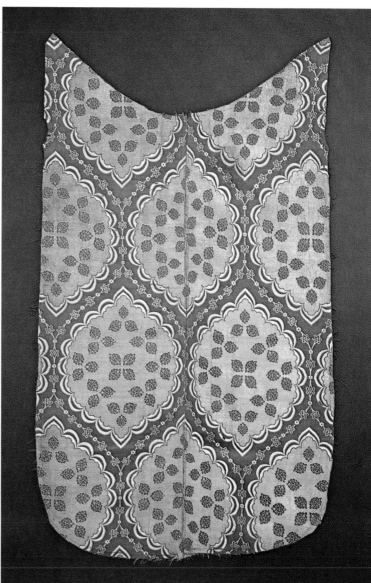

Cover
Persia,1600-1650
Compound weave, twill ground, silk,
gilt on a yellow silk core,
silver on a white silk core
31 x 26½ in. (79.0 x 67.5 cm.)
The Nasli M. Heeramaneck Collection
Gift of Joan Palevsky,1973

Canopy
Persia, late 16th-early 17th century
Twill tapestry, silk and metallic threads
107 x 83 in. (272.2 x 210.8 cm.)
Costume Council Fund,1971

Fragment of a Dress or
Furnishing Fabric
Persia, second half 17th century
Brocaded compound twill, silk, silver
on a white silk core
59½ x 20½ in. (115.1 x 52.1 cm.)
The Nasli M. Heeramaneck Collection
Gift of Joan Palevsky,1973

Covered Ting (tripod cauldron)
China (Late Chou dynasty), 1st quarter
5th century B.C.
Bronze
13½ x 15½ in. (32.2 x 39.3 cm.)
Gift of Mr. and Mrs. Eric Lidow, 1974

Horse
China (T'ang dynasty),
early 8th century
Buff white earthenware with brown,
green, and straw-colored glaze
h: 29⅜ in. (75.1 cm.)
Gift of Nasli M. Heeramaneck, 1973

38

Petal-Form Bowl
China (Northern Sung dynasty),
960-1126
Ting ware, porcelain with
ivory tone glaze; unglazed rim
h: 2¼ in. (5.5 cm.);
d: 7⅞ in. (20.2 cm.)
Gift of Nasli M. Heeramaneck, 1973

39

Tripod Incense Burner
China (Ming dynasty),
early 15th century
Cloisonné enamels on bronze
h: 4½ in. (11.5 cm.);
d: 5⅛ in. (13.0 cm.)
Gift of Taft and Rita Schreiber, 1973

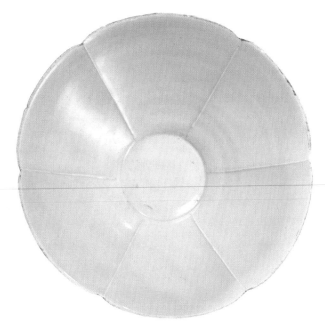

40

Large Covered Box with Floral Scrolls
Thailand (Sawankoloke),
14th-15th century
Stoneware painted with underglaze iron
h: 5½ in. (13.9 cm.);
d: 7 in. (17.8 cm.)
Far Eastern Art Council Fund,1972

41

Dish with Peonies in Relief
Korea (Koryŏ dynasty),12th century
Celadon ware, grayish porcelain with
gray green celadon glaze
h: 1½ in. (4.0 cm.);
d: 6⅞ in. (17.6 cm.)
Gift of Nasli M. Heeramaneck,1973

42

Jizo Bosatsu
Japan (late Heian period),12th century
Carved wood
h: 57⅝ in. (146.5 cm.)
Gift of Anna Bing Arnold,1974

43

Amida Buddha
Japan (Kamakura period),1185-1334
Bronze with carved wood hands
h: 18¾ in. (47.6 cm.)
Promised gift of Mr. and Mrs.
William T. Sesnon, Jr.

Hishikawa Moronobu, attributed
(ca.1625-1694)
Pleasuring on the Sumida River,
ca.1690
Six-panel screen, ink, colors,
and gold on paper
37⅝ x 96 in. (93.0 x 243.8 cm.)
Los Angeles County Funds,1965

Soga Shōhaku (1730-1781)
Taoist Immortal
Hanging scroll, ink on paper
33½ x 61½ in. (85.0 x 156.2 cm.)
Gift of the Art Museum Council,1974

Nobleman Plaque
Nigeria (Benin City), late 17th century
Bronze
18¾ x 7¼ in. (47.6 x 18.4 cm.)
Gift of Anna Bing Arnold,1974

Cycladic Figure
Probably from Naxos or Amorgos,
ca. 2200-2000 B.C.
Marble
h: 34⅝ in. (87.9 cm.)
Gift of Anna Bing Arnold,1967

48

Chasuble
Italy, 14th century
Compound brocaded satin,
silk and metallic threads
Costume Council Fund, 1964

49

Orphrey
Italy (Florence), last half 14th century
Embroidery, silk and metallic threads,
linen ground
Los Angeles County Funds, 1972
Costume Council Fund, 1972

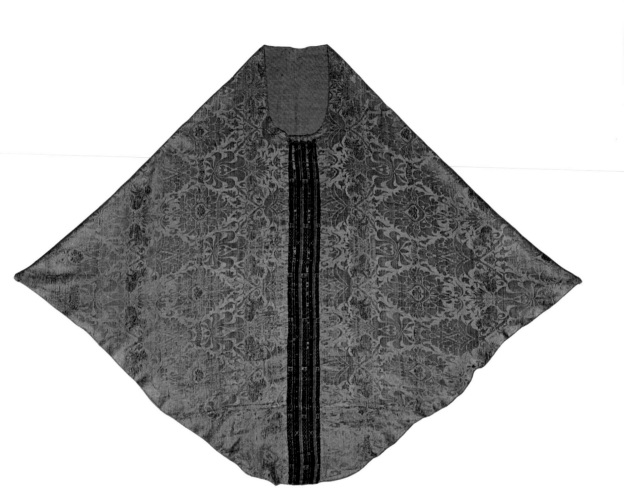

Cope with Orphrey
Cope: Italy, 15th century
Cut voided ferronnerie velvet, silk
Orphrey: Flanders, 15th century
Embroidery, silk and metallic threads
on linen ground
Costume Council Fund, 1964

Master of the St. Lucy Legend
(active ca.1480-1501)
Triptych, before 1483
Donor with His Patron,
St. Peter Martyr; Madonna and Child
with Angels; St. Jerome and His Lion
Oil on oak panels
Center panel: 32¼ x 27¼ in.
(82 x 69.5 cm.)
Side panels: 32¼ x 11¼ in.
(82 x 28.5 cm.)
Gift of Anna Bing Arnold,1969

Albrecht Dürer (1471-1528)
The Martyrdom
*of St. John the Evangelist,*1498
Pl. I from the *Apocalypse of St. John*
Woodcut, proof without text
15 x 11 in. (38.1 x 27.9 cm.)
Los Angeles County Funds,1969

Albrecht Dürer (1471-1528)
The Vision of St. Eustache, ca.1501
Engraving
14 x 10¼ in. (35.6 x 26.0 cm.)
Graphic Arts Council Fund,1966

Albrecht Dürer (1471-1528)
*Adam and Eve,*1504
Engraving
9¾ x 7½ in. (24.8 x 19.2 cm.)
Gift of the Art Museum Council,1966

Albrecht Dürer (1471-1528)
Knight, Death, and Devil,1513
Engraving
9¾ x 7⅜ in. (24.8 x 18.7 cm.)
Graphic Arts Council Fund,1970

Lucas Cranach the Elder (1472-1553)
Portrait of a Young Man
with a Short Beard
Oil on linden panel
16½ x 11⅛ in. (42 x 28 cm.)
Promised gift of R. Stanton Avery

Christoph Amberger (ca.1505-1562)
Portrait of Hans Jacob Fugger ,1541
Oil on panel
37¾ x 31¼ in. (95.9 x 80.7 cm.)
Gift of the
Michael J. Connell Foundation,1968

Fra Bartolommeo (Baccio della Porta)
(1472-1517)
Holy Family
Oil on canvas
59½ x 36 in. (151.0 x 91.3 cm.)
Gift of The Ahmanson Foundation,
1973

59

Baccio Bandinelli (1493-1560)
Colossal Head, ca.1534
Marble
h: 23⅝ in. (60.0 cm.)
Museum purchase: Mr. and Mrs.
Allan C. Balch Endowment,1967

60

Jean Duvet (1485-after 1561)
The Fall of Babylon, ca.1555
Engraving
11⅞ x 8⅜ in. (30.0 x 21.0 cm.)
Gift of the Graphic Arts Council
in memory of Hilda Hunter,1973

61,62

Paolo Caliari, called Veronese
(ca.1528-1588)
Allegory of Navigation
(holding astrolabe)
Allegory of Navigation
(holding cross-staff)
Oil on canvas
81 x 46 in. (206 x 117 cm.) each
Gift of The Ahmanson Foundation,
1974

Il Morazzone (Pier Francesco
Mazzuchelli) 1571/3-1626
St. Francis' Vision of the Musical Angel
Oil on canvas
46½ x 62 in. (108.1 x 157.5 cm.)
Gift of The Ahmanson Foundation,
1973

Peter Paul Rubens (1577-1640)
Young Woman with Curly Hair,
ca.1618-1620
Oil on panel
17 x 13⅛ in. (43.3 x 33.5 cm.),
enlarged to 26⅜ x 20⅝ in.
(67 x 52.4 cm.)
Promised gift of the
Armand Hammer Foundation

71

65

Peter Paul Rubens (1577-1640)
*The Israelites Gathering Manna
in the Desert,*1625-1628
Oil on panel
25½ x 20¾ in. (64.8 x 52.7 cm.)
Frances and Armand Hammer
Purchase Fund,1969

66

Rembrandt van Rijn (1606-1669)
Raising of Lazarus, ca.1630
Oil on panel
37½ x 32½ in. (93.7 x 81.1 cm.)
Gift of H. F. Ahmanson & Co.
in memory of Howard F. Ahmanson,
1972

Rembrandt van Rijn (1606-1669)
*Portrait of a Man
of the Raman Family*,1634
Oil on oval panel
25½ x 19⅞ in. (64.8 x 50.5 cm.),
enlarged to rectangle
27⅛ x 20⅞ in. (68.8 x 53.2 cm.)
Frances and Armand Hammer
Purchase Fund,1969

Frans Hals (1580-1666)
Portrait of Pieter Tjarck (?)
Oil on canvas
33½ x 27½ in. (85 x 70 cm.)
Gift of The Ahmanson Foundation,
1974

69

Jusepe de Ribera (1591-1652)
Ancient Greek Philosopher, 1637
Oil on canvas
49 x 39 in. (124.3 x 99.1 cm.)
Promised gift of R. Stanton Avery

70

Rembrandt van Rijn (1606-1669)
Clement de Jonghe, 1651
Etching and drypoint
8¼ x 6¼ in. (21.0 x 15.9 cm.)
Gift of the Graphic Arts Council, 1967

Giovanni Battista Foggini (1652-1725)
Time Ravishing Beauty
Bronze, dark brown varnish over
red brown natural patina
h: 21⅜ in. (54.3 cm.)
Gift of the
Michael J. Connell Foundation,1974

Jan van Huysum (1682-1749)
*Flowers,*1724
Oil on panel
31½ x 23½ in. (80 x 59.5 cm.)
Promised gift of
Mr. and Mrs. Edward W. Carter

73

Dresses for Ecclesiastic Lay Figures
Italy (Venice), ca.1725
Brocaded silk and metallic threads
Los Angeles County Funds,1965

74

Paul de Lamerie (1688-1751)
Pair of Wall Sconces, ca.1725
Silver gilt
h: 22 in. (55.8 cm.);
comb. wt.: 228 oz., 12 dwts.
Promised gift of
Mr. and Mrs. Arthur Gilbert

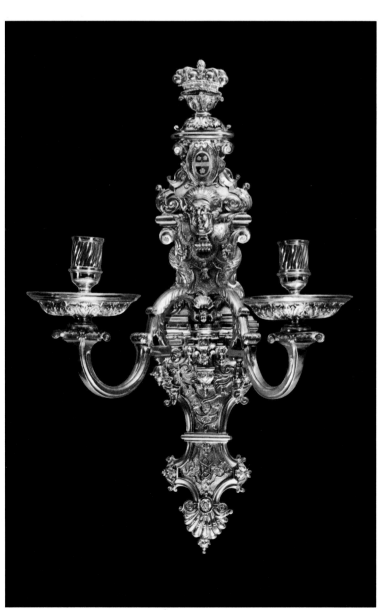

75	76	77

Paul de Lamerie (1688-1751)
*Sideboard Dish and Ewer,*1742
Silver
d: 29 in. (73.6 cm.), dish;
h: 18½ in. (47 cm.), ewer;
comb. wt.: 442 oz. 10 dwts.
Promised gift of
Mr. and Mrs. Arthur Gilbert

Jacques Angot (maître 1753,
active through 1788)
Commode sans traverse,
Louis XV style,1745-1749
Oak with tulipwood and mahogany;
marquetry of kingwood, satinwood,
rosewood, greenwood, and others
Fitted with chased gilt-bronze mounts
Rouge royal marble top
h: 34½ in. (87.6 cm.);
w: 50½ in. (128.2 cm.)
d: 23½ in. (59.7 cm.)
Gift of
Mr. and Mrs. Jerome K. Ohrbach,1967

Woman's Gown
England,1775-1785
Brocaded silk taffeta
Gift of
Mrs. Delmar Lawrence Daves,1964

Royal Gates
Church of the Nativity of the
Mother of God
Kiev, Ukraine, 1784
Silver and silver gilt
91½ x 40½ in. (232.3 x 102.8 cm.);
wt: 74 lbs. 9 oz.
Promised gift of
Mr. and Mrs. Arthur Gilbert

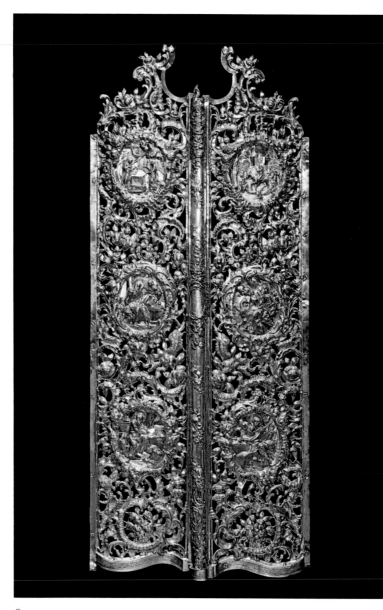

Royal Gates
Church of the Elevation of the
Holy Cross
Kiev, Ukraine, 1784
Silver gilt
106 x 49½ in. (269.2 x 125.1 cm.);
wt: 88 lbs. 8 oz.
Promised gift of
Mr. and Mrs. Arthur Gilbert

Giovanni Battista Tiepolo (1696-1770)
The Holy Family with St. John
Brown ink and wash over
black lead drawing
11¾ x 8½ in. (29.8 x 21.6 cm.)
Gift of Cary Grant, 1969

Giovanni Domenico Tiepolo
(1727-1804)
Centaur Arrested in Flight,
a Female Faun on His Back
Bister
7⅝ x 10⅞ in. (19.3 x 27.6 cm.)
Museum Purchase, 1965

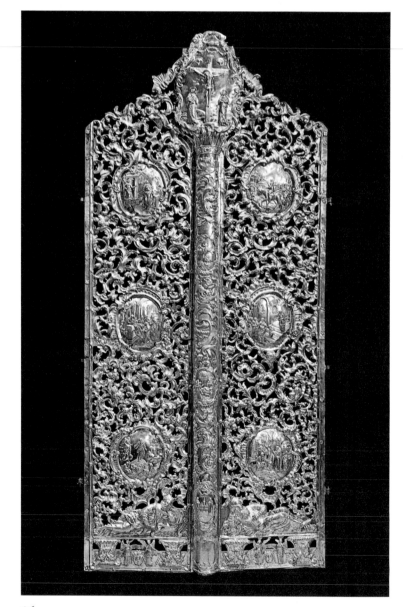

Selection of Mosaic Boxes
Collection of
Mr. and Mrs. Arthur Gilbert

*Faustulus Discovering Romulus
and Remus*
Late 18th century
Mosaic
d: 2¾ in. (7.1 cm.)

Profile of Bacchus
1804
Gold and enamel with mosaic
h: ¾ in. (2.0 cm.); d: 3¼ in. (8.2 cm.)

View of the "Basilica" at Paestum
Ca.1830
Gold and tortoise shell with mosaic
h: 1⅞ in. (4.9 cm.);
2⅜ x 3⅛ in. (5.9 x 8.1 cm.)

View of Berchtesgaden
Mid-19th century
Gold with mosaic
h: 1⅞ in. (4.9 cm.);
2⅜ x 3⅞ in. (5.9 x 9.9 cm.)
Promised gift of
Mr. and Mrs. Arthur Gilbert

Circular Table
19th century
Gilt bronze with marble mosaic top,
mirrored base
d: 31¼ in. (79.4 cm.), top;
h: 36½ in. (92.7 cm.)
Promised gift of
Mr. and Mrs. Arthur Gilbert

Théodore Géricault (1791-1824)
Portrait of a Gentleman
Oil on canvas
25⅝ x 21¼ in. (65.1 x 54.0 cm.)
Promised gift of the
Armand Hammer Foundation

Ingres Del.
rom. 1816

90

Jean Auguste Dominique Ingres
(1780-1867)
Portrait of Thomas Church,1816
Graphite
7⅜ x 6¼ in. (18.9 x 15.9 cm.)
Loula D. Lasker Estate Fund,1967

Claude Monet (1840-1926)
The Beach at Honfleur,1867
Oil on canvas
23½ x 32 in. (59.7 x 81.3 cm.)
Gift of Mrs. Reese Hale Taylor,1964
Life tenancy

Henri Fantin-Latour (1836-1904)
Peonies in a Blue and White Vase, 1872
Oil on canvas
23⅞ x 19⅝ in. (60.8 x 49.9 cm.)
Promised gift of the
Armand Hammer Foundation

Gustave Moreau (1826-1898)
Salome Dancing Before Herod, 1876
Oil on canvas
56⅝ x 41⅛ in. (143.8 x 104.2 cm.)
Promised gift of the
Armand Hammer Foundation

93

Paul Cézanne (1839-1906)
Still Life with Cherries and Peaches,
ca.1883-1887
Oil on canvas
19¾ x 24 in. (50.4 x 61 cm.)
Gift of the Adele R. Levy Fund and
Mr. and Mrs. Armand S. Deutsch,1961

Paul Gauguin (1848-1903)
*Thatched Cottages at Pont-Aven,*1886
Oil on canvas
23⅜ x 36¼ in. (72.0 x 92.0 cm.)
Promised gift of
Mr. and Mrs. Hal B.Wallis

Paul Gauguin (1848-1903)
*Bonjour, M.Gauguin,*1889
Oil on canvas
29½ x 21½ (74.9 x 54.6 cm.)
Promised gift of the
Armand Hammer Foundation

Vincent van Gogh (1853-1890)
*Hospital at Saint-Rémy,*1889
Oil on canvas
35½ x 28 in. (90.2 x 71.1 cm.)
Promised gift of the
Armand Hammer Foundation

Auguste Rodin (1840-1917)
*Head of Iris, No. 4,*1890-1891
Bronze
24 x 13 x 13 in. (61 x 33 x 33 cm.)
Gift of the B. G. Cantor
Art Foundation,1969

Auguste Rodin (1840-1917)
Study of Nude for Balzac C, No. 4, 1893
Bronze, Rudier cast
50¼ x 20½ x 24¾ in.
(127.6 x 52 x 62.8 cm.)
Gift of the
B. G. Cantor Art Foundation, 1967

Auguste Rodin (1840-1917)
Monument to Balzac, 1897
Bronze
117 x 47¼ x 47¼ in.
(297.1 x 120.0 x 120.0 cm.)
Promised gift of the
B. G. Cantor Art Foundation

Aubrey Beardsley (1872-1898)
Enter Herodias, 1893
Pen, black ink, and wash on
Whatman paper
8¾ x 6⅜ in. (22.3 x 16.3 cm.)
Gift of the Graphic Arts Council, 1973

Jean Worth (1856-1926)
Afternoon Dress, 1896
Printed silk taffeta
Gift of Mrs. Murray Ward, 1971

Edvard Munch (1863-1944)
*Seascape,*1899
Color woodcut, hand-colored with
yellow and white gouache
14¾ x 22¼ in. (37.4 x 56.5 cm.)
Gift of Mr. and Mrs. Felix Juda,1966

Pierre Bonnard (1867-1947)
Bridge in Paris, ca.1903
Oil on canvas
28⅛ x 39⅜ in. (71.5 x 100.0 cm.)
Gift of
Mr. and Mrs. Sidney F. Brody,1967

Pablo Picasso (1881-1973)
*Portrait of Sebastian Juñer Vidal,*1903
Oil on canvas
49¾ x 37 in. (126.4 x 94.0 cm.)
Bequest of David E. Bright,1967

101

Henri Matisse (1869-1954)
*Heads of Jeannette,*1910-1913
Bronze
Jeannette I, h: 13 in. (33.0 cm.)
Jeannette II, h: 10⅜ in. (26.4 cm.)

Jeannette III, h: 23¾ in. (60.3 cm.)
Jeannette IV, h: 24⅛ in. (61.3 cm.)
Jeannette V, h: 22⅞ in. (58.1 cm.)
Gift of the Art Museum Council
in memory of Penelope Rigby,1968

102

Frank Kupka (1871-1957)
Irregular Forms: Creation,1911
Oil on canvas
42½ x 42½ in. (108.0 x 108.0 cm.)
Bequest of David E. Bright,1967

103

Jacques Villon (1875-1963)
*Yvonne in Profile,*1913
Drypoint on Delâtre paper
21⅝ x 16⅞ in. (54.9 x 41.4 cm.)
Los Angeles County Funds,1965

104

Raymond Duchamp-Villon
(1876-1918)
*The Large Horse,*1914
Bronze, second cast of nine,1966
h: 59 in. (149.9 cm.)
Gift of Anna Bing Arnold,1968

Lyonel Feininger (1871-1956)
Vollersroda, 1918
Black pen and wash
7⅞ x 9⅞ in. (20.0 x 25.1 cm.)
Gift of the Graphic Arts Council, 1968

Fernand Léger (1881-1955)
Discs, 1918-1919
Oil on canvas
51⅛ x 38¼ in. (129.8 x 97.1 cm.)
Bequest of David E. Bright, 1967

Henri Matisse (1869-1954)
Tea,1919
Oil on canvas
55 x 83 in. (139.7 x 210.8 cm.)
Bequest of David L. Loew in memory
of his father, Marcus Loew,1974

Henri Matisse (1869-1954)
*Warrior Costume and Design for
"Le Chant du Rossignol,"* 1920
Costume: wool felt, velvet, silk
Costume Council Fund, 1968
Design: pencil on paper
16¾ x 8½ in. (42.5 x 21.6 cm.)
Costume Council Fund, 1968

Mariano Fortuny (1871-1929)
Coat, ca.1925
Beige silk stenciled in brown,
glass beads
Gift of Mrs. Harry D'Arrast,1973

Käthe Kollwitz (1867-1945)
Self-Portrait, 1934
Charcoal
13 ¼ x 17 in. (33.7 x 43.2 cm.)
Los Angeles County Funds, 1969

Joan Miró (b.1893)
Animated Forms, 1935
Oil on canvas
76½ x 68 in. (194.3 x 172.7 cm.)
Bequest of David E. Bright, 1967

Pablo Picasso (1881-1973)
Young Woman in Striped Dress, 1949
Oil on canvas
45⅝ x 35 in. (115.9 x 88.9 cm.)
Bequest of David E. Bright, 1967

Pablo Picasso (1881-1973)
*Woman with Hairnet,*1949-1956
Color lithograph, fourth and final state;
edition: 36/50
26 x 19¼ in. (66.0 x 48.9 cm.)
Gift of Mr. and Mrs. Harry Lenart,1966

Burial Mantle (see detail, overleaf)
Peru (Paracas Necropolis),
300 B.C.-A.D. 300
Embroidery, stem, buttonhole, and
knit stitches on plain weave ground,
alpaca
97⅛ x 51⅜ in. (247.6 x 130.5 cm.)
Los Angeles County Funds, 1967

115

Feather Tunic
Peru (Inca, central coast?),1100-1400
Rows of feathers knotted on cords,
stitched to plain weave cotton ground
71 x 33 in. (180.5 x 83.5 cm.)
Gift of Mr. and Mrs.
William T. Sesnon, Jr.,1974

John Singleton Copley (1738-1815)
Portrait of Hugh Montgomerie,
*12th Earl of Eglinton,*1780
Oil on canvas
94½ x 59¾ in. (238.7 x 151.8 cm.)
Gift of the Andrew Norman Foundation
and Museum Acquisitions Fund,1968

Gilbert Stuart (1755-1828)
Portrait of Richard,
4th Viscount Barrington
Oil on canvas
30 x 25 in. (76.2 x 63.5 cm.)
Museum Purchase,1968

Gilbert Stuart (1755-1828)
Portrait of George Washington, 1822
Oil on canvas
44⅛ x 34½ in. (112.0 x 87.6 cm.)
Promised gift of the
Armand Hammer Foundation

Thomas Cole (1801-1848)
L'Allegro, 1845
Oil on canvas
32 x 48 in. (81.3 x 121.9 cm.)
Art Museum Council and the
Michael J. Connell Foundation, 1974

Ball Dress
United States, 1865
Silk taffeta
Gift of
Mr. and Mrs. Parker Huntington, 1969

Jasper Francis Cropsey (1823-1900)
Sidney Plains—With the Union of the
*Susquehanna and Unadilla Rivers,*1874
Oil on canvas
42 x 72 in. (106.6 x 182.9 cm.)
Jessie R. McMahan Memorial and
Museum Acquisitions Fund,1970

John Singer Sargent (1856-1925)
*Doctor Pozzi at Home,*1881
Oil on canvas
80½ x 43⅞ in. (204.5 x 111.5 cm.)
Promised gift of the
Armand Hammer Foundation

William Michael Harnett (1848-1892)
*Still Life,*1885
Oil on panel
13¾ x 10¼ in. (34.9 x 26.2 cm.)
Promised gift of the
Armand Hammer Foundation

John Singer Sargent (1856-1925)
*Portrait of Mrs. Edward L. Davis and
Her Son, Livingston Davis,*1890
Oil on canvas
86 x 48 in. (218.4 x 121.9 cm.)
Frances and Armand Hammer
Purchase Fund,1969

Thomas W. Eakins (1844-1916)
*Portrait of
Sebastiano Cardinal Martinelli,*1902
Oil on canvas, mounted on panel
78¼ x 59⅞ in. (198.9 x 152.3 cm.)
Promised gift of the
Armand Hammer Foundation

126

Mary Cassatt (1844-1926)
Reine Lefebvre and Margot, ca.1902
Pastel on brown paper,
mounted on canvas
32¾ x 26½ in. (83.2 x 67.5 cm.)
Promised gift of the
Armand Hammer Foundation

127

Gaston Lachaise (1882-1935)
*Floating Figure,*1927
Bronze, edition 2/7
51¾ x 96 in. (131.4 x 243.8 cm.)
Promised gift of Mr. and Mrs. Ray Stark

Josef Albers (b.1888)
Homage to the Square:
*Beyond Focus,*1969
Oil on masonite
48 x 48 in. (121.9 x 121.9 cm.)
Promised gift of
Mr. and Mrs. Taft Schreiber

Jackson Pollock (1912-1956)
Black and White Number 20,1951
Duco on canvas
57⅛ x 64 in. (45 x 62.4 cm.)
Bequest of David E. Bright,1967

130

Gertrude and Otto Natzler
(1908-1971 and b.1908)
Selection of Natzler Ceramics
Collection of Mrs. Leonard M. Sperry
Gift of the
Rose A. Sperry Revocable Trust,1972

131

Franz Kline (1910-1962)
*The Ballantine,*1948-1960
Oil on canvas
72 x 72 in. (182.9 x 182.9 cm.)
Bequest of David E. Bright,1967

Mark Rothko (1903-1970)
White Center, 1957
Oil on canvas
84 x 72 in. (213.4 x 182.9 cm.)
Bequest of David E. Bright, 1967

David Smith (1906-1965)
Cubi XXIII, 1964
Stainless steel
76¼ x 172⅞ in. (193.7 x 439.1 cm.)
Contemporary Art Council Funds, 1967

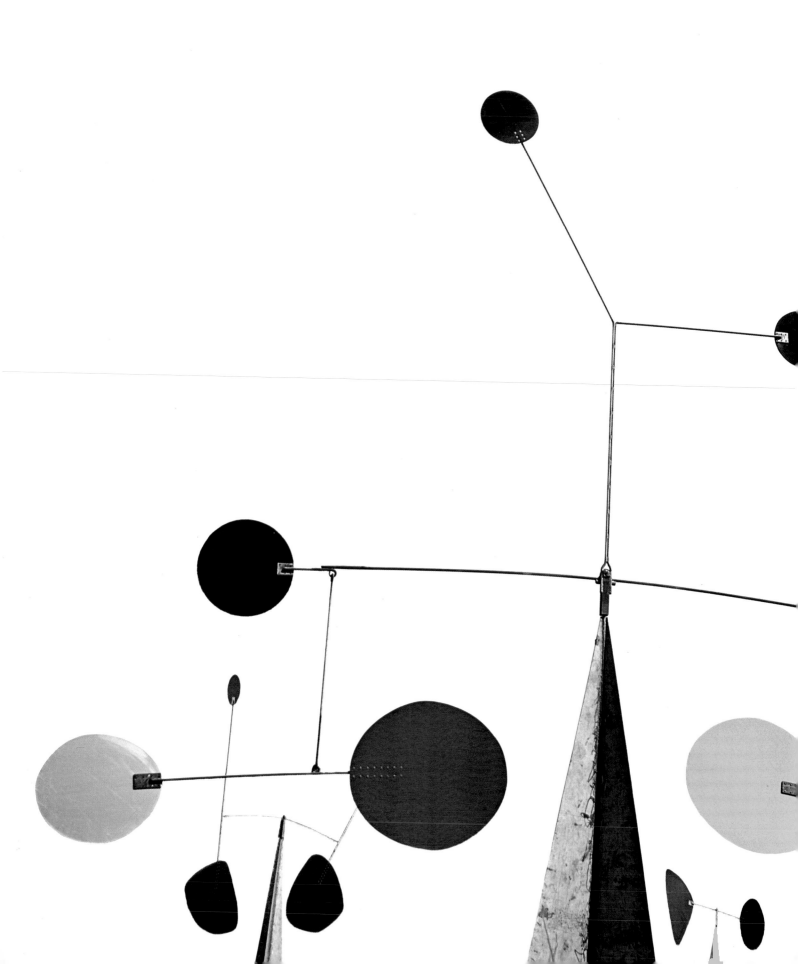

Alexander Calder (b.1898)
*Hello Girls,*1964
Three mobiles, painted metal
h: 8 ft. 9 in. (2.67 m.); 15 ft. (4.57 m.);
22 ft. 11 in. (6.98 m.)
Commissioned by the
Art Museum Council,1964

Claes Oldenburg (b.1929)
*Giant Pool Balls,*1967
Sixteen plexiglass balls,
24 in. each (61.0 cm.)
Wood rack, 120 x 120 x 108 in.
(304.8 x 304.8 x 274.3 cm.)
Anonymous gift through the
Contemporary Art Council,1969

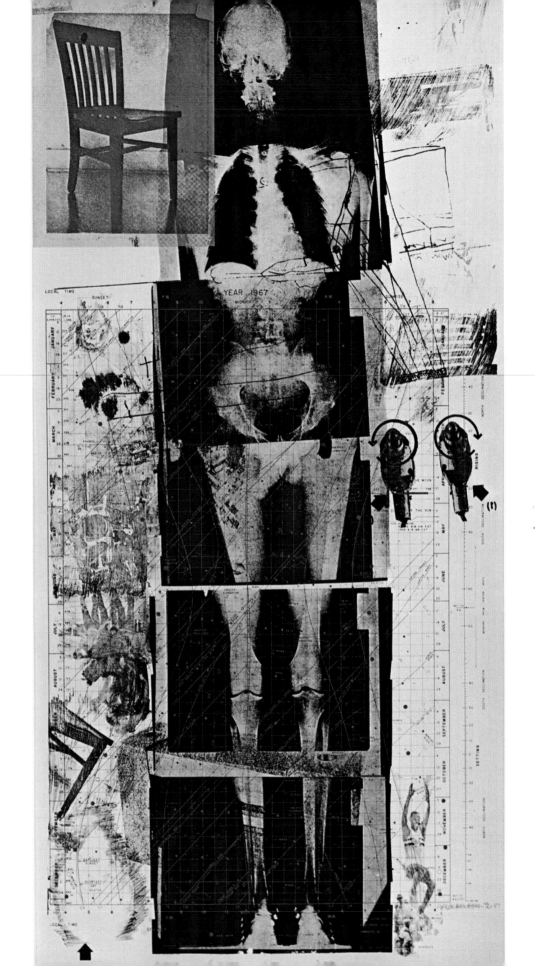

Robert Rauschenberg (b.1925)
*Booster,*1967
Color lithograph and silkscreen
Printed on Curtis Rag by Gemini Ltd.,
Los Angeles, from two stones in black,
two aluminum plates in white, and
silkscreen in red enamel
72 x 36 in. (182.9 x 91.4 cm.)
Gift of the
Times-Mirror Company,1973

Frank Stella (b.1936)
*Protractor Variation,*1969
Fluorescent-alkyd on canvas
10 x 20 ft. (3.05 x 6.1 m.)
Museum Purchase,1969

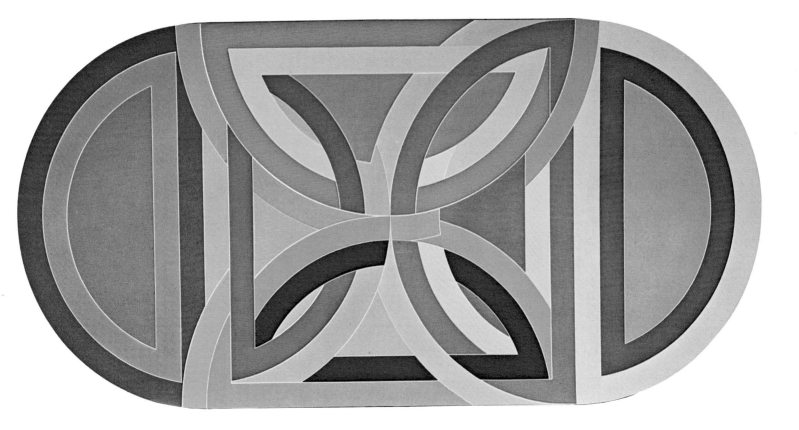

Larry Bell (b.1939)
*Untitled,*1971
Coated glass, two panels
Each panel: 108 x 60 x ⅜ in.
(274.3 x 152.9 x 1.0 cm.)
Gift of the Kleiner Foundation,1973

Richard Diebenkorn (b.1922)
*Ocean Park Series #49,*1972
Oil on canvas
93 x 81 in. (236.2 x 205.7 cm.)
Museum Purchase,1973

Ellsworth Kelly (b.1923)
Blue Curve III,1972
Oil on canvas
67¾ x 166½ in. (172.1 x 422.9 cm.)
Museum Purchase,1973

1

Palace Reliefs of Ashurnasirpal II
Assyria (Kalah), 9th century B.C.
Gypseous alabaster
Tree of Life, Panels 1 and 2
92 x 33⅛ in. (233.7 x 84.1 cm.)
and 91 x 42½ in. (231.1 x 108.0 cm.)
The King and a Winged Genius, Panel 3
90¾ x 83 in. (230.5 x 210.8 cm.)
Eagle-headed Daemon, Panel 4
88 x 70⅜ in. (223.5 x 178.8 cm.)
Winged Genius, Panel 5
93 x 77¼ in. (236.2 x 196.2 cm.)
Los Angeles County Funds donated by
Anna Bing Arnold, 1966
66.4.1-5

Collections: William Kennett Loftus, Newcastle-upon-Tyne;
Literary and Philosophical Society, Newcastle-upon-Tyne;
Spink and Company, Ltd., London; Kimbell Art Foundation,
Fort Worth

Literature: A. H. Layard, *Monuments of Nineveh,* London,
1849 and 1853; idem, *Nineveh and Its Remains,* London,
1849 and 1854; W. K. Loftus, *Travels and Researches in
Chaldea and Susiana,* London, 1857; E. F. Weidner,
Die Reliefs der Assyriaschen Konige, Berlin, 1939;
R. D. Barnett, *Assyrian Palace Reliefs,* London, n.d.;
J. B. Stearns, *Reliefs from the Palace of Ashurnasirpal II,*
Graz, 1961; R. Stead, "Assyrian Reliefs in the Los Angeles
County Museum of Art," *The Burlington Magazine,*
London, Nov. 1968; idem, *Reliefs from Nimrud,* Los Angeles
County Museum of Art, 1968

Inspired by the earlier Hittites, the Assyrians developed
more fully the use of carved stone panels in royal building
construction. Carved in both high and low relief—and
generally also painted—with scenes of battles and sieges,
religious rituals, and lion hunts, their most important
function was to emphasize the god-sanctioned power of
the king.

These reliefs, by unknown sculptors whose work followed
rigid canons, are of differing quality and were found in
royal palaces at the changing Assyrian seats of government.

In 1848, the ninth century B.C. royal residence of
Ashurnasirpal II (reigned 883-858 B.C.) at Kalah was
discovered by Austen Henry Layard. Known as "the North
West Palace," Ashurnasirpal's great complex was a maze
of courtyards, royal apartments, reception halls, tablet
rooms, sanctuaries, garden areas, and administrative and
service quarters.

The Los Angeles reliefs, despite necessary minimal
restoration, are equal in quality to the best Kalah examples
in the vast Assyrian collections of The British Museum,
the Louvre, and the Bagdad Museum. The five panels do not
form a continuous scene and in fact came from different

parts of the North West Palace. Based on Layard's original
notes and drawings, it would appear that the Los Angeles
sections are from two principal areas: an antechamber for
the royal throne hall and the "living room" of the king's
private apartment.

The subject matter of the Los Angeles panels is, unlike
so many other extant reliefs, devoid of commemorative
military material. The Tree of Life, an old Near Eastern
theme that has both sustaining and religious connotations,
appears on corner panels 1 and 2, and again on panel 4,
where it is being annointed or pollinated with a fir-cone
applicator by an eagle-headed daemon. The daemon, a
beneficent creature, derives from much earlier Mesopotamian representations, of baked clay, that were buried
under household floors, apparently to bring good fortune.
The bared foreleg suggestive of action is an iconographic
tradition found in much Mesopotamian work. It gives
life to what would otherwise be heavy with rigid and static
form. This artistic device is seen again on the winged
genius guardian of panel 5 and on a similar protective figure
immediately behind the king in panel 3. Ashurnasirpal
himself is shown holding a libation bowl, perhaps an offering to the gods, while with his other hand he clenches a
bow, a symbol of strength and prowess.

The panels themselves are surcharged with identical
"royal standard inscriptions." This incised cuneiform statement, almost a liturgy, gives incessant emphasis to
Ashurnasirpal's conquests, his protection by the gods, his
wrath and might.

It is known that Layard discovered and recorded the
Los Angeles reliefs. Yet, another English archaeologist and
historian, William Kennett Loftus, continued the excavations when Layard retired to write, and it was Loftus who
presented the Los Angeles reliefs to the Literary and
Philosophical Society at Newcastle-upon-Tyne.

2

Worshiper Figure
Sumer (Mari ?), first half 3rd millennium B.C.
Alabaster
h: 11½ in. (30.1 cm.)
Gift of Phil Berg, 1971
M.71.73.5

Collections: K. Rabenou, Ltd., New York; Phil Berg,
Los Angeles

Exhibition: Los Angeles County Museum of Art,
Man Came This Way: The Phil Berg Collection,
Mar. 9-May 30, 1971, no. 4, repr. in cat. p. 21

Although most extant Sumerian male worshiper
figures have extensive and elaborately coiffed beards, this
clean-shaven example is closer to those produced before
the reign of Sargon, the Akkadian ruler who conquered the

Sumerians. Its attitude of supplication suggests that it was placed in a temple by its owner, presumably reflecting his likeness, to perform necessary prayers for him. A contemporary comparison might be the lighting of a candle in a Catholic church.

A great many such figures have been found, notably near modern Tell Hariri in the middle Euphrates region. The hollow eyes may have once been inlaid with bone corneas and the eyelids with bitumen. The highly intricate design of the worshiper's garment, called a *kaunake,* represents a practical and warming garment of cloth strips that simulate or may actually have been sheep's fleece.

3

Ceremonial Beaker
Northwest Iran, ca. 1000-900 B.C.
Gold
h: 4¼ in. (10.8 cm.)
Gift of the Art Museum Council, 1968
M.68.25

Collection: K. Rabenou, Ltd., New York

Shaped about 3,000 years ago from a thin sheet of gold, this cup probably comes from the Dailaman region below the Caspian Sea. The vigorous repeat design of a grazing gazelle was then peened from within, doubtless using a carved wood mold. Die-stamped decorative registers around the top and bottom of the vessel accent the major design and are typical of many Iranian metal productions. Originally ascribed to a first millennium royal tomb at Marlik, a site in Gilan Province often confused with nearby Amlash, it is now apparent that the type of gold material excavated there in recent years under official Iranian Government supervision is of a similar but clearly different style. The Marlik culture, apparently short lived, was more Assyrian-oriented, and the Museum's object falls somewhere between Marlik and Kalar Dasht types. The admittedly broad attribution to "Northwest Iran" appears reasonable in terms of its overall style and in the absence of precise field documentation.

4

Whetstone Finial (?)
Iran, before 7th century B.C.
Gold
l: 2¾ in. (6.9 cm.)
Gift of Phil Berg, 1971
M.71.73.18

Collection: Phil Berg, Los Angeles

Exhibitions: Paris, Musée du Petit Palais, *Sept Mille Ans d'Art en Iran,* Oct. 1961-Jan. 1962; Los Angeles County Museum of Art, *Man Came This Way: The Phil Berg Collection,* Mar. 9-May 30, 1971, no. 15, repr. in cat., p. 25

Found at Ghaflantou, Iran, not far from the Kurdistan Province site of the spectacular "Ziwiye Treasure" discovered in 1947, this gold ibex head must have been a prototype for the later and better known Achaemenid works that appear both in this scale in gold, silver, and bronze as handle ends, and in larger scale in metal and pottery as rhytons.

The ibex motif, done here in repoussé technique, is an old Iranian form that has both religious and economic implications. It is also known to us from both Assyrian and Scythian art. André Godard believed that its design origin might be Mannaean (the Old Testament Manni). The Mannaeans formed a type of buffer state between the Urartians and Assyrians until the Medean conquest.

5

Śālabhañjikā (Tree Dryads)
India (Madhya Pradesh, Sanchi), A.D. 10-25
Sandstone
h: 25 in. (63.5 cm.)
The Nasli and Alice Heeramaneck Collection, 1969
L.69.24.285

Exhibitions: Boston, Museum of Fine Arts, *The Arts of India and Nepal: The Nasli and Alice Heeramaneck Collection,* Nov. 21, 1966-Jan. 8, 1967, no. 1, repr. on cover and p. 24 of cat.; traveled to Los Angeles County Museum of Art, Feb. 8-Apr. 2, 1967; Detroit Institute of Arts, June 20-Aug. 6, 1967; Richmond, Virginia Museum of Fine Arts, Sept. 18-Oct. 14, 1967; Toronto, Royal Ontario Museum, Jan. 23-Mar. 10, 1968; Los Angeles County Museum of Art, *The Art of India, Nepal and Tibet: The Nasli and Alice Heeramaneck Collection,* Sept. 24-Nov. 15, 1970

Literature: *Los Angeles County Museum of Art Annual Report 1968-1969,* vol. XIX, no. 1, repr. p. 8

The area of Sanchi is one of the oldest Buddhist sites in the world, with one of the *stūpas* (reliquary mounds) dating to the second century B.C. In addition to this relief of tree dryads, there are only two other early sculptures from this site known outside of India; they are at the Boston Museum of Fine Arts and The British Museum.

The Los Angeles sculpture once served as a bracket on one of the gateways located at the four cardinal points around *Stūpa* No. 1, the most recent of the three *stūpas* at Sanchi.

On one side of the relief a dryad holds the leaves of a mango tree, while on the other side another holds the stems of a flowering plant. Both women, richly adorned with headbands, necklaces, bracelets, girdles, and anklets, pose provocatively, displaying their physical charms. This representation of the female, conceived in rounded volumes with special emphasis on her fertility, was to remain the standard female type in Indian sculpture throughout its history.

6

Head of a Bodhisattva
Pakistan (Jellalabad district), 4th-5th century
Stucco with polychrome
h: 10½ in. (26.7 cm.)
The Nasli and Alice Heeramaneck Collection, 1969
L.69.24.244

Exhibitions: Rochester, New York, Memorial Art Gallery
of the University of Rochester, *The Art of India,* Apr. 7-30,
1961, no. 9, repr. in cat.; Boston, Museum of Fine Arts,
*The Arts of India and Nepal: The Nasli and Alice
Heeramaneck Collection,* Nov. 21, 1966-Jan. 8, 1967,
no. 21, repr. in color in cat.; traveled to Los Angeles County
Museum of Art, Feb. 8-Apr. 2, 1967; Detroit Institute of
Arts, June 20-Aug. 6, 1967; Richmond, Virginia
Museum of Fine Arts, Sept. 18-Oct. 14, 1967; Toronto,
Royal Ontario Museum, Jan. 23-Mar. 10, 1968; Los Angeles
County Museum of Art, *The Art of India, Nepal and Tibet:
The Nasli and Alice Heeramaneck Collection,* Sept. 24-
Nov. 15, 1970

Originally this head formed part of a full figure of a
Bodhisattva. It comes from the ancient area of Gandhāra,
which was composed of the northwest area of modern
Pakistan and parts of southern Afghanistan. This area was
a provincial Roman trading center and, like other sculpture
from this region, this piece shows marked characteristics
of the Greco-Roman tradition. Traces of polychrome remain
on the head, outlining the eyes and lips. Most Indian
sculpture originally was painted; however, few examples
have survived with the colors still visible.

In the Buddhist pantheon, a Bodhisattva is a being who
has achieved enlightenment and, therefore, is able to become
a Buddha but has chosen to remain a Bodhisattva in order
to save less fortunate mortals. Two of the outstanding
qualities of a Bodhisattva are compassion and sympathy for
human frailties and imperfections. In this remarkably
sensitive stucco head these qualities are conveyed in a
poignant fashion through the half-closed eyes and the sad,
gentle expression.

7

Buddha Śākyamuni
North India (Uttar Pradesh?), 6th century
Gilt bronze
15½ x 6¾ in. (39.4 x 17.1 cm.)
Gift of the Michael J. Connell Foundation, 1970
M.70.17

Literature: *Archives of Asian Art,* vol. XXV, 1971-1972,
New York, p. 98, fig. 22; *Los Angeles County Museum of
Art Bulletin 1973,* p. 50, fig. 46

The age of the Guptas, a dynasty that ruled much of
northern India from A.D. 320 until about the mid-sixth
century, is generally regarded as the classical period in the
history of Indian sculpture. While stone sculptures from
this period are abundant, only a handful of bronzes—
of which the present example is one of the finest—have
survived. This sculpture also demonstrates that the artists of
Gupta India were accomplished in the art of bronze casting.

The figure represents the historical Buddha Śākyamuni
in a classic image type. His right hand is raised in the
gesture of protection and the left gathers up the ends of the
monk's robe with an elegant sweep. The folds of the
garment are indicated by a series of concentric ripples
beginning at the shoulders and continuing down to the hem,
where pleats are formed at the outer edges. Below the
garment, the idealized though supple body of the Buddha
stands out prominently, as if the cloth were diaphanous.
Typical of the Gupta style, the figure of the Buddha combines austere form with sensuous grace. Although
Śākyamuni was a historical person, this image is an idealized
one modeled after a prototypical and perfect yogī. Hence
the limbs appear pliant but firm, his eyes are half-shut and
suggestive of inner serenity, the expression beatific and
compassionate. Among the supranormal signs of divinity
are his webbed fingers, elongated earlobes, boneless limbs,
his short hair curling to the right, and the cranial bump
symbolizing extraordinary wisdom.

8, 9

The River Goddesses Gaṅgā and Yamunā
India (Madhya Pradesh), 8th century
Red sandstone
h: 27 in. (68.6 cm.)
The Nasli and Alice Heeramaneck Collection, 1969
L.69.24.238 a, b

Exhibition: Los Angeles County Museum of Art, *The Art of
India, Nepal and Tibet: The Nasli and Alice Heeramaneck
Collection,* Sept. 24-Nov. 15, 1970

Literature: *Los Angeles County Museum of Art Annual
Report 1968-1969,* vol. XIX, no. 1, repr. in color on the cover

Over the millennia the rivers of India have acquired a
peculiar sanctity in the Indian mind. Each river is
considered to be a sacred entity, but perhaps the most
venerated are Gaṅgā and Yamunā. The former, called
the Ganges in English, dominates the plains of northern
India. The Yamunā is a tributary of the Gaṅgā, but is
almost equally sacred because of its specific association with
the popular god Krishna. Because of their sanctity and
auspicious character, it is customary to place personified
images of the two rivers at the entrance of a temple.
Since rivers enhance the fertility of the land, all rivers are
conceived as goddesses, as in these two exceptionally
beautiful reliefs.

In both reliefs the largest females represent the goddesses. The two are almost identically conceived, except for their mounts; Gaṅgā's is the mythical *makara* and Yamunā's, the tortoise. Each goddess is accompanied by an elegant attendant carrying a bag of cosmetics, a female dwarf balancing a cushion on her head, and a young girl holding the staff of an umbrella. A celestial couple carrying a garland of flowers and a male guardian placed as a deterrent to evil forces also accompany both goddesses. Thus, although these reliefs were used symbolically at the entrance of a temple, their depiction has a lively genre quality. Except for the *makara* and the tortoise, these representations might well be regarded as idealized portrayals of royal ladies going to their baths accompanied by their servants.

Crisply and deeply carved from their backgrounds, these figures stand out in unusually bold relief. What is further remarkable about these sculptures is the delightful fusion of abundant volume and linear grace. The female form is unquestionably treated with an almost baroque exuberance, and yet the figures seem to be infused with unusual buoyancy. Indeed, this buoyant, linear rhythm flows continuously from one figure to another, suggesting the rippling surface of a river.

10

Buddhist Altar
India (Madhya Pradesh, Sirpur) 8th-9th century
Bronze with copper and silver inlay
h: 15 in. (38.1 cm.)
The Nasli and Alice Heeramaneck Collection, 1969
L.69.24.277

Exhibition: Los Angeles County Museum of Art, *The Art of India, Nepal and Tibet: The Nasli and Alice Heeramaneck Collection,* Sept. 24-Nov. 15, 1970

Literature: M. D. Dikshit, *Sirpur and Rajim Temples,* Bombay, 1960, repr. pl. 56

This Buddhist altar represents the epiphany of the goddess Tārā. One of the principal female deities in the Buddhist pantheon, Tārā is the saviour who removes fear and apprehension and fulfills the wishes of believers. She is also a fertility goddess and is usually depicted carrying a lotus, the Indian symbol of grace and beauty.

The main figures of the shrine are placed within its central portion and in front of an intricately designed set of pillars capped by a lintel or cross bar. Tārā sits on a double lotus cushion, supported by a lion throne. Her drapery is exquisitely detailed and inlaid with bands of silver and lotus designs of copper. Elaborate jewelry adorns both her torso and her tiara-like crown, which is interwoven with her long, cascading hair. Flanking Tārā are two female

attendants each carrying a lotus and displaying a jewel while making the gesture of munificence. Attention to detail is further apparent in the treatment of the attendants' garments, which are incised with patterns emulating textile designs. They also wear elaborately ornamented headbands for their chignons. The eyes of all three females would have been inset with silver; however, the metal has now been lost and only depressions in the surface remain.

At the apex of this shrine, where now only the staffs remain, there would have been three umbrellas, symbolic of divinity. In the central portion, Tārā's parent Buddha, Amitābha, is seated in the meditating posture and is flanked on the left by the Bodhisattva Vajrapāṇi and on the right by the Bodhisattva, Avalokiteśvara. All three are seated on lotus pedestals in front of delicate flame mandorlas. At the base of the shrine, two *Nāgas* (snake kings) hold bowls of jewels as offerings to the goddess, while the figure of the shrine's donor kneels in adoration.

During the late eighth and the early ninth centuries, an excellence in metal casting was achieved in Sirpur which equaled that of Nalanda, the major Buddhist artistic center of eastern Indian. This Tārā shrine is an example of this superb level of quality.

11

Dancing Gaṇeśa
India (Uttar Pradesh), 9th century
Red sandstone
h: 28½ in. (72.4 cm.)
Gift of Nasli M. Heeramaneck, 1974
L.74.39

Collection: Nasli and Alice Heeramaneck, New York

Gaṇeśa, the elephant-headed son of Śiva, is one of the most popular Hindu deities. Regarded as the god of auspiciousness and good fortune, he is worshiped universally in India and Nepal. Even the Buddhists and the Jainas venerate him and include him in their pantheons.

Like his father, Śiva, Gaṇeśa loves to dance, and his bulky volume is remarkably infused with rhythmic grace. The sculptor has chosen to accentuate the corpulent volume of the god by using rounded forms throughout the sculpture. Gaṇeśa is framed at the top by a curvilinear garland composed of snake bodies, while at each side the rounded form is continued in the axe handle and the mace held in his hands.

That the dance is a formal performance is evident from the inclusion of the musicians who are playing various instruments. In the texts, Gaṇeśa is often said to dance for the amusement and delight of his indulgent parents. Ordinarily, he is portrayed with four arms, but here the number of arms has increased to eight, indicating the image's tāntric affiliation. The sculpture probably once graced a side niche in a Śaiva temple.

12

Śiva, the Lord of Dance (Naṭarāja)
India (Tamilnadu), ca. 10th century
Bronze with green patina
h: 30 in. (76.2 cm.)
Anonymous gift, 1974

The art of dance in India is not only regarded as a form of
yoga, but it is associated with the very act of creation.
As the ancient texts tell us:

> When, ye, O Gods, in yonder deep embrace of
> one another stood,
> Thence, as of dancers, from your feet a thickening
> cloud of dust arose.

Few sculptural traditions have so joyously explored the
relationship between form and rhythm as has that of India.
In no other human activity is movement so rhythmic and
spontaneous as in dance; no doubt this is why Indian
sculpture so vividly mirrors the postures and gestures of
the dancer.

As the Lord of Yoga, Śiva is also the source of the dance,
the cosmic dance that creates the universe in endless
rhythmic cycle. Of all the many different images of dancing
Śiva or Naṭarāja invented by the Indian artist, perhaps
the most complete and graphic visual statement is that
created by the Tamil sculptors during the Chola period in
South India (ca. tenth century). This classic form of
Naṭarāja, as exemplified by the Museum's bronze, has
become symbolic of Indian civilization itself.

Surrounded by a ring of flame symbolizing the universe,
the serene and elegant lord dances in perfect equipoise with
his left leg raised and the right trampling a dwarf. The
remarkably alert dwarf is symbolic of the desire that
characterizes the phenomenal world. The fire in one of his
left hands is the fire of destruction, while from the drum
arises creation. The second right hand displays the gesture
of reassurance, and the remaining left hand points to the
uplifted foot which gives refuge to the soul. His flying hair
creates a lively visual design, with the strands of hair spread
out symmetrically like branches of a tree and garnished
with flowers and leafy sprigs. The implication here seems
to be the identification of Śiva with the wish-fulfilling
tree *(kalpavriksha)*. The tiny figure of the river goddess
Gaṅgā is added to one of the strands on the god's right.
His crown of matted hair, adorned with the crescent moon,
is treated in a most unusual fashion, and contributes in a
very large measure to the imperious bearing of the dancing
god. Indeed, some Naṭarājas are impressive for their size,
others for their grace, still others for their liveliness; but few
are characterized by such compelling majesty as this example.

13

The Bodhisattva Maitreya
India (Bihār), 11th century
Gray sandstone
h: 33 in. (83.8 cm.)
Formerly the Nasli and Alice Heeramaneck Collection
Museum Associates Purchase, 1969
M.69.13.7

Maitreya is the Buddha of the future whose arrival on
earth is still awaited by pious Buddhists. In Buddhist art,
therefore, he is represented at times as a Buddha and
at others, as in this instance, as a Bodhisattva. A Bodhisattva
is a compassionate being who is ready to achieve his own
nirvāṇa, but has postponed it in order to save less fortunate
sentient beings.

Regally ornamented, yet sporting the chignon of an
ascetic, the svelte and elegant figure of Maitreya is seated
on a lotus in a relaxed manner. A smaller lotus flower is
provided at an unnatural angle to support his right foot. His
principal emblem is the *nāgakeśara* flower held by his left
hand. Almost hidden in this flower is a small water pot which
is said to contain the elixir of life. Inset in his matted hair
is a tiny *stūpa* which symbolizes the religion *(dharma)*
he will preach.

In the beatific expression of the figure the unknown
artist has captured the Bodhisattva's basic quality of
compassion. Atypically, he has completely cut away the stone
immediately behind the figure. This not only adds to the
sense of volume, but emphasizes the rhythmic flow of the
outline. The proportions are idealized, and yet typical
of Indian sculpture, the form is imbued with a sensuous
grace that seems to echo the pliancy of the flower he holds.

A companion piece representing the Bodhisattva
Avalokiteśvara is in the Museum of Fine Arts, Boston (see
J. Fontein and P. Pal, *Museum of Fine Arts, Boston:
Oriental Art,* Boston, 1969, pl. 127).

14

Krishṇa Rājamannār
South India (Tamilnadu), 12th century
Bronze
Krishṇa—h: 34 in. (86.4 cm.)
Rukmiṇī—h: 27 in. (68.6 cm.)
Satyabhāmā—h: 28 in. (71.1 cm.)
Garuḍa—h: 19¼ in. (48.9 cm.)
Gift of Mr. and Mrs. Hal B. Wallis, 1970
M.70.69.1-4

Collection: Belmont Collection, Basel, Switzerland

Literature: P. Pal, *Krishṇa: The Cowherd King,* Los Angeles
County Museum of Art, Monograph Series, No. 1, 1972

In his human aspect of Rājamannār, leader of the
people, the divine Krishṇa is portrayed as a regal personage,
accompanied by his two wives and his avian mount.

Krishna's majesty is emphasized by his graceful stance and his elaborate jewels and ornaments. His high crown, interlaced with precious jewels, further indicates his royal character. To his right stands his principal wife, Rukmiṇī, slim and elegant, while his more sumptuous consort, Satyabhāmā, occupies the position to his left and is the recipient of his gentle touch. The fourth figure of this group is the celestial bird, Garuḍa, who serves as Krishna's mount. He stands in humble adoration with his hands clasped in worship.

Although each of the principal figures, except Garuḍa, reflects a standard of beauty that is essentially humanized, the figures conform to a conceptual ideal, following the general Indian practice. There is no attempt to delineate idiosyncratic human musculature. Rather, the physical structure is one of unmitigated smoothness with none of the imperfections of a mortal corpus. The unknown sculptor of this group could hardly have displayed a better sense of composition or proportion, whether in the individual figures or in the group as a whole.

15

Bichitr
Indian, active early and mid-17th century
Shah Shuja Enthroned with Gaj Singh of Marwar
Mughal style, ca. 1633
Opaque watercolors and gold on paper
9⅞ x 7¼ in. (25.2 x 18.5 cm.)
The Nasli and Alice Heeramaneck Collection, 1969
L.69.24.246

Exhibitions: New York, Asia House Gallery, *The Art of Mughal India,* 1964, no. 44, repr. in color in cat.; Boston, Museum of Fine Arts, *The Arts of India and Nepal: The Nasli and Alice Heeramaneck Collection,* Nov. 21, 1966-Jan. 8, 1967, no. 216, repr. in cat.; traveled to Los Angeles County Museum of Art, Feb. 8-Apr. 2, 1967; Detroit Institute of Arts, June 20-Aug. 6, 1967; Richmond, Virginia Museum of Fine Arts, Sept. 18-Oct. 14, 1967; Toronto, Royal Ontario Museum, Jan. 23-Mar. 10, 1968; Los Angeles County Museum of Art, *The Art of India, Nepal and Tibet: The Nasli and Alice Heeramaneck Collection,* Sept. 24-Nov. 15, 1970

Shah Shuja, born in 1616, was the second son of the fifth Mughal emperor, Shah Jahan. In 1633, Shah Shuja was made the governor of the Deccan so that he might aid the emperor in his military campaigns in that area. When he arrived in the Deccan the Mughal army was being led by Raja Gaj Singh, the ruler of Marwar (later known as Jodhpur). The scene depicted in this painting, probably commissioned by the Mughal prince himself, commemorates the formal meeting of the Mughal viceroy and the general, probably soon after Shuja's arrival in the Deccan and before Gaj Singh's return to Delhi. The gentlemen sit in Indian

fashion on a lavish throne of embossed gold set upon a floral carpet. Gaj Singh is about to accept a *pān* (betel nuts wrapped in leaves) from the Imperial Prince as a gesture of his amicable intentions for their meeting. The imperial grandeur of the occasion is further emphasized by the two angels who hold a canopy above. Interestingly, the canopy shows designs that are more Persian than Indian.

Bichitr was one of the most prominent members of the court atelier under the emperors Jahangir, Shah Jahan, and Aurangzeb. He is particularly noted for his excellence in portraiture, expressed here with almost photographic realism. His fascination with pigment textures also seems to have been a characteristic of his as is evident in the jewelry and turban ornaments of the two nobles depicted in this painting.

16

Part of a Hanging or Curtain
India (Gujarat), early 17th century
Satin, with weft-patterned figures and
warp-patterned stripes, silk
67¾ x 43⅝ in. (172.1 x 110.8 cm.)
The Nasli and Alice Heeramaneck Collection, 1969
L.69.24.344

Exhibitions: New York, Museum of Modern Art, *Textiles and Ornaments of India,* 1956, detail p. 55; Boston, Museum of Fine Arts, *The Arts of India and Nepal: The Nasli and Alice Heeramaneck Collection,* Nov. 21, 1966-Jan. 8, 1967; traveled to Los Angeles County Museum of Art, Feb. 8-Apr. 2, 1967; Detroit Institute of Arts, June 20-Aug. 6, 1967; Richmond, Virginia Museum of Fine Arts, Sept. 18-Oct. 14, 1967, no. 262 (detail), repr. in cat., p. 177

Almost no textiles that date from before the early seventeenth century have survived in India, though there are countless literary references to a silk textile tradition of scope and quality dating back to the fourth to third century B.C. This example is therefore an important link as it is one of the few surviving examples of a textile in the Indian court tradition, scarcely touched by the influence of the Mughals.

Under the Mughal emperors, *kārkhānās* or workshops were established as suppliers to the royal courts. Many of these were established in traditional weaving centers, as Ahmadabad in Gujarat. The earliest reference to weaving in Gujarat comes from an inscription dated A.D. 473 (Mandasor, central India); it records that members of a silk weavers guild had built and restored a sun temple there. It is possible that the Gujarat weavers had seen Sassanian textiles, and that weavers from Sassanian workshops were part of the migrations that took place to western India during the beginning of the Christian era. The affronté deer under the tree with birds in this hanging seem to continue a theme popular in Sassanian fabrics, as do the eight-petaled lotus flowers enclosed in the roundels that make up the border.

The Āīn-i-Ākbarī, a chronicle on the reign of Akbar, mentions Ahmadabad as particularly famous for the weaving of silks, including brocades and velvets. Akbar conquered the city in 1572, and probably established an imperial workshop there sometime afterward; however, it is likely that it took some time to achieve the level of excellence represented by this textile. The costume worn by the figures in the fragment gives more specific evidence for the dating of this piece. Both the four-pointed *chakdār jāmah* (coat) and the flat form of the *atpati pagrī* (turban) are frequently seen in paintings of the Akbar period, and could be placed at the beginning of the seventeenth century, though some time might be added since Ahmadabad was a provincial capital.

The sumptuous Safavid style with its languidly elegant figures and graceful floral motifs was to supplant this earlier, more forceful Indian style. The powerful treatment of the swordsman and the mounted horseman are distinctly a part of the strong visual folk tradition of Gujarat which is apparent in both their wood carvings and embroideries. Colors are both simple and direct: red (madder), yellow (tumeric), and white (natural silk color). Combined with the horizontal arrangement of the design, they emphasize the two-dimensionality of the textile. This style connects it with both the mainstream of miniature painting in western India and with the tradition of resist-dyed textiles produced in this area for centuries. Many of these resist fabrics have been preserved in graves in Egypt. As yet there is no definite dating of the resist prints, but many examples are presumed to date to the fifteenth century and were made in Gujarat to be exported in bulk rather than as luxury fabrics. The resemblance of this silk textile to the simple cotton resist fabrics lies in its clear linear design—a result of applying the resist to the fabric before the dyeing. This method also makes the design appear to be cut out of the background.

17

Fragment of a Dress or Furnishing Fabric
India (Mughal), mid-17th century
Voided cut velvet, silk and gilt threads
72 x 21-23 in. (182.9 x 53.3-58.4 cm.)
Costume Council Fund, 1971
M.71.13

Exhibition: Los Angeles County Museum of Art, *Fabric and Fashion,* May 14-Oct. 16, 1974, no. 14, repr. in cat.

Literature: M. Kahlenberg, "A Mughal Personage Velvet in the Los Angeles County Museum of Art Collection," *The Burlington Magazine,* no. 848, vol. CXV, Nov. 1973, pp. 722-727

Of all fabrics, velvet is the one most synonymous with luxury. Woven with a pile, velvet is a three-dimensional

fabric. A distinct characteristic of Islamic velvets is the use of the pile for the design and a gold or metallic flat weave for the background. The two different types of weave contrast and emphasize each other: the pile or velvet area absorbs the light in a variety of rich and subtle color changes and the metallic area reflects the light to produce a shimmering effect.

Most personage-figured velvets have been automatically attributed to Persia because Persian tradition is more widely known and better preserved. There are indications, however, that some of these velvets were actually produced in India for the Mughal court. Such pieces obviously carry on the grand Persian velvet-weaving tradition of the Safavid period in both technique and design.

Visual and written sources give us information about seventeenth-century Indian velvets. Paintings not only show precise renderings of patterns and figural decoration but also the uses of textiles as horse trappings, pillows, coats, canopy covers, and court standards. These accurate representations of the velvets give evidence of the fact that velvets used at the Mughal court came from every area of the world where velvets were produced. The *Āīn-i-Ākbarī* confirms this with a list of places that provided gold brocaded and plain velvets for Akbar's court in the late sixteenth century. At that time gold velvets came from Yazd in Persia, Europe (described as Firangi), Bursa in Turkey, and Gujarat and Lahore in India. The inclusion of these last two names indicates that although the Mughal court imported velvets from great distances, they were also produced in their own court workshops. It is clear, however, that Mughal ostentation required the widest range of costly fabrics, and the court resources were devoted to obtaining them from every possible source in a calculated attempt to create the maximum impression of power and wealth.

In this velvet from the Textiles and Costumes collection, gracefully swaying figures accompanied by a playful dog are set against a garden background. The design appears to have drawn its elements from two other personage velvets which are distinctly Persian. One velvet from the first half of the seventeenth century shows silver-tuniced male figures enjoying the scent of a flower while pondering a cypress tree growing alongside a pond.

A second velvet shows ladies swaying in rhythmic pairs in the midst of a floral landscape. The Los Angeles piece shows the same design format as these two velvets: paired female figures in a garden setting of cypress trees and flowers which spring from central ponds. A distinct difference, however, is in the less sensuous curves of the overall patterns made by the figures and the drawing of the heads. The turned heads are handled in full profile, as they are in many Indian paintings, and the eyes are characteristically depicted from an almost frontal view, in a manner particularly reminiscent of the Golconda style. The 1649 war between India and Persia followed by a cessation of diplomatic contact for the next ten years may well have prevented temporarily the import of fine Persian fabrics. While Shah Jahan may have ordered velvets woven at his own workshop in this interim period, such a venture might not have proven to be a complete success. Though weavers could be found with a mastery of the technique, the languid elegance of the Persian style was unnatural to most Indian draftsmen.

18

Krishna and Rukmiṇī Riding a Celestial Chariot
India (Rajput style, Bundi school), ca. 1675
Opaque watercolors on paper
11¼ x 9 in. (28.6 x 22.8 cm.)
Gift of Edwin Binney, 3rd, 1974
M.74.13

The passengers in this celestial chariot are Krishṇa and his wife Rukmiṇī, whose elaborate attire and particular headdresses suggest that they have just come from their wedding ceremony. Behind them stands a maidservant with a flywhisk, and before them Gaṇeśa, the elephant-headed god of auspiciousness, as divine charioteer.

In the seventeenth century Bundi was a semi-independent Rajput state with ties to the Mughal rulers in Delhi. Emulating their imperial overlords, the Bundi rulers became patrons of painting. As a result, an active school developed which derived its subdued, subtle palette and shaded modeling from Mughal models. In contrast to most Rajput painting which was restricted to traditional themes, the Bundi artist occasionally departed into unusual dramatic subject matter or composition, as in this painting. The royal chariot appears to float miraculously against the flat blue background, producing a curiously surreal effect.

19

Tathāgata Ratnasambhava and Acolytes
Nepal, 12th century
Opaque watercolors on cloth
16⅛ x 13 in. (41.0 x 33.0 cm.)
The Nasli and Alice Heeramaneck Collection, 1969
L.69.24.294

Exhibition: Los Angeles County Museum of Art,
The Art of India, Nepal and Tibet: The Nasli and Alice Heeramaneck Collection, Sept. 24-Nov. 15, 1970

Literature: *Archives of Asian Art,* vol. XXVI, 1972-73, repr. p. 72

The Tathāgata Ratnasambhava, dressed as a prince complete with jewels and a crown rather than in the usual monk's robe, is seated in the center of this delicately rendered painting. Ratnasambhava is designated as the Buddha of the south; his color is yellow and his right hand is in *varada mudrā,* the gesture of bestowing gifts.

Also associated with Ratnasambhava are the jewel, which he holds in his left hand, and his vehicle, the horse, which can be seen in a double representation at the base of the throne.

Flanking the Buddha are two attendant Bodhisattvas—Mañjuśrī on his right carrying the manuscript atop the lotus, and Avalokiteśvara on his left carrying the open lotus. Six other Bodhisattvas are placed on either side of the elaborate throne, suggesting that the painting was originally made for a particular sect of Buddhism that favored the worship of the Eight Bodhisattvas. At the top is a panel of eight seated Buddhas, dressed in monks' robes, while at the base is a row of four female and three male deities.

Originally forming one of a set of five or eight paintings, a companion to it is now in the Museum of Fine Arts in Boston. Perhaps the earliest group of such religious paintings from Nepal, these works are distinguished both by their sparkling, vibrant colors and exquisitely rendered details. The workmanship is jewellike and the colors have been applied with a view to achieving dramatic contrast.

20

Sambara and Vajravārāhī
Nepal, ca. 1500
Opaque watercolors on cotton
54 x 45 in. (137.1 x 114.2 cm.)
Formerly the Nasli and Alice Heeramaneck Collection
Museum Associates Purchase, 1970
M.70.1.3

Remarkably well preserved for a work over four-and-a-half centuries old, this is one of the largest known paintings to have survived in Nepal. It portrays the esoteric Buddhist deities Sambara and Vajravārāhī engaged in copulation against a sea of leaping tongues of flame representing the fiery field of wisdom. This union is regarded as the symbol of ultimate bliss and the non-duality of divine nature. The dark figure of Sambara is given multiple heads and arms which are symmetrically disposed to create a harmonious visual pattern. His many weapons are appropriate to his wrathful nature, for he is ever alert to destroy the evil that lurks in the human heart as well as in the universe. His red partner brandishes a chopper in her right hand and embraces her lord with passionate abandon. The fiery field is surrounded by eight cemeteries symbolizing the phenomenal world. Each cemetery is distinguished by a narrow band of water and is peopled with corpses, funeral pyres, scavenging animals, ghosts, and goblins as well as gods and humans.

This painting is remarkable for both the harmony of its composition and the richness of its colors. Each area is characterized by intense activity; yet the total expression is one of innate calm. The painting is a tour de force as much for its abstract visual design as for its sensuously delineated details.

21

A Tathāgata Surrounded by Bodhisattvas
Tibet, 13th century
Opaque watercolors on linen
102 x 59 in. (245.1 x 149.8 cm.)
The Nasli and Alice Heeramaneck Collection, 1969
L.69.24.281

Exhibitions: Boston, Museum of Fine Arts, *The Arts of India and Nepal: The Nasli and Alice Heeramaneck Collection,* Nov. 21, 1966-Jan. 8, 1967, no. 121, repr. in color in cat.; traveled to Los Angeles County Museum of Art, Feb. 8-Apr. 2, 1967; Detroit Institute of Arts, June 20-Aug. 6, 1967; Richmond, Virginia Museum of Fine Arts, Sept. 18-Oct. 14, 1967; Toronto, Royal Ontario Museum, Jan. 23-Mar. 10, 1968; New York, Asia House Gallery, *The Art of Tibet,* Apr. 10-June 8, 1969, no. 1, repr. in cat.; traveled to Washington, D.C., National Collection of Fine Arts, July 3-Sept. 1, 1969, and Seattle Art Museum, Oct. 2-Nov. 16, 1969; Los Angeles County Museum of Art, *The Art of India, Nepal and Tibet: The Nasli and Alice Heeramaneck Collection,* Sept. 24-Nov. 15, 1970

Occupying the major portion of this painting is a Tathāgata, or Buddha, of green complexion, seated in meditation and holding a vase. He is surrounded by a number of Bodhisattvas, principally Maitreya and Avalokiteśvara who flank him, while above are eight other Bodhisattvas and two monks. At the base of the painting are five figures; three placid Bodhisattvas and the fierce protectors of the faith, Mahākāla and Vajrapāṇi. The vase is usually associated with Amitābha, the Buddha of endless light, but his complexion is generally red. Because this figure is green, he may therefore be identified with the healing Buddha.

This tankā is one of the most monumental as well as one of the earliest examples of Tibetan painting, and shows strong influences both of the Indo-Nepali and central Asian traditions. Usually such large tankās were rolled for storage in monasteries and brought out to be hung on exterior walls for public worship on festive occasions. Indeed, the somewhat earlier Nepali painting (see no. 19), or one like it, may well have served as a stylistic forbear. Despite its monumental composition, details are rendered with incredible precision and care. Because the work is primarily a religious icon, the composition is governed by strict laws of symmetry as geometrical perfection in Tibetan religion is essentially associated with cosmic order.

22

Arhat Vajrīputra in Landscape
Tibet, 14th century
Opaque watercolors on cotton
25½ x 21¼ in. (64.8 x 54 cm.)
The Nasli and Alice Heeramaneck Collection, 1969
L.69.24.187

Exhibitions: Boston, Museum of Fine Arts, *The Arts of India and Nepal: The Nasli and Alice Heeramaneck Collection,* Nov. 21, 1966-Jan. 8, 1967, no. 1, repr. on cover and p. 24 of cat.; traveled to Los Angeles County Museum of Art, Feb. 8-Apr. 2, 1967; Detroit Institute of Arts, June 20-Aug. 6, 1967; Richmond, Virginia Museum of Fine Arts, Sept. 18-Oct. 14, 1967; Toronto, Royal Ontario Museum, Jan. 23-Mar. 10, 1968; New York, Asia House Gallery, *The Art of Tibet,* Apr. 10-June 8, 1969; repr. frontispiece and p. 132 of cat.; traveled to Washington, D.C., National Collection of Fine Arts, July 3-Sept. 1, 1969, and Seattle Art Museum, Oct. 2-Nov. 16, 1969; Los Angeles County Museum of Art, *The Art of India, Nepal and Tibet: The Nasli and Alice Heeramaneck Collection,* Sept. 24-Nov. 15, 1970

Literature: M. W. Meister, "The Arts of India and Nepal," *Oriental Art,* n.s. XIV, 2 (1968), p. 109; P.Pal, "The Art of Tibet," *The Connoisseur,* May 1969, vol. 171, no. 687, p. 48

Vajrīputra (Tibetan: *rDorje moi bu*) is an *arhat,* or Buddhist saint, and may actually have been a historical figure, though the only information available about him is that he was the son of King Jatrayana and Queen Vajrī of Kauśāmbī. He is one of a group of eighteen *arhats* or *Lohans* who were especially venerated both in China and Tibet. The depiction is idealized rather than realistic and the *arhat* is represented in a landscape.

The landscape elements in this work are undoubtedly derived from Chinese paintings. But unlike the academic landscape paintings of China in which nature predominates, here the figures retain primary significance, following the Indian Buddhist tradition.

The mountains, flowers, trees, and clouds are added to enhance the decorative and symbolic function of the painting rather than as a response to the sensuous appeal of nature. This is also apparent in the expressionistic use of reds, greens, and blues which not only reveals the artist's predilection for bright, rich surfaces, but also imbues the work with unusual warmth.

23

Portrait of an Abbot
Tibet, 15th century
Gilt bronze
h: 11¼ in. (28.6 cm.)
Promised gift of Christian Humann

Apart from the gods and goddesses, the Tibetan pantheon—and hence the artist's repertoire—was considerably enriched by the inclusion of apotheosized monks. Important monks, known as *lamas* in Tibet, were regarded as reincarnations of earlier religious figures as well as of gods. The proclivity for representing such historical figures can be considered a distinguishing feature of the Tibetan aesthetic tradition. In fact, neither in Chinese nor in Indian Buddhist art do we find such a strong impulse to portray and perpetuate the likenesses of important teachers.

Most such portraits were executed posthumously as memorial images. There can be no doubt, however, that the artists studied their models from life, especially as far as the facial features were concerned. In this portrait the physiognomical features have been rendered with unusual sensitivity, and the personality of the abbot is expressed with remarkable forcefulness. At the same time, however, his posture and the gesture of his hands follow the Indian tradition of idealistic portraiture and are symbolic of a yogī and a teacher. Especially masterful is the delineation of the garments. Such naturalistic depiction of the folds as well as the volume of the garment is not only unusual, but also makes the portrait remarkably animated despite the hieratic posture.

24

Bowl with Flaring Sides and Ring Foot
Persia (Nishapur), 10th century
Ceramic
h: 3¼ in. (8.3 cm.); d: 9 in. (22.8 cm.)
The Nasli M. Heeramaneck Collection
Gift of Joan Palevsky, 1973
M.73.5.203

Exhibition: Los Angeles County Museum of Art,
Islamic Art: The Nasli M. Heeramaneck Collection,
Dec. 17, 1973-Mar. 3, 1974, no. 16, repr. in cat.

This striking Nishapur bowl is exemplary of the slip-painted wares produced at this major ceramic center in northeastern Persia under the Samanid dynasty (847-999). Unlike the fine-grained red clay employed by the contemporaneous Samarkand potters, a fine-grained buff earthenware was used in the formation of Nishapur ceramics. While the wares of Samarkand more commonly incorporated simulated bands of Kufic script into their decoration, those of Nishapur typically display, as in this bowl, primitively rendered figural and animal motifs outlined in manganese purple and highlighted with yellow, rust brown, and green pigments under a transparent lead glaze.

The obverse of this bowl, painted in a colorless slip, features an imperious figure holding a blossoming bough in one hand and a beaker from which he is about to drink in the other. Two birds perch on the figure's long tresses which fall to either side. The herringbone pattern of the figure's garment, the additional asterisk forms and the unidentifiable animal and vegetable motifs which fill the remaining surface area illustrate the *horror vacui* that is typical of Nishapur slip-painted pottery. While the figure, animal, and foliate forms are outlined in a rich black, the overall composition is strikingly highlighted by abstract washes of green and yellow.

The forms depicted on the obverse of this bowl are characteristically shown as composites of several viewpoints, each of which reveals the object represented in its most recognizable form. The physical features of the figure, for example, are shown either frontally, as are the single eye, the shoulders, and the upper torso, or in profile, as are the head, hips, and feet. Similarly, the birds are drawn in profile, while one eye is represented frontally. Even the stool combines an aerial view of its top and a side view of its legs.

The reverse of this bowl, as opposed to the figural decoration on the obverse, displays a systematic alternation of vertical bands of yellow or green with bands of calligraphic spirals.

25

Bracelet
Persia, 10th-11th century
Gold
h: 2 in. (5.1 cm.); d: 5 in. (12.7 cm.)
The Nasli M. Heeramaneck Collection
Gift of Joan Palevsky, 1973
M.73.5.371

Exhibition: Los Angeles County Museum of Art,
Islamic Art: The Nasli M. Heeramaneck Collection,
Dec. 17, 1973-Mar. 3, 1974, no. 275, repr. in color in cat.

This hand-tooled gold bracelet, almost identical to the one in The Metropolitan Museum of Art, represents a major development in the history of Islamic jewelry. Although relying strongly upon the established bird and cone motifs as they were used in the pre-Islamic Near East, the Islamic artisan brought new freshness to their interpretation in jewelry design. The bracelet itself is comprised of two semi-circular gold plaques, attached on one side by a hinge and secured at the other with a pin crowned by a rosette. On its outer surface are displayed alternating rows of cone shapes fashioned from twisted wire and three-dimensional birds highlighted by repoussé detail. Like the Metropolitan bracelet, the Los Angeles one displays rows of four birds with alternating rows of three cones, a total of twelve rows of each motif. The disposition of each of these rows on the bracelet's upper section is a mirror image of that on the lower one, so that the birds on the upper plaque face in the reverse direction of those on the lower. Thus, the birds are symmetrically arranged, all facing the direction of the clasp. At the hinge two rows of cones appear without an alternate row of birds; and at the clasp two rows of birds confront each other without an alternate row of cones.

So similar is this bracelet to that of the Metropolitan in the arrangement and treatment of the motifs, that one might conclude that both were created by the same atelier, if not by the same artist. It is certain that because of their sumptuous quality and exquisite craftsmanship, they both must have been designed for royal patrons.

26

Mihrab
Persia (Kashan), 1200-1225
Ceramic
40½ x 46⅞ in. (102.9 x 119.0 cm.)
The Nasli M. Heeramaneck Collection
Gift of Joan Palevsky, 1973
M.73.5.1

Collection: Kevorkian Foundation, New York

Exhibition: Los Angeles County Museum of Art,
Islamic Art: The Nasli M. Heeramaneck Collection,
Dec. 17, 1973-Mar. 3, 1974, no. 70, repr. in cat.

Originally part of a *mihrab* (prayer niche), this tile would have been placed on the side of a mosque wall which faces the holy Muslim city of Mecca. It has been suggested that the origins of the *mihrab* are traceable to earlier apse forms of Roman and early Christian basilicas.

Kashan craftsmen are particularly noted for their work in ceramics and especially for their luster tiles on which they use two types of glazes. First the tiles are painted in turquoise and blue under-glaze, then the tile is over-glazed in a brownish gold luster.

The central portion of the Los Angeles *mihrab* is recessed and adorned with a bold arabesque executed in low relief, while the background is filled with spirals, blossoms, and branches. A wide band of inscription from the *Koran* serves as a border to this central area.

27

Folio from a Shah Nama Manuscript:
Isfandiyar Attacks the Simurgh
Persia (Shiraz), ca. 1490
Opaque watercolors on paper
8⅞ x 6 in. (22.5 x 15.2 cm.)
The Nasli M. Heeramaneck Collection
Gift of Joan Palevsky, 1973
M.73.5.410

Exhibition: Los Angeles County Museum of Art,
Islamic Art: The Nasli M. Heeramaneck Collection,
Dec. 17, 1973-Mar. 3, 1974, no. 197a, repr. in cat.

Isfandiyar, the son of the Persian King Gushtasp, is one of the heroes in the *Shah Nama* (Book of Kings), the tenth-century Persian epic written by the poet Firdousi. Isfandiyar's principal feat was the rescue of his sister who had been confined in the Brazen Hold. To achieve this feat

Isfandiyar had to accomplish seven tasks that required extraordinary strength and cunning. One of these was to kill the great mythical phoenix, the *simurgh*. This miniature depicts Isfandiyar slashing his sword at the *simurgh's* wing from which blood is flowing. The Persian warrior has devised an armored box to protect himself from the ferocious bird.

Persian painting is primarily typified by book illustrations such as this *Folio from a Shah Nama*. Despite their relatively small scale, such manuscript paintings typically achieve a striking monumentality through the use of complex compositional and coloristic effects. Noteworthy also is the effective fusion of both stylized and naturalistic techniques which produces an overall decorative pattern.

28

Dish with Lobed Rim and Flaring Body
Turkey (Isnik), 1550-1560
Ceramic
h: 2¾ in. (7.0 cm.); d: 13⅜ in. (34.0 cm.)
The Nasli M. Heeramaneck Collection
Gift of Joan Palevsky, 1973
M.73.5.381

Exhibition: Los Angeles County Museum of Art,
Islamic Art: The Nasli M. Heeramaneck Collection,
Dec. 17, 1973-Mar. 3, 1974, no. 128, repr. in color in cat.

This Isnik dish represents the second phase of the ceramic tradition under the patronage of the Ottoman Turks. Unlike the earlier blue and white porcelains which were closely fashioned after Chinese Ming models, this phase of Isnik ceramic production typically displays a wider palette of brilliant colors—cobalt blue, bolus red, copper green, turquoise, and black—on a white slip ground. Although yet dependent upon Chinese motifs, as is evidenced in the lobed rim and the cloud-scroll pattern, the general style of this plate is typical of later Ottoman taste. The three peonies arranged around two interlocking tulips reflect a basic symmetry, but because of the spiraling effect of the stem supporting two of them, the overall design becomes both asymmetrical and wind blown. The boldness of this design is further enhanced by the effective use of strikingly vibrant enamel glazes which have been applied to this floriate composition. The featherlike treatment of both the stems and the tulip blossoms creates an elegant, curvilinear composition that is well suited to the shape of the dish. Decoration, however, is not solely restricted to the obverse of the dish. Even the reverse displays on its slightly flaring body a row of five abstract blossoms which alternate with groupings of three tulips.

29

Folio from a Shah Nama Manuscript:
Firdousi in a Bathhouse Receiving Wages
for Having Written the Shah Nama
Persia (Shiraz), 1550-1575
Opaque watercolors on paper
17¼ x 11¼ in. (43.7 x 28.5 cm.)
The Nasli M. Heeramaneck Collection
Gift of Joan Palevsky, 1973
M.73.5.591

Exhibition: Los Angeles County Museum of Art,
Islamic Art: The Nasli M. Heeramaneck Collection,
Dec. 17, 1973-Mar. 3, 1974, no. 207, repr. in cat., p. 122

Islamic painting was primarily a court art produced by
the royal ateliers for the aesthetic fulfillment of their patrons.
One of the most popular histories to be illuminated was
that of the *Shah Nama* (Book of Kings), written for Sultan
Mahmud (986-1030) by the court poet Firdousi.
This epic recounts the mythical adventures of the legendary
rulers of Persia.

This isolated folio depicts a particularly frustrating
episode from the life of Firdousi—his payment by the sultan
for having written the epic. After having received the
commission from Sultan Mahmud to compose this history
of the Persian kings, Firdousi was unable to exact financial
compensation for his work. Periodically he would make
personal appeals to the sultan for the earnings due him.
The subject of this folio is one such appeal. To impress the
sultan with his acute financial need, Firdousi has followed
him to the bathhouse. The painting is in itself a remarkable
and detailed study of a sixteenth-century Turkish bathhouse. Such genre depictions are relatively uncommon in
Persian painting, which more typically concerns itself
with legendary and religious narratives.

30

Horizontal Tile
Turkey (Isnik), 1550-1600
Ceramic
29½ x 52¾ in. (75.0 x 134.0 cm.)
The Nasli M. Heeramaneck Collection
Gift of Joan Palevsky, 1973
M.73.5.6

Exhibition: Los Angeles County Museum of Art,
Islamic Art: The Nasli M. Heeramaneck Collection,
Dec. 17, 1973-Mar. 3, 1974, no. 124, repr. in cat.

The Isnik ceramic tradition, as exemplified by tiles
produced for the embellishment of religious structures,
achieved its greatest flowering under the patronage of
the Ottoman Turks. In contrast to the earlier decorative
tiles made by the Seljuks, which were either octagonal or
star-shaped, Ottoman tiles were generally square or

rectangular so that large-scale patterned panels could be
more easily designed. The actual tile designs typically
combine calligraphy with realistic flower and leaf motifs
painted in brilliant glazes—cobalt blue, copper green,
turquoise, bolus red, and white—over which a transparent
glaze was applied. While the more stylized floriate patterns
of red and blue have been relegated to the borders of this
tile, the bold white Thulth script is set off against an inner
blue rectangular region. Lightly punctuated with additional
floriate motifs similar to those of the border, this bold
calligraphic design is indicative of the Islamic artist's genius
in combining these two types of artistic motifs into a
unified overall composition.

The inscription on this tile has been translated as follows:
"This world is the bridge to the next," suggesting that
man's actions in this world will secure him a place in the
next. Hence, although essentially decorative, the tile
originally served a didactic purpose as well.

31

Flat-rimmed Dish with Narrow Foot
Persia (Kubachi ?), ca. 1600
Ceramic
h: 2½ in. (6.3 cm.); d: 13⅜ in. (34.0 cm.)
The Nasli M. Heeramaneck Collection
Gift of Joan Palevsky, 1973
M.73.5.244

Exhibition: Los Angeles County Museum of Art,
Islamic Art: The Nasli M. Heeramaneck Collection,
Dec. 17, 1973-Mar. 3, 1974, no. 115

This delicately delineated polychrome dish represents
a transitional phase in the development of "Kubachi"-style
ware that was produced under the Safavid dynasty
(1502-1736). Although a great number of plates and dishes
have been uncovered at Kubachi on the western bank of
the Caspian Sea, there is no concrete evidence to prove that
this site was responsible for the actual production of this
ware which bears its name. In fact, some scholars believe
this so-called Kubachi ware to have been exported from the
Tabriz region in northwestern Persia in exchange for
metalwork, a craft in which Kubachi artisans are known
to have excelled.

While the respective designs of the early and late
phases of Kubachi-style ware are predominantly either
figural or foliate, the composition enhancing the surface of
this transitional-style dish is an unusual fusion of the two.
The decoration, which appears in two of the three
concentric circles delineated, is painted in polychromatic
glazes under a thick transparent crackle glaze, the technique of which probably derives from Chinese celadons.
Within the central medallion of this dish two figures are
depicted walking from left to right in a landscape, as if
in procession. The figures themselves are represented in

profile, their hands outstretched, their faces featureless—an aspect which in itself is unusual. Because the bright cobalt of their kaftan-like robes and conical-shaped caps is the only solid expanse of any one color, it not only enhances the stability of this composition but also serves to accentuate the blue highlights which appear in the foliate design of the rim. By contrast, the landscape which serves as a background for these figures is painted in more subtle tones of mustard yellow, rust brown, and varying shades of green, thus permitting the figures to dominate the composition. The careful organization of the decorative scheme of this plate is further indicated by the undulating forms of the foliage which reiterate the S-curves of the figures, and again by the restraint exhibited in allowing the inner ring of the dish to remain plain, its only decoration being the crackle glaze itself.

32

Part of a Garment
Turkey (Bursa or Istanbul)
Second half 16th century-early 17th century
Compound satin with supplemental twill weave,
silk and gilt on a yellow silk core
53 x 30¾ in. (134.7 x 78.0 cm.), seamed in center
Gift of Edwin Binney, 3rd, 1974
M.74.6

Collection: Kelekian, New York

Exhibition: Philadelphia, *Persian Exhibition,*
Oct. 11-Nov. 25, 1926

Literature: *La Collection Kelekian, Etoffes et Tapis d'Orient et de Venise,* Paris, n.d., pl. 49, left

Bold designs and vivid color contrasts are the identifying marks of Turkish fabrics. In this example gold medallions on a red ground create the dynamic effect typically achieved with a limited color palette. A thin white double scallop outlines each medallion emphasizing the contrast between the two colors, and the juxtaposition of large and small elements reinforces this contrast. The ogival design is enriched by interior clusters of smaller, finely drawn ogives, each enclosing an arabesque, while intricate strapwork forms an interlacing among the medallions.

Few Turkish fabrics are known before the consolidation of the Ottoman Empire in the fifteenth century. The ogival design, however, is not new to the area, for it appears in Byzantine silks produced in Asia Minor, as well as in the Chinese damasks imported to the West in the thirteenth and fourteenth centuries. A design connection can also be made with versions produced in Mamluk Egypt. The ogival pattern begins to appear in decorative arts including textiles, ceramics, and tiles during the second quarter of the sixteenth century and in many more variations into the seventeenth century.

Commerce between Venice and the Ottoman Empire encouraged an exchange of designs, and in particular the development of the double ogival system into the pomegranate designs of the Italian Quattrocento. During the seventeenth century the detailed areas of the designs of this type were eliminated, leaving only the broad outline.

The textiles of the ogival style from the second half of the sixteenth century to the middle of the seventeenth form a stylistic group. Many are woven in what contemporary records refer to as *kemha,* a compound satin with supplemental twill weave. This technique, requiring a highly sophisticated loom, allowed the weaver to copy exactly the fine line drawings of patterns made for textiles as well as for other arts. Since there is little variation in the techniques employed in weaving silks, few places of manufacture have been positively identified. They all, however, are contained within a limited area. Bilajik, Adrianople, and Hereke all have weaving traditions extending back to the Byzantine period. Adrianople and Scutari, known also for their sericulture, produced most of the silk used in the Turkish fabrics. The broad flowing designs of the fabrics lend themselves to the voluminous kaftan robes that were constructed with a minimum of seams. They were also suited for covering the large pillows or "ottomans" which were a major component in Turkish domestic furnishings. Many examples found their way to the West where they were not as easily converted to the elaborately seamed garments. Western ecclesiastical garb of large unseamed shapes, however, were suitable means of display for these fabrics, and their use in this manner accounts for the preservation of many pieces known today. This piece is cut at the sides and bottom to the shape of a chasuble; the cut of neck, however, is far too deep and a slight indenture reveals what might at one time have been armholes. There seems to be no way to find its exact use, though very likely it was used twice, each time having the opportunity to display its powerful design qualities.

33

Cover
Persia, 1600-1650
Compound weave, twill ground, silk, gilt on a yellow silk core, silver on a white silk core
31 x 26½ in. (79.0 x 67.5 cm.)
The Nasli M. Heeramaneck Collection
Gift of Joan Palevsky, 1973
M.73.5.658

Exhibition: Los Angeles County Museum of Art, *Islamic Art: The Nasli M. Heeramaneck Collection,* Dec. 17,1973-Mar. 3, 1974, no. 443, repr. in cat., p. 208

Drawing on the centuries-old weaving traditions and techniques of Persia, the weavers of the Safavid dynasty produced fabrics unequaled at the time and still considered marvels of the craft. Under the patronage of Shāh Tahmāsp, Shāh 'Abbas, and subsequent Safavid rulers, textiles not only enjoyed unparalleled popularity, but weavers themselves were elevated to positions of prestige and status; a few even began to sign their works.

Floral patterns such as this have always been part of the Persian design tradition, and many of the floral motifs predominant in western textiles, such as the pomegranate, may have had their beginnings in Persia. While the floral forms have been subjected to a stylization characteristic of many of the arts of Islam, the grace and refinement of the design removes any rigidity that might be expected from such stylizing tendencies.

The dyes developed in the Safavid period were in a wide range of colors, with perhaps the greatest variety in shades of red and pink. The nuances of those shades found in this piece testify to the skill and sophistication Persian dyers brought to the art of textiles.

The main field of this cover imitates designs such as those used to decorate walls or *mihrabs* in mosques. The central motif is an eight-pointed star decorated by a large four-lobed flower with floral appendages which reach out to fill the points of the star. In tile design, these octagonal star-shapes were fitted together in such a way that the spaces between them formed a cross with pointed arms, just as they do in the cover.

34

Canopy
Persia, late 16th-early 17th century
Twill tapestry, silk and metallic threads
107 x 83 in. (272.2 x 210.8 cm.)
Costume Council Fund, 1971
M.71.52

Collections: Count Ludwek Tadeuse; Prince Czartorysky, Cracow

Literature: A. E. Pope and P. Ackerman, *A Survey of Persian Art,* 6 vol., London: Oxford University Press, 1967, vol. 6, figs. 1090, 1091

Ackerman describes this highly unusual tapestry as follows: "The first (of two sixteenth-century figural tapestries known) in the private collection of Prince Czartorysky of Cracow, translates into a complex but very light and fragile twill tapestry weave a large variety of themes from a book-decorator's repertoire: angels, birds, animals. Each motif is an elegantly drawn and painted decorative portrait of the subject, executed with the most exquisite detail of line and in minutely fragmented colours, yet sufficiently broadly treated withal to constitute a proper textile ornament. In the center is the Prince himself on his

takht, almost certainly Shāh Tahmāsp, and though rendered with painstaking finish, the figure conveys regal authority. Moreover, the whole composition is as effective at a distance as it is astonishing on close examination, presenting a mosaic of brilliant tones in sufficiently varied units to constitute a striking geometrical pattern."

The tapestry was most likely woven for use as a canopy, as both the perspective and mirrored images suggest that it is best seen from below. It was undoubtedly made in honor of the important personage though not necessarily Shāh Tahmāsp as suggested by Dr. Ackerman. This person pictured in the center star sits on a low, six-sided platform wearing a conical hat with a tassel and a narrow upturned brim. In one hand is a scarf, in the other an open book; before him is a tray with a wine bottle and two cups. The book suggests that he may be a poet or even a painter of book illustrations, or more likely a patron of both.

As in tiled decoration, the octagons alternate with cruciforms, and tiles of Kashan, an important tile production center in central Iran in the thirteenth and fourteenth centuries, may have influenced the design of this canopy. Kashan products were decorated with flowers, animals, personages—a large repertoire of motifs which continued as a tradition long after the decline of the Kashan workshops themselves in the fifteenth century. Kashan was also known to be a textile center, though little is known about the kinds of fabrics produced there.

The arrangement of the angels, often companions of deities or participants in apotheoses, making offerings to the central personage undoubtedly has iconographic meaning, as do the deer and the feline which exist in proximity yet do not engage in combat. The theme of the preying feline and the hunted deer is common in Persian art, particularly in this period when such struggles were frequently depicted as part of the design of a textile or carpet. Normally combatants, only rarely are they shown at peace with one another, as in this silk tapestry canopy.

35

Fragment of a Dress or Furnishing Fabric
Persia, second half 17th century
Brocaded compound twill, silk, silver
on a white silk core
59½ x 20½ in. (115.1 x 52.1 cm.)
The Nasli M. Heeramaneck Collection
Gift of Joan Palevsky, 1973
M.73.5.783

Exhibition: Los Angeles County Museum of Art, *Islamic Art: The Nasli M. Heeramaneck Collection,* Dec. 17, 1973-Mar. 3, 1974, no. 456, repr. in cat., p. 216

When the Safavid dynasty was founded in 1502, a tradition of high artistic and technical achievement had already existed in Persia since the Sassanian period

(224-642). Royal Safavid patronage of the arts began early in the dynasty, and the ensuing national renaissance coincided with a period of great luxury and elegance. The sumptuous Safavid silks required complicated weaving techniques, such as this brocaded compound twill, and also a considerable number of dyes that produced a wide spectrum of colors and shades. Because the Muslim faith theoretically prohibited artists from depicting the visual world, the Islamic artist tended to seek inspiration within himself rather than in natural phenomena. As a result his subjects became stylized as the choice of shape or color owed little to the laws of nature. In this textile the flowering vines have become arabesques; a variety of blossoms stem from the same vine; and birds and parakeets are arranged to carry out the rhythm of the repeat. Decorative intent rather than botanical accuracy has determined the design.

Floral motifs have long enjoyed an important place in the Persian textile tradition, though most frequently they are even less realistically interpreted than in this textile. The style of this fabric with its recognizable flowers and birds appeared during the second half of the seventeenth century. It has been hypothesized that the naturalistic floral motif developed in Persia as a result of the designs of Shafī 'Abbāsī whose plant drawings, obviously intended for use in textiles, were directly inspired by European herbals. Though Shafī 'Abbāsī's drawings are of a singular floral element rather than a flowering vine as in this example, the shape and color of the plants, and in particular the birds, are easily identified from his drawings. His plant designs date from 1640 to 1674, and from this time well into the eighteenth century, we find a selection of fabrics all using the theme of the flowering plant. Usually each plant holds a variety of blossoms, and there is a bird either beside it on the ground or perched within the plant itself. Though this fabric contains the same images as those attributed to Shafī 'Abbāsī it retains the arabesque style that is better known in the sixteenth and early seventeenth centuries.

36

Covered Ting (tripod cauldron)
Chinese (Late Chou dynasty), 1st quarter 5th century B.C.
Bronze
13½ x 15½ in. (34.2 x 39.3 cm.)
Gift of Mr. and Mrs. Eric Lidow, 1974
M.74.103

Collections: Yamanaka & Company, New York;
Mrs. Christian R. Holmes, New York;
Mr. and Mrs. Eric Lidow, Los Angeles

Exhibition: Los Angeles County Museum of Art (extended loan)

Literature: S. Umehara, *Shina-kodō Seikwa or Selected Relics of Ancient Chinese Bronzes from Collections in Europe and America,* Osaka: Yamanaka & Co., 1933, part I, vol. III, repr. pl. 179; idem, *Sengoku shiki dōki no kenkyū,* Kyoto: Tōhō-bunka-gakuin Kyōto kenkyūsho, 1936, Memoire, vol. 7, repr. pls. 30-33; S. Mizuno, *Bronzes and Jades of Ancient China,* Tokyo: The Nihon Keizai, 1959, repr. pl. 138; J. A. Pope, R. J. Gettens, J. Cahill, N. Barnard, *The Freer Chinese Bronzes,* Washington, D.C.: Smithsonian Institution, 1967, vol. I, p. 492; M. Loehr, *Ritual Vessels of Bronze Age China,* New York: The Asia Society, Inc., 1968, p. 144

Anarchy and constant warfare plagued the Eastern Chou period (770-256 B.C.); yet in the works of the Chou metalsmiths a combination of fertile artistic imagination and technical mastery produced bronzes that are still unequaled. Fine bronzes were prized objects, used in ceremonies to commemorate important events or to grace royal tombs; they also served as sumptuous gifts to visiting rulers, as valued rewards, or even as bribes.

With the perfecting of bronze casting techniques during Eastern Chou, the crude but vital designs of the preceding late Western Chou were refined. The hieratic and symbolic birds and animals of the earlier Shang and Western Chou periods became finely stylized or developed into linear, decorative abstractions. The old ritual vessels whose forms and designs were strictly governed by the requirements of ceremony were in part supplanted by objects created for pleasure and adornment. This secularization encouraged a new vitality in design and innovations in casting methods. Several artistic currents can be observed in Eastern Chou bronzes. On some pieces composite animal and human forms are sculpturally rendered with increasing naturalism, while others are embellished with a lively rococo pattern of curls and commas. In still others, typified by the Lidow *ting,* a geometric interlacery of zoomorphic elements covers the surface of the vessel.

The Lidow *ting,* or ceremonial cauldron, is an exemplary specimen of the Li-yü style of Eastern Chou which flourished during the decades around 500 B.C. In 1923 a cache of magnificent bronzes was discovered in Li-yü, a site in Northern Shansi province; more recent archaelogical excavations at Hou-ma-chen in Shansi have unearthed mold fragments with designs similar to the Los Angeles *ting* (Ref. *Wen Wu,* 1960, nos. 8-9, p. 9, fig. 9). This cauldron consists of several parts individually cast; the two handles and the three legs were made first and then attached to the body in casting. The lid, with its three loop handles, was produced in one piece.

Except for the bottom, the entire surface of the Lidow bronze is decorated with five horizontal bands of continuous interlacing forms. These occur in two types of zoomorphic patterns—one based on a ramlike head alternately set among intertwining elements and the other seemingly derived from birds and felines. The frieze of overlapping images, rendered in a flat two-layer relief which creates an illusion of layers, is a principal element of the Li-yü style. Arranged somewhat rectilinearly, the forms are rounded at the corners, and turn at right angles at all endings. Within these ribbon-like shapes are a rich variety of spirals, triangles, S-spirals, and striations, augmented by scales and pseudo-granulations which are framed by plain borders. On the three cabriolet legs appear traces of an inlaid design of a highly abstracted animal mask. On the top and sides of the handles are metallic inlay patterns in C-shaped curves and spirals. The rich surface patina is a smooth gray green with malachite formations under the lid.

37

Horse
China (T'ang dynasty), early 8th century
Buff-white earthenware with brown, green,
and straw-colored glazes
h: 29⅜ in. (75.1 cm.)
Gift of Nasli M. Heeramaneck, 1973
M.73.48.79

Collections: Yamanaka & Company, New York;
Alice and Nasli M. Heeramaneck, New York

Exhibition: Los Angeles County Museum of Art,
Chinese Ceramics: The Heeramaneck Collection,
Dec. 18, 1973-Mar. 3, 1974, p. 24, repr. in color on cat. cover

Literature: W. E. Cox, *The Book of Pottery and Porcelain,*
New York: Crown, 1956, vol. I, p. 112, repr. pl. 29

Although the practice of interring elaborate tomb furniture with the dead reached such proportions by the T'ang dynasty that proscriptions limiting their number and size were frequently announced, so many of these pieces have been excavated from T'ang tombs that one can hardly believe the sumptuary laws were strictly followed. Most were mass-produced stock figures but numerous ceramic sculptors of extraordinary ability created funerary figures which reveal perceptive observation and sensitive modeling.

The Heeramaneck horse, an example of T'ang mortuary art, is a marvel of observed naturalism in its well-balanced proportions and clarity of form. This monumental steed is richly caparisoned with a saddle and trappings adorned with palmette medallions of Iranian inspiration, attesting to the international character of the T'ang empire. The horse is made of fine white earthenware covered with brown, green, yellow, and cream glazes that are applied with great flair and imagination. The art of polychrome glazing called *san-ts'ai* was one of the major technical achievements of the T'ang potter. Copper, iron, or cobalt was mixed with a colorless lead-silicate glaze to produce a rich range of greens, browns, yellows, and blues. Recent archaeological excavations in China serve to date this horse to the early eighth century and possibly to the ceramic sculptors of Sian (T. C. Ma and C. L. Chang, "Brief report on the excavation of three T'ang tombs in the suburbs of Sian" [text in Chinese], *Kaogu,* 1958, no. I, pp. 42-52; Shensi Province Cultural Preservation Association, "T'ang Yung-t'ai kung-chu mu fa-chüeh Chien-hsi," *Wen Wu,* 1964, no. I, repr. pl. 4, nos. 3, 4; T'ang tombs excavation team, the Shensi Provincial Museum, "Brief report on the excavation of the tomb of Crown Prince Chang Huai of the T'ang" [text in Chinese], *Wen Wu,* 1972, no. 7, pp. 13-25; idem, "Brief report on the excavation of the tomb of Crown Prince I-te of the T'ang" [text in Chinese], ibid., pp. 26-31; M. Traeger, ed., "Neolithic Cultures to the T'ang Dynasty," *Arts of China,* vol. I, Tokyo & Palo Alto: Kodansha International, 1968, p. 155, repr. pl. 254).

38

Petal-Form Bowl
China (Northern Sung dynasty), 960-1126
Ting ware, porcelain with ivory tone glaze; unglazed rim
h: 2¼ in. (5.5 cm.); d: 7⅞ in. (20.2 cm.)
Gift of Nasli M. Heeramaneck, 1973
M.73.48.108

Collection: Alice and Nasli M. Heeramaneck, New York

Exhibition: Los Angeles County Museum of Art,
Chinese Ceramics: The Heeramaneck Collection,
Dec. 18, 1973-Mar. 3, 1974, no. 19, p. 28, repr. in cat., pl. 10

Ting ware, a refined and elegant white porcelain, is one of the classic imperial wares of Sung. There is literary evidence to indicate its use at court as early as the tenth century. The Ting-yao kilns were first discovered in 1941 by Fujio Koyama in Ch'u-yang hsien, Hopei Province, in an area which fell under the jurisdiction of Ting-chou during the Sung period. Since Koyama's investigation, further Chinese archaeological activity has confirmed Chien-ts'u-ts'un, Hung-t'u-nien, Pei chen, and East and West Yen-shan-ts'un, as important Ting sites in Ch'u-yang hsien. Production of Ting wares seems to have continued into the succeeding Chin dynasty (1115-1234) at Chien-ts'u-ts'un.

This bowl typifies the elegant simplicity of Northern Sung Ting ware. It is modeled with six curving sides marked by ribs and ending in a foliate rim defined by six notches. The shape is analogous to the opening of a flower and reflects the Sung interest in organic forms. It stands on a small low footring enclosing a glazed base. Ting wares were fired upside down, leaving an unglazed rim which was concealed by metallic bands of gold, silver, or bronze. Like most northern Chinese wares, Ting was fired in a level kiln with coal that produced an oxidizing flame resulting in a white ware notable for its smooth lustrous surface. On cooling, the fluid glazes often congeal into running "tear drops," which is diagnostically characteristic of Ting. The enduring fame and popularity of Ting wares derive from the classic simplicity of their shapes and the warm ivory tone of their glaze.

39

Tripod Incense Burner
China (Ming dynasty), early 15th century
Cloisonné enamels on bronze
h: 4½ in. (11.5 cm.); d: 5⅛ in. (13.0 cm.)
Gift of Taft and Rita Schreiber, 1973
M.73.95

Collection: Sir Harry Garner, Beckenham, England

In China the art of enameling was probably known as early as the first millennium A.D. but did not flourish until its reintroduction from the Islamic Near East or eastern Europe under the Mongol emperors of the Yüan dynasty (1280-1368). The earliest extant and clearly datable Chinese examples of cloisonné originate in the Hsüan-te period (1426-1435) with a number of inscribed pieces. Hsüan-te cloisonné represents the apogee of the Chinese enameler's art. Vessels were cast of bronze rather than shaped from thin sheets as in later centuries. Bronze cloison wires were laboriously hammered into fine thin strips which were soldered into position. These hammered wires have split in the course of time and serve to date and differentiate Ming cloisonné from Ch'ing examples in which the cloisons were copper wires extruded through dies. Hsüan-te cloisonné vessels were embellished with carefully composed designs that filled the whole field of decoration, but in later periods a neutral background filler, usually of spiral patterns, was widely used to fill the composition. The rather simple palette includes a brilliant lapis blue, turquoise blue, yellow, white, tomato red, and a blackish green. The characteristic Hsüan-te blue is a stunning deep color tinged with purple and does not occur again in the Ming period after the fifteenth century.

The Schreiber incense burner, an excellent example of Hsüan-te cloisonné, is one of the few existing in America. This tripod vessel may have once graced a Buddhist altar and its cast bronze body is decorated with a lotus scroll below a fret border (Fitzwilliam Museum, Cambridge, England, mate to Schreiber Tripod; repr. in R. S. Jenyns and W. Watson, *Chinese Art,* London: Oldbourne Press, 1963, pl. 75, and in H. Garner, *Chinese and Japanese Cloisonné Enamels,* London: Faber and Faber Ltd., 1962, pl. 17A). The floral motifs, analogous to those found on

imperial blue and white porcelain of the Hsüan-te reign, vary in their dominant colors from flower to flower against the turquoise blue background. Each foot is decorated with lotus scrolls and a gilt bronze boss of lotus leaves. The two side handles are inlaid with red, lapis blue, and blackish-green enamel executed in champlevé.

40

Large Covered Box with Floral Scrolls
Thailand (Sawankoloke), 14th-15th century
Stoneware painted with underglaze iron
h: 5½ in. (13.9 cm.); d: 7 in. (17.8 cm.)
Far Eastern Art Council Fund, 1972
M.72.39

Collection: Robert P. Griffing, Jr., Honolulu

Exhibition: Los Angeles County Museum of Art, *Ceramics of Southeast Asia,* Feb. 15-Apr. 30, 1972, repr. in cat. p. 7

Literature: G. Kuwayama, "Ceramics of Thailand," *Los Angeles County Museum of Art Bulletin,* Los Angeles: Los Angeles County Museum of Art, 1973, vol. XIX, no. 2, pp. 28-35, fig. 1

The ceramics of Thailand with their qualities of unaffected simplicity and spontaneity have aroused the interest of ceramic collectors in recent years. Thai wares have been preserved in kiln waster heaps or treasured through the centuries as ancestral heirlooms and temple relics. Large quantities of exported Thai ceramics remain in the graves of Indonesia and the Philippines as a result of the funerary practices of interring ceramic pieces with the dead.

Ceramics were produced in Thailand from neolithic times but the wares known as Sawankoloke are the most famous. They were made during the fourteenth and fifteenth centuries in Sri Sajjanalai, or Old Sawankoloke, reflecting strong influences from the Chinese potters of Tz'u-chou and Lung-ch'üan.

The shape of this unusually large, round Sawankoloke box and the knob on its cover was inspired by the fruit of the mangosteen. The stoneware body is covered with a gray slip and decorated with deftly drawn floral scrolls which meander in iron black designs beneath a clear glaze. A light blue color which occasionally occurs on Sawankoloke wares tinges the glaze on the cover. Sawankoloke ceramics are usually heavy-bodied stonewares with finely textured, well-levigated clay bodies, and fired on tall tubular pontils which leave a characteristic dark circular ring on the base.

41

Dish with Peonies in Relief
Korea (Koryŏ dynasty), 12th century
Celadon ware, grayish porcelain with gray green
celadon glaze
h: 1½ in. (4.0 cm.); d: 6⅞ in. (17.6 cm.)
Gift of Nasli M. Heeramaneck, 1973
M.73.48.117

Collections: Warren E. Cox, New York;
Alice and Nasli M. Heeramaneck, New York

Exhibition: Los Angeles County Museum of Art,
Chinese Ceramics: The Heeramaneck Collection,
Dec. 18, 1973-Mar. 3, 1974, no. 59, repr. in cat., pl. 19, p. 40

Literature: W. E. Cox, *The Book of Pottery and Porcelain,*
New York: Crown, 1956, repr. vol. I, p. 223, fig. 405

During the flourishing Koryŏ period (918-1392), new
developments in Korean ceramics were stimulated by
influences of the Yüeh potters of China. Contacts between
the two countries led to the establishment of celadon kilns in
Kangjin and Puan at the end of the tenth century, and
new forms and designs inspired by Chinese Sung wares
were produced for the court and for the Buddhist temples.

Korean celadons were usually fired in a reducing
atmosphere, resulting in a variety of greenish shades.
The most highly prized have a subtle gray green tone
produced by a thinly applied clear glaze which reveals the
gray body beneath.

This shallow bowl is supported by a low glazed footring.
At its base are three whitish spur marks produced by
clay kiln spurs when they were broken off after firing. The
mouth rim has six small notches and the outside surface
is decorated with six radial lines, creating an analogy
between the lobes of the bowl and the petals of a flower.
The form is thus integrated with the graceful peony design
engraved on the body. Fine combed lines within the
symmetrical outline of the flower reinforce a sense of
vegetal life. The single peony spray is a design inspired by
Chinese wares of the Northern Sung Dynasty and became
a dominant and enduring motif in Korean ceramics. Here
in its Koryŏ form it is given new vitality with a directness
and an austere refinement that is distinctly Korean.

42

Jizo Bosatsu
Japan (late Heian period), 12th century
Carved wood
h: 57⅝ in. (146.5 cm.)
Gift of Anna Bing Arnold, 1974

Collections: Ryo Hosomi, Saga, Japan; T. Yanagi, Kyoto

Literature: S. Mochizuki, ed., *Nihon Bukkyo Bijutsu Hiho,*
Tokyo: Sansaisha, 1973, p. 283, repr. pl. 75

The Heian period (784-1185) saw the importation of
Esoteric Buddhist culture from China into Japan. This
doctrine and its iconography brought radical changes in
Japanese Buddhist art.

The cult of Jizo Bosatsu was introduced into Japan in the
mid-eighth century. He was widely worshiped as a deity
concerned with the needs of suffering humanity and the
souls of the misguided who had been sent to Hell. As the
patron saint of children he acts as a guide to lead them
to piety. Usually depicted as a simple monk, Jizo has a
shaven head and no adornment except a jewel, carried in
the left hand, symbolizing his power to attain any
material or spiritual goal.

Noteworthy changes also took place in the materials
and techniques of sculpture during the Heian period.
Wood became the principal medium, and in the course of
four hundred years Japanese sculpture freed itself from
continental influences and culminated in the gentle, graceful
wa-yō ("Japanese style") established by the great sculptor
Jōchō in the eleventh century. The purely Japanese aesthetics
appears in the feeling for the intrinsic properties of the
wood and in the expressive use of the chisel that comes from
an organic understanding of the material. This virtuosity
is particularly apparent in the adroit carving of Jizo's
drapery which permits the play of light over the surface.

Jizo was a popular deity when this sculpture was made.
It is carved out of *kaya* wood in the *yosegi* technique
("joined wood blocks"), an important technical development of the Heian period. The head and body are
composed of front and rear halves, and are attached at the
neck. The hands and feet are later additions; the head and
body are original. The impressive mass and inner tension of
the full round torso and face impart a quality of elemental
strength and vitality to the sculpture.

43

Amida Buddha
Japan (Kamakura period), 1185-1334
Bronze with carved wood hands
h: 18¾ in. (47.6 cm.)
Promised gift of Mr. and Mrs. William T. Sesnon, Jr.

Collections: Ryo Hosomi, Saga, Japan; Harry Packard,
Tokyo: Mr. and Mrs. William T. Sesnon, Jr., Los Angeles

The cult of Amida Buddha became increasingly popular
during the Fujiwara period (897-1185) and flourished
in the Kamakura period (1185-1334). It provided an easier
path for salvation than the arduous metaphysics of Shingon
or the strict meditative practices of the Tendai sects.
Salvation by faith and the repetition of the name of Amida
became the key to his paradise.

One of the two main currents of Kamakura sculpture is
a dynamic realism typified by the vigorous naturalistic
work of Unkei. The other, of which this statue is an example,

relates to the *wa-yō* style created by Jōchō in the eleventh century. In the Sesnon Amida the modeling and the treatment of the drapery reflect the Fujiwara style, as does the hair rendered in traditional snail shell curls. This essentially Heian treatment is modified by the trend toward realism in the succeeding age and by elements of the Nara period revival which are particularly evident in the face. The drapery folds are unostentatious, fluid, and shallow, especially on the sleeves, and fall in rhythmic, symmetrical folds. The hand position, in *vitarka mudra,* symbolizes compassion and the offering of salvation.

Imperturbable with a benign smile and serene with downcast eyes, this Buddha epitomizes the compassion of Amidaism. This figure was most likely made in the Kyoto-Nara area, where the court style of the Fujiwara period never died. There are echoes of the late Heian style in the rather feminine quality of elegance and grace. The scarcity of bronze sculpture from this period and the fineness of execution of this Amida make it all the more exceptional.

44

Hishikawa Moronobu, attributed
Japanese, ca. 1625-1694
Pleasuring on the Sumida River, ca. 1690
Six-panel screen, ink, colors, and gold on paper
37⅝ x 96 in. (93.0 x 243.8 cm.)
Los Angeles County Funds, 1965
65.12

Collection: Hayato Ikeda, Tokyo

This screen, a rare example of early *Ukiyo-e* painting from the Genroku era (1688-1704), is attributed to Hishikawa Moronobu, one of the formative masters of this school. He was trained in the techniques of *Kano* and *Tosa* painting, and, after settling in Edo about 1660, he soon mastered the new medium of wood-block illustration. Moronobu consolidated the disparate stylistic tendencies of *Ukiyo-e* and set it on the course it was to follow for the next two centuries.

Executed with elegantly drawn lines and brilliant colors, *Pleasuring on the Sumida River* is a genre scene celebrating the amusements of city life. In this harmonious circular composition, several groups of people are engaged in a variety of activities at the Sumida River. Each group is unified by its own internal tension, yet relates to the others as well; this ability to integrate multiple figures into a composition is a quality that sets Moronobu apart from his imitators. The people are individualized in their poses and dress and are rendered with great animation. The artist imbues each of them with a sense of vitality that is concentrated particularly around the eyes. The women embody the idealized beauty emerging in the Edo period, with the imaginative treatment of the kimono patterns and delicacy of their poses. Moronobu's paintings bustle with activity

and vigor, revealing how the people of the period responded to the joys of city life. The focal point of the screen is a large boat whose occupants are engaged in conversation and games of *go.* This section is comparable to a similar Sumida River screen in the Freer Gallery that is also attributed to Moronobu (Freer Gallery of Art, Washington, D.C., Hishikawa Moronobu, *Autumn at Asakusa Temple, Cherry Blossoms at Ueno.* Reproduced in *Freer Gallery of Art: II, Japan,* Tokyo: Kodansha, 1972, pl. 47 and pp. 167-168 and H. P. Stern, *Freer Gallery of Art, Fiftieth Anniversary Exhibition, I. Ukiyo-e Painting,* Washington, D.C.: Smithsonian Institution, 1973, no. 22, pp. 52-55).

45

Soga Shōhaku
Japanese, 1730-1781
Taoist Immortal
Hanging scroll, ink on paper
33½ x 61½ in. (85 x 156.2 cm.)
Gift of the Art Museum Council, 1974
M.74.80

Collections: Shohei Kumita, Tokyo; Joseph Brotherton, San Francisco

Exhibition: Los Angeles County Museum of Art, *Japanese Paintings of the Edo Period,* Nov. 1971-Jan. 23, 1972

In recent years the Kyoto eccentrics of the eighteenth century have aroused great interest in the field of Japanese painting. One of the most individual, bizarre, and fascinating masters of this group is Soga Shōhaku. Inspired by the Chinese *Che* School and the fifteenth-century monk-painter Soga Dasoku, whose works were accessible to him at the Daitoku-ji temple, Shōhaku created intense, violently expressive works.

The subject of this painting is a Taoist Immortal or *Sennin,* a being who attained supernatural powers through Taoist practices. *Sennin* originated in China, and these immortals became popular subjects of Japanese painting in the Muromachi period (1392-1573).

In this scroll, one is immediately struck by the strength of the brushwork, and the bold, impetuous lines charged with movement. The turbulent rhythms in the waves and the *Sennin's* grotesque expression intensify the macabre fantasy of the painting. In the Koshō-ji temple in Kyoto there are paintings of Kanzan and Jitoku similar in style to this work which is attributable to Shōhaku's mature period ("Kanzan" and "Jitoku," Koshō-ji temple, Kyoto; Y. Yonezawa, ed., *Suiboku Bijutsu Taikei,* Tokyo: Kodansha, 1973-74, vol. IV, pl. 72, 73; *Nihonga Taisei,* Tokyo: Toho Shoin, 1932, vol. XV, pl. 51, 52; "The Art of Recent Individualists—Jakuchu, Shōhaku, Rosetsu," *Nihon Keizai Shimbun,* Tokyo: 1973, pl. 10).

46

Nobleman Plaque
Nigeria (Benin City), late 17th century
Bronze
18¾ x 7¼ in. (47.6 x 18.4 cm.)
Gift of Anna Bing Arnold, 1974
M.74.90

Collections: K. J. Hewitt, London; Eugene V. Thaw,
New York

In 1897 the British Punitive Expedition was sent to
Benin City, capital of one of the oldest "Yorubaland"
aristocracies, to avenge the 1896 ambush-slaying of 248
British traders who had defied a prohibition of the *Oba*
of Benin to enter his royal capital. The expedition laid waste
to the city and seized a vast amount of booty, including
ceremonial objects of bronze, brass, ivory, and wood.

The objects taken were of varying aesthetic quality.
The more notable works, designated by art historians
as in the "Benin Court Style," came largely from the palace
of the *Oba,* a lavish building which, according to a Dutch
observer in 1668, contained numerous wood columns, the flat
sides of which were faced with rectangular bronze reliefs.

William Fagg of The British Museum suggests that
out of some several hundred plaques from the palace, about
twenty can be dated to the late sixteenth century. These
are of unusual refinement and are generally in low relief.
They probably reflect earlier life styles and casting
techniques. With increased access through the Portuguese
to European tin bronze, heavier sculpture was cast,
deeper relief work came into vogue, and indeed foreign
design elements, principally Portuguese, appeared in
Benin work.

The Los Angeles Benin plaque probably dates to the
latter half of the seventeenth century. Its subject appears
to be a nobleman (or perhaps a warrior of high rank),
suggested by the coral necklace and other accoutrements
which, despite the unadorned pot helmet, indicate even
a possible kinship to the *Oba.* The ground of the plaque is
ornamented with incised quatrefoils.

By the early eighteenth century a French observer noted
that the plaques had been removed for restoration of the
palace. There is speculation that the plaques were never
replaced—but simply stored somewhere within the *Oba's*
compound—and thus were readily available to the 1897
Expedition. The Los Angeles bronze, probably from the
"middle period" of Benin Court Style, though done in relatively deep relief, nonetheless has a delicacy of execution
which represents a continuation of earlier styles.

47

Cycladic Figure
Probably from Naxos or Amorgos, ca. 2200-2000 B.C.
Marble
h: 34⅝ in. (87.9 cm.)
Gift of Anna Bing Arnold, 1967
M.67.6

Collections: Munzen und Medaillen A.G., Basel; Mr. and
Mrs. Harold Bache, New York; André Emmerich, Inc.,
New York

Exhibition: New York, André Emmerich Gallery,
Early Art in Greece, May 7-June 11, 1965, no. 10,
repr. in cat., p. 9

Literature: *Los Angeles County Museum of Art Bulletin,*
vol. XVIII, no. 1-2, 1968, repr. p. 13

This unusually large and perfect marble figure of a
woman seems to represent that moment when Bronze Age
Cycladic art first evidences a transition to a more self-
consciously abstract style. It employs all the conventions of
the female "idols" from the Cyclades: traditional simplification of the human form, a tilted spatulate head, modeled
nose and breasts, folded arms, incised pubic triangle,
slightly flexed legs, and down-pointed feet. Yet the thin
ribbonlike profile, the geometricized but highly
proportionate body denote the skillful sophistication of an
individual artist moving a step beyond these norms.

Very little is known about the intent of prehistoric
sculpture from the Cyclades. Female figures are most
frequently found in tombs and were apparently made to
accompany the dead in a future life—whether as goddess,
concubine, servant, or protector of the soul is still a matter
of speculation. They are, however, markedly different
from female figures of two nearby cultures, the Minoan and
the Helladic. Exaggeratedly female in their proportions
female idols from both Crete and the Greek mainland
express fecundity overtly. By contrast, Cycladic figures
suggest restraint or even austerity. Continuous in line, they
are often small-breasted, waistless, and slim-hipped,
characteristics further enhanced by geometrization. While
the figures cannot stand alone and both posture and align-
ment of body parts imply a reclining position, they are also
described as hovering. Indeed they convey a resilience
not usually associated with grave sculpture.

Traces of pigment on many of the Cycladic figures
indicate that they were originally painted, at least partially,
some with linear eyes and tattooed cheeks in red and blue
pigments. While the Los Angeles figure bears no paint traces,
its golden-hued patination lends the warmth of a painted
image. Archaeologically the type of patina relates the figure
to those found in tombs near the sea on the island of Naxos.

Outstanding in both conception and scale this Cycladic marble appeals to a vision trained by Arp and Brancusi. A fine rhythmic interplay of flat and modeled forms, grooves, incisions, and perforation distinguishes it; only two examples in the National Museum of Athens and one in the Ashmolean Museum at Oxford exceed it in size. Together they constitute the beginning of monumental sculpture in the West.

48

Chasuble
Italy, 14th century
Compound brocaded satin, silk and metallic threads
Costume Council Fund, 1964
M.64.82.1

Literature: O. von Falke, *Decorative Silks,* New York: W. Helburn, Inc., 1922, fig. 349 (fabric detail) and fig. 284 (orphrey fabric)

Silk textiles from northern Italy were the first of the European textiles to gain a reputation for their beauty and quality, and were sought by the church and royalty alike. Commercial fairs of the twelfth and thirteenth centuries introduced them to distant places. Through these fairs northern Italian fabrics traveled as far as England, Scandinavia, and Flanders. By the end of the thirteenth century merchants had developed more formal trade that gave them direct access to the nobility, and most important, to the church.

Raw silk from China as well as finished fabrics that began to appear in Italy in the early fourteenth century influenced the design of northern Italian textiles. Previously the fabrics were characterized by paired heraldic animals, frequently lions and birds enclosed in either a roundel or some other geometric shape; between the enclosures were geometrical floral motifs, evidence of Byzantine influence. With the arrival of the Chinese fabrics, the northern Italian motifs began to expand and adapt more freely, using a depiction of natural motion to carry the overall pattern. The appearance of new animal forms, based on the Chinese *lungma* (a dragon-headed horse), the *khilin* (a kind of griffin), and the *Fong-Hueng* (a fantastic birdlike form), signaled the beginning of a more freely drawn style. And the more naturalistic floral designs led to curving, often asymmetrical patterns.

The freely interpreted pomegranate design in this chasuble was to become highly stylized in subsequent centuries. The pomegranate here with carnations shows an apparent absorption of design motifs and overall patterns found in Turkish textiles. Since practically no Turkish textiles of this period exist now, we can only speculate on influences. Certainly there were strong commercial ties between Turkey and the Italian states that affected textile design. The silver affronté lions originally appeared as

shimmering highlights. While they are based on the heraldic Byzantine animals, instead of being stiff representations they appear in a playful pose.

The black strip down the front of the chasuble is a fourteenth-century Chinese brocade and the Arabian-like script on this strip is similar to that found on Italian silks of the fourteenth century (including the silk of the chasuble) which imitated Chinese textiles. In China, such inscriptions appeared on fabrics which were intended for an Islamic market. The existence of this small piece of fabric on the chasuble is evidence that it has not been altered since the mid-fourteenth century. Both the fabric design and the cut of the chasuble confirm this date.

49

Orphrey
Italy (Florence), last half 14th century
Embroidery, silk and metallic threads, linen ground
Los Angeles County Funds, 1972
72.3
Costume Council Fund, 1972
M.72.46.2

Exhibition: Los Angeles County Museum of Art, *Fabric and Fashion: 20 Years of Costume Council Gifts,* May 14-Oct. 13, 1973

An orphrey is a decorative band affixed to an ecclesiastical vestment. This orphrey exemplifies *opus florentinium,* embroidery of an exceptionally high quality known throughout Europe, which sought to imitate the subtle color gradations of fourteenth-century Florentine paintings. Like this one, most examples of *opus florentinium* were carried out primarily in extremely fine split stitch, with backgrounds and decorative highlights filled in with metallic gold threads—usually made up of very thin strips of metal wound around a cloth core. Here the gold background is further ornamented by the design of six dots arranged flowerlike and worked at varying angles so that the light catches them from different directions and sets them apart from their background.

Originally, the two orphrey bands were together on a cope. The right band has undoubtedly been altered on the bottom panel, where only a portion of the figure remains and three separate panels of female heads have been joined together, then added to fill out the panel to its normal length. Possibly parts of the embroideries were destroyed or damaged, and the three small female heads salvaged from another section of the vestment to repair the orphrey.

The saints on the orphrey are common ones, and there does not appear to be a predominating theme. The right panel begins with the Virgin who receives the Annunciation from the angel on the opposite panel; below her is St. John the Baptist and next the apostle St. Andrew; St. Paul follows him; and in the altered bottom panel are a prophet or apostle and three female figures, probably representing the three Marys.

The left panel begins with the Angel of the Annunciation; below him is St. Peter; in the next two panels are St. Bartholomew and St. James Major; the bottom panel again contains a prophet or apostle.

Stylistically, the orphrey relates to other Florentine embroideries of the fourteenth century as well as to painting styles of those years. Geri Lapi, the Florentine embroiderer whose masterwork is the altar frontal (second quarter of the fourteenth century) of the Collegiate Church of Santa Maria in Manresa, Spain, certainly is a source for this piece. Lapi's hand, or at least his influence, has been discerned in a number of Florentine embroideries, and though there is no question of his workmanship here, certain figures, notably the Virgin and the three Marys, show that his style was of great importance in Florence for many decades.

Another set of embroideries must be mentioned in relation to this orphrey: those of the altar curtain of Jacopo Cambi, worked in Florence and dated 1336 (Florence, Palazzo Pitti, Museo degli Argenti). In the scene of the Annunciation is an angel who almost seems to be a model for the angel of the orphrey, similar as it is in such details as the treatment of the wings, the gesture, and a peculiar patchlike area on the upper arm.

Despite their basis in the decorative, miniaturistic style of the earlier masters, these embroideries show a distinct evolution toward the more monumental style of Giotto and his followers in Florence. The bulk of the draperies and the sense of anatomical mass argues for an awareness, if not a complete understanding, of Giotto's innovations in the early years of the fourteenth century.

50

Cope with Orphrey
Cope: Italy, 15th century
Cut voided ferronnerie velvet, silk
Orphrey: Flanders, 15th century
Embroidery, silk and metallic threads on linen ground
Costume Council Fund, 1964
M.64.82.3

Exhibition: Los Angeles County Museum of Art, *Velvets East and West,* Mar. 21-May 15, 1966, no. 2, repr. in cat., p. 18

Copes of this magnificence were worn only for the most splendid ecclesiastical functions. This cope is semicircular in shape, the straight edge embellished with embroidered orphreys, or decorative bands. Six widths of velvet have been used to complete the semi-circle. The design of cinquefoils enclosing pomegranates is precisely cut from the velvet ground. This particular type

of velvet with a linear design is generally known as *ferronnerie,* a name connecting it with the wrought-iron work of Florence. The thinly cut lines give the feeling that the design is inlaid on the rich garnet colored pile. The actual design is a simple repeat in alternating rows, organized so gracefully that one is aware only of the overall rhythm.

The orphrey is embroidered with both gold and multicolored silk threads. The gold used for the background, architectural elements, and certain details of the costume is laid on, then couched with yellow silk to form a pattern. The background has a diamond pattern and the borders have a zigzag motif. The ridges around the architectural niches are covered with gold thread drawn over silk ropes and couched at the sides. The embroidery of the figures is carried out almost entirely in an overlapping satin stitch. The use of this stitch is frequently referred to as "needlepainting" because of the great subtleties in color gradations.

The orphrey is divided into seven panels, each containing a saint or other divinity. God the Father occupies the center panel; St. Michael the Archangel and St. Peter face each other below, followed by St. John the Baptist on the left and St. Andrew on the right; at the bottom are St. Jerome and St. Sebastian. Due to the similarity of embroidery techniques throughout Europe, iconography and drawing styles must be considered in discussion of provenance. In this case, the attributes and costumes of the saints provide clues which suggest a northern origin. In addition, several of the figures appear to have prototypes in Flemish fifteenth-century painting. The X-shaped cross in the middle panel on the right band identifies the figure as St. Andrew. The X-shaped cross argues for a northern origin, because it occurs as the attribute of St. Andrew much more frequently there than in the south where the Latin cross is far more common.

Copes with embroidered orphreys are often worn by figures in paintings of the fifteenth century. Though they are only details, the painstaking realism of many of the paintings permits some observations to be made. The orphrey worn by a bishop in van der Weyden's *Lamentation after the Deposition* (The Hague, Mauritshuis) provides a very close comparison, including the architectural niches with a diagonal grid floor in which the saints stand. Another example is depicted in Gerard David's *Canon Bernardinus de Salviatis and Three Saints* (London, National Gallery). Though they may be inventions of the artist, it can nevertheless be assumed that the painter would normally reproduce existing orphreys.

51

Master of the St. Lucy Legend
Flemish, active ca. 1480-1501
Triptych, before 1483
*Donor with His Patron, St. Peter Martyr; Madonna and
Child with Angels; St. Jerome and His Lion*
Oil on oak panels
Center panel: 32¼ x 27¼ in. (82 x 69.5 cm.)
Side panels: 32¼ x 11¼ in. (82 x 28.5 cm.)
Gift of Anna Bing Arnold, 1969
M.69.54

Collections: Flemish woman who married into the Cittadella
family; Marchese Cittadella, Lucca; Cav. Giuseppe
Toscanelli, Pisa/Lucca (Sale, Florence, Apr. 9, 1883);
Sedelmeyer Gallery, Paris, 1900; Henri Heugel and heirs,
Paris, until 1968; Galerie Heim, Paris, 1969

Exhibitions: London, Burlington House, *Flemish and
Dutch Art,* 1927, no. 73 in cat. edited by Sir Martin Conway
(lent by Henri Heugel, Paris); Antwerp, *Exposition
internationale coloniale, maritime et d'art flamand,* June-
Sept. 1930, no. 179, cat. p. 69 (lent by Mme. Henri
Heugel, Paris)

Literature: Sale catalog, *Catalogue de tableaux, meubles
et objets d'art formant la galerie de M. le Chev. Toscanelli,
redigé par Gaetano Milanese,* Florence, Giulio Sambon
Gallery, Apr. 9-23, 1883, p. 40, no. 152, repr. pl. XXXVII a
and b in album accompanying catalog (as Hugo van der
Goes); *Illustrated Catalog of the Sixth Series of 100
Paintings by Old Masters...of the Sedelmeyer Gallery,* Paris,
1900, no. 14, repr. p. 21 (as Flemish School, 15th century);
S. Reinach, *Répertoire des Peintures du Moyen-Age et
de la Renaissance, 1280-1580,* Paris: E. Leroux, vol. 1 (1905),
pp. 182 and 566; M. J. Friedländer, *Die Altniederländische
Malerei,* Berlin: P. Cassirer, vol. III (1925), p. 126, no. 91 a,
vol. VI (1928), p. 140, no. 140; W. Schöne, *Dieric Bouts
und seine Schule,* Berlin/Leipzig, 1938, p. 212, no. 140 a;
N. Veronee-Verhaegen, "Le Maître de la Légende de
S. Lucie. Précisions sur son oeuvre," *Bulletin de l'Institut
Royal du Patrimoine Artistique,* vol. II (1959), pp. 73-82;
M. J. Friedländer, *Early Netherlandish Painting,* with
commentary and notes by N. Veronee-Verhaegen, New York:
Praeger, vol. III (1968), p. 72, no. 91 a, and vol. VI, p. 62,
no. 140, repr. pl. 151

Max Friedlaender, in a critical commentary in 1903
on the exhibition of early Flemish painting in Bruges the
preceding year, noted the stylistic affinity between two
anonymous paintings, the *Legend of St. Lucy* in the church
of St. James in Bruges, dated 1480 but not signed, and
the *Virgin and Child with Eleven Female Saints* in the
Fine Arts Museum of Brussels (M. J. Friedlaender, "Die
Brügger Leihaustellung von 1902," *Repertorium für
Kunstwissenschaft,* XXVI [1903], p. 84-85). This was the

beginning of the reconstruction of the artistic personality
of the painter Friedlaender first called "Master of 1480"
and soon after "Master of the Saint Lucy Legend." By 1928
Friedlaender could list twenty-two paintings by the Master,
including the Arnold triptych (VI, nos. 139-158), and by
1937 he had increased the number to twenty-seven (XIV,
p. 105). In her recent edition of Friedlaender, Dr. Nicole
Veronee-Verhaegen has added eleven works, bringing
the total to thirty-eight (VI, pt. 2, 277-278), and has presented a summary of the literature on the Master
from 1937 to 1971 (VI, pt. 2, p. 123-124).

Dr. Veronee-Verhaegen *(Bulletin de l'Institut Royal du
Patrimoine Artistique,* 1959) has offered proof that the
Master worked in Bruges from before 1483 to after 1501
and established a chronology for a critical body of his
work on the basis of representations of the Belfry of Bruges,
which he painted with great fidelity in the backgrounds
of more than fifteen of his pictures. During those years the
Belfry underwent a series of changes. Before 1483 the
tower was square with a small roof awaiting the addition of
the octagonal tambour; from 1483 to 1487 the octagon
and its steeled roof were under construction; when completed it did not change until 1493 when a fire destroyed
the roof and left the skeleton of the octagon standing without
covering; between 1499 and 1501 the damage to the
octagon was repaired, the roof was replaced, and a balustrade
was added atop the octagon, all of which remained
unchanged until 1741.

In the left panel of the Arnold triptych the city of Bruges
is represented with two of its prominent towers: Notre
Dame on the left and the Belfry on the right. Between them
is the turret of the House of the Burghers (Poortersloge).
The Belfry is shown in its pre-1483 state. Even if indication
of date were not present, on stylistic grounds the triptych
would be dated close to the St. Lucy panels of 1480.

Max Friedlaender wrote that three things distinguish
the Master of the St. Lucy Legend, "an understanding of
architecture, intimate observation of the plant world, and a
pleasing decorative sense." These qualities are all present
in the Arnold triptych along with other specific characteristics—a liveliness of color, an immutability of form,
a love of pattern, and a scrupulousness in the rendering of
details. The central portion of the triptych is based on a
composition popular in Bruges in the second half of the
fifteenth century. The side panels are original creations of the
Master, and therefore can be best compared with the
St. Lucy panels of 1480.

In the left panel is the donor with his patron, St. Peter
Martyr. Of the donor, there is known only that he was named
Peter and was presumably unmarried at the time the
painting was made, since no companion donor is present.

St. Peter Martyr was a thirteenth-century Dominican from Verona who fought so valiantly against heresy that he received the title, "Glory of the Dominican Order." His attributes are the wound in his head and the sword of his martyrdom. The inscription "Maria Mater" on the sword refers to his having founded the Confraternity of Our Lady of Mercy in Florence in 1246. In the right panel is St. Jerome extracting a particularly conspicuous thorn from the paw of the lion, a subject popularized in Flanders by Roger van der Weyden. Jerome's defense of the perpetual virginity of Mary in his controversy with Helvidius makes his presence appropriate in a painting dedicated to the Madonna. The large, statuesque figures of Jerome, Peter Martyr, and the donor with relatively small heads and arms are so similar to those in the St. Lucy panels that they may be considered hallmarks of the Master's style of the early 1480s. This aspiration to monumentality may well be an influence of Hugo van der Goes. It is curious that the Master did not continue in this direction in his later works, but rather proliferated stylized female figures, flowers, foliage, textiles, and design details to create brilliantly colored tapestries in paint.

The less monumental but more poetic central panel is based on a lost prototype which was apparently well known in Bruges in the late fifteenth century, since a number of versions of it exist, usually complete with details like the expulsion of Adam and Eve from Paradise atop the throne and the upward fold of the Madonna's outer garment. None of these paintings is a copy of the other. We are grateful to Dr. Veronee-Verhaegen for listing and commenting on them in a letter of January 12, 1970, summarized here.

There are four versions by the Master of the St. Lucy Legend of which the Los Angeles painting is of the highest quality: the so-called Boutsian version in Granada (Friedlaender III, no. 91) probably painted in the Ghent-Bruges circle before Memlinc; a free interpretation by Memlinc (Friedlaender, VI, no. 100) translating the elements into his personal style; a version attributed to the Bouts school (Friedlander III, no. 65) probably by Albert Bouts (d. 1548); and a panel in the Bode Museum in East Berlin (Friedlaender I, pl. 97 a in 1967 ed.) which uses the same background, but with Madonna and Child adopted from the *Madonna van der Peale* of Jan van Eyck.

In its simple, uncomplicated manner and psychology, the Arnold triptych is a joyous painting, communicating the artist's delight in the purity of the Madonna in her heavenly surroundings, the virility of her saints, the skill of architects and craftsmen, the clarity of light, the brilliance of color, and the manifoldness of nature.

52

Albrecht Dürer
German, 1471-1528
The Martyrdom of St. John the Evangelist, 1498
Pl. 1 from the *Apocalypse of St. John*
Woodcut, proof without text
Watermark: Large Imperial orb
15 x 11 in. (38.1 x 27.9 cm.)
Los Angeles County Funds, 1969
69.4

Collection: R. G. Michel, Paris

Literature: A. Bartsch, *Le peintre graveur,* Leipzig: J. A. Barth, 1876, vol. 7, no. 61; J. Meder, *Dürer Katalog,* Vienna: Gilhofer and Ranschburg, 1932, no. 164, watermark no. 53; E. Panofsky, *The Life and Art of Albrecht Dürer,* 3rd ed., Princeton, 1948, vol. 2, no. 281

The first two woodcuts of the series of fifteen illustrations of the *Apocalypse* were, according to Panofsky, undertaken last and thus "represent the utmost in grandeur of scale, concentration on essentials, and graphic economy." At the same time this first print is among the most monumental and theatrical of the subjects in the series. The majestic richly robed and jeweled Oriental emperor set amid all his decorative luxury was purposely made the antipodal contrast to the prayerful martyr, emphasizing the drama of their confrontation. With the low wall serving as a kind of barrier for the throng of spectators, the act takes on the character of a medieval public spectacle; the canopy drawn over the clustered buildings in the background further contributes to the theatrical effect of the scene. In addition to these features, the artist makes abundant use of Renaissance ornamental details. Drawn by an engraver trained as a goldsmith, the properties of richly carved and chased accoutrements as well as jewels, brocaded hangings, and architectural ornaments are observed with the greatest precision and fidelity.

Together with the *Vision of the Seven Candlesticks,* the second print of the series, the *Martyrdom of St. John* is the most striking example of Dürer's brilliant execution of engraved ornament in the *Apocalypse.*

53

Albrecht Dürer
German, 1471-1528
The Vision of St. Eustache, ca. 1501
Engraving
Watermark: High Crown
14 x 10¼ in. (35.6 x 26.0 cm.)
Graphic Arts Council Fund, 1966
M.66.89

Collections: James Reiss, London (Lugt 1522, 1523); Hellmut Wallach, New York

Literature: A. Bartsch, *Le peintre graveur*, Leipzig:
J. A. Barth, 1876, vol. 7, no. 57; C. Dodgson, *Albrecht Dürer, Engravings and Etchings,* New York: Da Capo, 1967, no. 32; J. Meder, *Dürer Katalog,* Vienna: Gilhofer and Ranschburg, 1932, 60b; E. Panofsky, *The Life and Art of Albrecht Dürer,* 3rd ed., Princeton, 1948, vol. 2, no. 164; C. W. Talbot, ed., *Dürer in America, His Graphic Work,* Washington, D.C.: National Gallery of Art, 1971, p. 127, no. 24, fig. 24

This masterful work was inspired by the legend of St. Eustache who had been a valorous general under the Roman emperor Trajan as well as a passionate hunter. Dürer portrayed Placidius (the general's Roman name) at the moment of his conversion. Between the antlers of a stag he was hunting, St. Eustache beheld the vision of Christ crucified; the stag then spoke to him in the voice of God. According to legend the general fell from his horse as had St. Paul, but Dürer depicted St. Eustache kneeling before the apparition.

St. Eustache was Dürer's largest and, in a sense, most ambitious engraving. In size and finish the work approximates a small painting while conveying the allover detailed effect of a meticulously worked tapestry. With intense concentration, the artist depicted nature with the most precise gradations of line and tone, creating perhaps the single finest landscape passage among his prints. While Dürer's study of proportion was not yet perfected at this time, as is visible in the articulation of the left front leg of the stalwart horse, the group of hounds in the foreground comprises one of the most felicitous motifs of the composition.

54

Albrecht Dürer
German, 1471-1528
Adam and Eve, 1504
Engraving
Watermark: Bull's head with five-petaled flower
(Meder 62)
9¾ x 7½ in. (24.8 x 19.2 cm.)
Gift of the Art Museum Council, 1966
M.66.33

Collections: Baron Edmond de Rothschild, Paris; J. Thorel, Paris (Lugt, 1542); Louis Silver; William Schab, New York

Literature: A. Bartsch, *Le peintre graveur*, Leipzig:
J. A. Barth, 1876, vol. 7, no. 1; J. Meder, *Dürer Katalog,* Vienna: Gilhofer and Ranschburg, 1932; E. Panofsky, *The Life and Art of Albrecht Dürer,* 3rd ed., Princeton, 1948, vol. 2, no. 39; C. Dodgson, *Albrecht Dürer, Engravings and Etchings,* New York: Da Capo, 1967, no. 39

Adam and Eve is probably Dürer's most renowned print and possibly the most easily read subject in his graphic oeuvre. This is not to overlook the several symbolic motifs in the composition that relate to the biblical story of the Fall of Man which Dürer included to compensate for the nudity of the figures.

The engraving best represents Dürer's concept of the canon of human proportions as represented by the antique and the ideals of the Italian Renaissance. The slim, gracefully proportioned figures of Adam and Eve are set in silhouette against the thickly wooded garden, enhancing their flowing lines and gleaming nudity; and Dürer's rich treatment of the foliage, a characteristic from his goldsmith's training and the influence of Schongauer, is equally evident in the intricate curls and wavy locks of his two protagonists. The pristine beauty of the human form as it is disclosed in this print became a model for many Northern artists. The Museum's engraving was printed on a fine thin paper with bull's head watermark, often used for the earliest and best impressions. In 1869 the Baron Edmond de Rothschild annotated his ownership on the back of the print.

55

Albrecht Dürer
German, 1471-1528
Knight, Death, and Devil, 1513
Engraving
9¾ x 7⅜ in. (24.8 x 18.7 cm.)
Graphic Arts Council Fund, 1970
70.1

Collections: O. Gerstenberg, Berlin (Lugt 2785); Hellmut Wallach, New York

Literature: A. Bartsch, *Le peintre graveur*, Leipzig:
J. A. Barth, 1876, vol. 7, no. 98; J. Meder, *Dürer Katalog,* Vienna: Gilhofer and Ranschburg, 1932; E. Panofsky, *The Life and Art of Albrecht Dürer,* 3rd ed., Princeton, 1948, vol. 2, no. 205; C. Dodgson, *Albrecht Dürer, Engravings and Etchings,* New York: Da Capo, 1967, no. 70

Generally classed among Dürer's three *meisterstiche, Knight, Death, and Devil* is the most graphic expression of the spirit of the German Reformation. The Christian knight symbolizes a faith inspired by Erasmus' manual, *Enchiridion Militis Christiani* (the *Pocket Dagger for the Christian Soldier*). Armed with this spiritual strength the traveler could pass unscathed and unshaken through the terrors of his journey unfrightened by Death (decay) and Devil (evil).

The print personifies Dürer's worship of truth as well as his embodiment of the Christian *vita activa,* in contrast to the *vita contemplativa* of *Melencolia* and *St. Jerome in His Study,* the engravings which, with *Knight, Death, and Devil,* form the triad of his philosophical ideas.

Dürer's double-sided drawing for the mounted knight, in the Ambrosiana, Milan, demonstrates his method of constructing the horse by means of ruler and compass to achieve its proper proportions according to his theory. The study also reveals the artist's drawing and re-drawing of the horse's right leg for its correct positioning. In the engraving, Dürer solved the problem of the melee of quadruped legs in the lower foreground with a complex positioning and rhythm that averts confusion or monotony. The Museum's impression of *Knight, Death, and Devil* is very finely wiped, thus creating translucent hatched areas that appear velvety in the shaded passages. Graded subtleties of tone and variations of line masterfully convey the coat of the Leonardesque horse, the knight's armor, the dog, and the repulsive figures of Death and Devil against the rugged background.

56

Lucas Cranach the Elder
German, 1472-1553
Portrait of a Young Man with a Short Beard
Oil on linden panel
16½ x 11⅛ in. (42 x 28 cm.)
Signed and dated above left shoulder with serpent with erect wings, 1518
Promised gift of R. Stanton Avery

Collections: Count Dohna, Germany; R. Zahn, Munich; Marczell von Nemes, Budapest; A. S. Drey, Munich, 1921; Samuel Untermeyer, New York, 1940; Morris Shapiro, Baltimore; Newhouse Galleries, New York

Exhibitions: New York, Van Diemen Galleries, *Exhibition of Paintings by Lucas Cranach the Elder,* Nov. 18-Dec. 5, 1929, p. 8, no. 22 in cat.; Basel, Kuntsmuseum, *Lukas Cranach,* June 15-Sept. 8, 1974, cat. vol. I (1974), p. 197, pl. 11, vol. II (1975), no. 603

Literature: Sale catalog, Galerie Hugo Helbig, Munich, *Sammlungen...R. Zahn...Versteigerung,* Nov. 20, 1917, no. 11; *Der Cicerone,* vol. XXII, Jan. 1930, p. 31, repr. p. 34; M. J. Friedländer and J. Rosenberg, *Die Gemälde von Lucas Cranach,* Berlin: Deutscher Verein für Kunstwissenschaft, 1932, p. 50, repr. pl. 106; C. L. Kuhn, *A Catalogue of German Paintings of the Middle Ages and Renaissance in American Collections,* Cambridge: Harvard University Press, 1936, no. 92, p. 37; Sale catalog, Parke-Bernet Galleries, New York, *Important Paintings...the Untermeyer Collection,* Sale, May 10-11, 1940, p. 48, no. 50, repr. p. 49

While Lucas Cranach (1472-1553) is usually thought of as a painter of elegantly stylized female figures with porcelainlike surfaces, his portraits reveal him as a member of that great generation of painters—Albrecht Dürer (1471-1528), Hans Burgkmair (1473-1545), and Hans Holbein (1495-1531)—who gave visual expression to Northern Humanism. In his portraits Cranach mirrors the interaction of classical learning and Protestantism through the entire first half of the sixteenth century.

His early portraits of scholars and humanists in Vienna before 1505 reflect an ideal of spiritual freedom and autonomy of the personality. Painted with dramatic intensity and with the figure usually in a landscape to which it is intimately related, they express forcefully the individuality of the sitter.

In the Avery portrait, painted in 1518 in Wittenberg, Cranach's view of man is considerably modified by his close relationship with Luther. The background is neutral—an almost abstract space—against which the subject is delineated with cool rationality, clarity, and a minimum of flattery. It is a work of an objective observer who paints a sober but vital portrait recording the individual with his strength and weaknesses. The mood is calmer, the lines quieter than in the early portraits. The figure is clearly and compactly structured, albeit in a more restricted space. While the painter retains the typical Northern meticulous accuracy of detail, the painting has acquired a more courtly polish and painterly refinement.

In late works, like Cranach's self-portrait of 1550 in the Uffizzi, Protestantism has submerged the follies and enthusiasms of Humanism. It is a stern portrait in which, in Otto Benesch's words, "Life had to be mastered and the human character had to be proved in it severely and harshly."

The relative dating of Cranach's paintings, even when not recorded on the panel, is indicated by the type of signature he used. Until 1508 Cranach signed with his initials L.C. On January 8 of that year Frederick the Wise granted him a coat of arms and Cranach began to sign his works with a serpent with erect wings, crowned and bearing a ring in his mouth, like that in the Avery painting. After 1537, he used a serpent with folded, birdlike wings, indicating in all probability that Cranach the Younger had taken over the workshop (Friedländer-Rosenberg, p. 20).

The esteem in which Cranch was held by his contemporaries was expressed as early as 1509 by Dr. jur. Johann Scheurl in a panegyric before a congregation of princes and scholars: "...in the long neglected, now reawakened art of painting, with the single exception of his fellow countryman Albrecht Dürer, an undoubted genius, Lucas Cranach alone holds the highest rank" (G. Fehr, *Lucas Cranach,* Bonn, 1972, p. 8).

57

Christoph Amberger
German, ca. 1505-1562
Portrait of Hans Jacob Fugger
Oil on panel
37¾ x 31¼ in. (95.9 x 80.7 cm.)
Dated upper right: MDXLI
Gift of the Michael J. Connell Foundation, 1968
M.68.33

Collections: Countess Isbary, Vienna; Princess
Windischgraetz (daughter), Vienna; Frederick Mont,
New York

The subject of this portrait is identified traditionally
as a member of the Fugger family of Augsburg, for which
Amberger executed a number of commissions in the 1540s.
No substantiating documents have yet been found, but a
comparison of his facial characteristics with well-documented
Fugger portraits, like Albrecht Dürer's *Jacob Fugger*
in the Alte Pinakothek, Munich, confirms the tradition.
The date 1541 restricts more precise identification to
one of three sons of Raymund Fugger: Hans Jacob, born in
1516; Georg, born in 1518; or Christoph, born in 1520.

On the basis of the inscribed age—twenty—a Fugger
portrait by Amberger in the Alte Pinakothek, Munich, also
dated 1541, has been identified as Christoph (W. D. Dube,
The Alte Pinakothek, Munich, New York, Abrams, n.d.,
repr. in color, p. 110). The subject is younger and much less
self-assured than the Los Angeles sitter. The Munich
painting, a companion in size and style to the Los Angeles
painting, was acquired in 1927 directly from the Fuggers
of Babenhausen. Georg's likeness is well known from a
wooden model for a medal attributed to Hans Kels in the
Fugger-Museum, Babenhausen (*Austellung Augsburger
Renaissance,* Augsburg, Schaezler-Haus, May-Oct. 1955,
p. 59, no. 311, enlarged, repr. fig. 13), and from a full-length
portrait attributed to Jacob Seisenegger in the collection
of Dr. Clemens Fugger-Kirchberg-Weissenhorn in Schloss
Oberkirchberg bei Ulm. The medal is inscribed GEORGIUS
FUGGER. ETATIS SUAE XXIIII. ANNO MDXLI; the painting is
also dated 1541. Both show a tall, slender young man
with a long, thin face, sharp features, and a short beard
trimmed to frame the face. By elimination, the Los Angeles
Fugger must, therefore, be the eldest—Hans Jacob,
twenty-five and already the head of the family enterprises,
described as "highly gifted and strong willed." Dr. Alfred
Stange first made this identification in a letter of February 21,
1968. Dr. Norbert Lieb, the foremost authority on the
Fuggers as patrons of the arts, arrived at the same conclu-
sion, but more tentatively, in a letter of September 25, 1968.

At the time the portrait was painted, the Fuggers were
at the height of their wealth and influence. The family
had started as weavers in the fourteenth century and became
bankers and merchants in the fifteenth. By the early sixteenth

century, they were bankers to the Hapsburgs, owners of
copper and silver mines in Austria, Hungary, Spain, and
South America, and of the largest aggregate of real estate in
Europe. They had offices in every important city in Europe.
In 1546 the chief accountant of the family estimated their
wealth as sixty-three million florins. In politics they provided
the greater part of the funds for the election of Charles V
as Holy Roman Emperor. In return they were created counts
by the emperor in 1530 and given the rights of princes.
In religion, they staunchly supported the Catholic Church
against Protestantism. They were patrons of the arts,
letters, and sciences. Raymund Fugger, who provided each
of his sons with a humanistic education and a love of
learning, was the first important collector of Greek and
Roman antiquities in Germany. This was the heritage
of our sitter.

Hans Jacob was educated in Italy, Spain, France, and
the Netherlands; he spoke the languages of those countries
as well as Latin and Greek. His father's early death in
1535 forced him to terminate his formal education and
assume the family business responsibilities. His greater
ambitions and abilities, however, were in historical scholar-
ship and public life. He represented the Fuggers at the
Hungarian and Bohemian courts for several years until his
marriage in 1540 to the aristocratic Ursula von Harrach
zu Roraw. The year before the Amberger portrait was made
Hans Jacob returned to Augsburg and became master of
his father's house. In 1542 he was elected city councilor and
in 1548 he was appointed by the emperor as first Burgomaster of Augsburg, a position he held for many years.
In 1570 he was named Privy Councilor and President of the
Royal Chamber of the Bavarian Court.

As a historian, he produced two major works, still
considered as source books, on the princes of the House of
Austria and on his own family.

Hans Jacob's lifelong passion for books and historical
research led him to sell lands and castles to assemble a
library of more than 12,000 manuscripts and printed books
on philosophy, theology, jurisprudence, the liberal arts,
and especially history—a collection which eventually became
the foundation for the Bavarian State Library.

The Fugger portraits of 1541 are unique in the work of
Amberger, combining the German character portrait
evolved by Dürer and Holbein with new Italian elements to
produce an aristocratic portrait type comparable to that
being developed concurrently by the Florentine Mannerists.
In the Los Angeles portrait, the background is simplified—
a section of undecorated palace wall and curtain. The figure
in a dark suit and hat of restrained fashion is silhouetted
against the slightly lighter background. The pose is elegant,
the facial expression commanding. It is a portrait of
aristocracy as a state of being; but, at the same time, the

artist has remained faithful enough to the German Renaissance tradition that it is also a penetrating portrait of a highly individual personality.

The painting is not yet included in the Amberger literature since it was not accessible even to scholars during the many years it was in the Isbary collection. When the historian of German art, Dr. Alfred Stange, did have the opportunity to see it shortly before it was acquired by the Los Angeles County Museum of Art, he wrote of it in the letter referred to above as "one of the most beautiful works of the full-blown Renaissance in Germany."

58

Fra Bartolommeo (Baccio della Porta)
Italian, 1472-1517
Holy Family
Oil on canvas
59½ x 36 in. (151.0 x 91.3 cm.)
Gift of The Ahmanson Foundation, 1973
M.73.93

Collections: Ferdinand Panciatichi Ximenes d'Aragona, Florence; Conte Alessandro Contini-Bonacossi, Rome and Florence; Thomas Agnew & Sons, Ltd., London

Exhibitions: Florence, Palazzo Strozzi, *Mostra del Cinquecento Toscano,* Apr.-Oct. 1940, no. 3, cat. pp. 21-22 (lent by Contini-Bonacossi); King's Lynn, Norfolk, Fermay Art Gallery, *Renaissance Painting in Tuscany 1300-1500,* 1973 (lent by Thomas Agnew)

Literature: B. Berenson, *Drawings of the Florentine Painters,* New York: Dutton, 1903, vol. I, p. 143, 2nd ed., Chicago: University of Chicago Press, 1938, vol. I, p. 162, 3rd ed., Milan: Electra Editrice, 1961, vol. I, p. 239; A. Venturi, *Storia dell' Arte Italiana,* Milan: Hoepli, vol. IX, part I, 1925, pp. 351-354, repr. fig. 253; H. Bodmer, "Opere giovanili e tardi di Mariotto Albertinelli," *Dedalo,* vol. IX (1928-29), p. 608; W. Haftmann, "Toskanische Malerei des Cinquecento...," *Pantheon,* XXVI (July-Dec. 1940), p. 186; B. Berenson, *Italian Pictures of the Renaissance, Florentine School,* London: Phaidon, 1963, vol. I, p. 23; E. Fahy, "The Earliest Works of Fra Bartolommeo," *Art Bulletin,* 1969, pp. 148-149, repr. fig. 20; idem, "A Holy Family by Fra Bartolommeo," *Los Angeles County Museum of Art Bulletin,* vol. XIX, no. 2 (1974), repr. frontispiece

The Ahmanson Fra Bartolommeo was first mentioned in art historical literature by Berenson in 1903 as "an old copy in the Panciatichi Collection of a lost original by Albertinelli, representing the Holy Family, all the figures standing—a fascinating work." It was next published by Adolfo Venturi in 1925 as an autograph work of Albertinelli, "a most original composition." Bodmer in 1929 called it Albertinelli's masterpiece of the first decade of the sixteenth century. It was not until three distinguished scholars of

Florentine painting, Bernard Berenson, Roberto Longhi, and Carlo Gamba were brought together during the period of catalog preparation to study the paintings to be exhibited in the *Mostra del Cinquecento Toscano* at the Palazzo Strozzi in 1940 that the picture was recognized as an unquestionable work of Fra Bartolommeo. The attribution has never since been questioned. In his article in the *Art Bulletin* (1969) and his more exhaustive study of the painting in the *Los Angeles County Museum of Art Bulletin* (1974), Everett Fahy has demonstrated the close typological and stylistic relationship between the Ahmanson painting and other works of Fra Bartolommeo of the last decade of the fifteenth century and has differentiated it from Albertinelli stylistically as having "a much firmer sense of design, a more talented handling of paint, and a far more elevated feeling of religious conviction." The earlier attribution to Albertinelli is understandable since he was a close colleague of Fra Bartolommeo's and often imitated his style.

In Florentine painting of the last quarter of the fifteenth century there developed concurrently the poetic imagery of Botticelli, the descriptive narrative of Domenico Ghirlandajo, and the innovations of Leonardo and Michelangelo. It was in this milieu that Baccio della Porta, who under the influence of Savonarola's teaching became a Dominican monk about 1500 and received the name Fra Bartolommeo, began his artistic career. He studied under Cosimo Roselli, but seems to have been formed by Ghirlandajo with whom he worked and by Leonardo whom he greatly admired. The Ahmanson *Holy Family,* painted only two or three years before the end of the century, indicates his grasp of the new High Renaissance style and foretells his role as the artist who brought the High Renaissance in Florence to its fruition. Each of the figures in the picture has a prototype in his own work or that of his immediate contemporaries, but it is the manner in which he has adapted and composed them which makes the picture significant. Everett Fahy has shown that the Madonna was without doubt made from the same cartoon which Bartolommeo used for the Virgin Annunciate of 1497 in the Cathedral of Volterra. The head of St. Joseph has a prototype in his own *Holy Family,* in the Borghese Gallery, Rome, of 1495. Both the figure of the Christ Child and of the Madonna have formal prototypes in works of Domenico Ghirlandajo, but Bartolommeo united them into a new image of formal and spiritual harmony. The Madonna has become an ideal of spiritual beauty reflected in human form; any trace of either human defect or individualizing facial feature has been eliminated. The mantle which had been over her shoulders in the Volterra painting now covers her head and unifies her outline as she stands in sculpturesque majesty before the open sky and ordered landscape. Her robes fall in gentle cadences. She gently touches the head of the Christ Child, a vigorous, young Herculean God. St. Joseph, again not an imitation of any single human model but a composite image of benign age, places his hand on the shoulder of the Child to protect him. The atmospheric light and the harmony between Joseph's inner concern for the Child and his external appearance, betray Bartolommeo's debt to Leonardo. The counter-movement of the Child and Joseph subtly balances the slight movement of the Madonna to the left. The architectural forms of pedestal and low wall are simple abstractions to define space, not to be themselves objects of attention. The light is clear and unvaried. The ordered landscape in the background parallels the serenity of the foreground. A narrative scene at the lower right in which St. Dominic welcomes St. Francis before a Dominican monastery is a link with daily reality. To the sixteenth-century viewer this would have recalled the dream of St. Dominic in which the Madonna tells the Christ Child that these two friars and their followers would fight valiantly against the vices of pride, luxury, and corruption. Since the High Renaissance style, while seeking to perfect nature, is nonetheless based on the study of nature, the Ahmanson picture is entirely credible as a natural representation, but is at the same time what Fahy calls a "vision of supernatural beauty." The off-center composition, the tall rectangular format, and the use of canvas all distinguish this painting from the traditional *Holy Family*. In Florence at this time, altarpieces were more nearly square and painted on wood. There were some tall rectangles with individual saints to be affixed to church columns, but they too were on wood panels. Fahy has therefore proposed that the Ahmanson *Holy Family* was not painted for permanent installation, but that it was more likely a processional banner commissioned by a confraternity or order dedicated to the Virgin. The central position of the Madonna and the complementary role of the Christ Child and Joseph indicate, he believes, that it is indeed not a Holy Family in the conventional sense, but an image of Mary, Queen of Heaven.

Mario Modestini, who was responsible for the cleaning of the picture, attested the excellence of its condition in a letter dated October 30, 1973.

59

Baccio Bandinelli
Italian, 1493-1560
Colossal Head, ca. 1534
Marble
h: 23⅜ in. (60.0 cm.)
Museum purchase: Mr. and Mrs. Allan C. Balch Endowment, 1967
M.67.39

Collections: Gioacchino Ferroni, Rome (Sale, Rome, Apr. 14-22, 1909); Luigi Galli, Milan; Adolph Loewi, Los Angeles

Literature: Sale catalog, *Catalogue de la vente...de M. Joachim Ferroni...aux maisons de vente Jandolo et Tovizzi-Galerie Sangiorgi,* Rome, Apr. 14-22, 1909, repr.

Eighteen years younger than Michelangelo and the great master's most jealous rival, Baccio Bandinelli belonged to the generation of Pontormo and Rosso. The colossal head, as might be expected, exemplifies the transition from High Renaissance to Mannerism in sixteenth-century Florence. The combination of classic nobility and study of nature in the construction of the head is still High Renaissance; the introspection, the elongation of proportions, and the elegant stylization of the hair and beard are already Mannerist.

Professor Ulrich Middeldorf, then Director of the Kunsthistorisches Institut in Florence, wrote of the sculpture in a letter of April 7, 1967: "The head seems to me to be a beautiful work of Bandinelli himself, from the period in which he executed the gigantic Hercules and Cacus in front of the Palazzo Vecchio (erected 1534). In the heads of this group one finds the same treatment of the hair and the characteristic modeling of the face. This head, however, is nobler and more classic than the group. The equilibrium of expression and of classic forms indicates a moment in which Bandinelli comes closest to the style of Michelangelo. The head must have been intended to be inserted into a colossal statue. But it stands very well by itself, being of exceptional quality." The gigantic sculpture into which this head was to have been inserted may have been an antique one, since Bandinelli had earlier achieved great fame for his reconstruction of the lost upper arm of Laocoön.

60

Jean Duvet
French, 1485-after 1561
The Fall of Babylon, ca. 1555
Apocalypse, pl. 18, ca. 1546-1555
Engraving
11⅞ x 8⅜ in. (30.0 x 21.0 cm.)
Gift of the Graphic Arts Council in memory of Hilda Hunter, 1973
M.73.13

Collections: A. P. F. Robert-Dumesnil, Paris (Lugt 2200); D. Karshan, New York; William Schab, New York

Literature: A. Bartsch, *Le peintre graveur,* Leipzig: J. A. Barth, 1876, vol. 7, p. 510, no. 30; A. P. F. Robert-Dumesnil, *Le peintre graveur français ou catalogue raisonné des estampes gravées par les peintres et les dessinateurs de l'école française...,* Paris: F. de Noble, 1967, reprint, vol. 5, p. 23, no. 44

The Fall of Babylon is an unusually fine impression with full margins from the artist's series, *The Apocalypse.* Duvet worked in France at a time when feelings against the forces of Protestantism ran very high. In contrast to the elegance and worldliness of the dominant Fontainebleau style, the expression evident in Duvet's prints communicates an intense mysticism which links him to the Middle Ages. *The Fall of Babylon* is derived from Dürer's woodcut, *The Whore of Babylon,* but the contrast is extreme. For his *Apocalypse* series Duvet adopted an arched format, suggestive of the shape of an altarpiece or of a Romanesque or early Gothic stained glass window; or he may possibly have derived it from *nielli paxes* by Maso Finiguerra. Duvet's composition in this engraving is also "Gothic" in its violation of the Renaissance canon of perspective. In contrast to Dürer, Duvet does not suggest depth as succeeding recessive planes; instead, he packs the whole composition into a pulsing foreground, rejecting classical order and the illusion of space in favor of a synoptic compression of elements.

It is the mass and density of the artist's pattern, the feverish intensity of the actions and emotions of the figures, and the unreal, composite architectural backdrop which create the great concentration of graphic force in this crowded surface. The composition represents the reactions of the spectators to the collapse of the symbolized Babylon. Duvet shows her downfall literally in a veritable *chute.* Monster-headed serpents writhe below while the legs of Babylon herself project forward in the artist's deliberate emphasis on grotesqueness, satirizing the evil city's doom in the very awkwardness of her tumble.

Undoubtedly influenced not only by Dürer but by Italian art as well, Duvet preserved his subjectivity and his visionary approach, remaining not only the solitary great engraver of the French Renaissance but also one of the most vivid and compelling graphic artists in the history of Western art.

61, 62

Paolo Caliari, called Veronese
Italian, ca. 1528-1588
Allegory of Navigation (holding astrolabe)
Allegory of Navigation (holding cross-staff)
Oil on canvas
81 x 46 in. (206 x 117 cm.) each
Gift of The Ahmanson Foundation, 1974
M.74.99.1
M.74.99.2

Collections: Hon. Robert Baillie-Hamilton, Langton near Duns, Berwickshire, Scotland, before 1881; Robert Goelet, Newport, R.I.; Salve Regina College, Newport, R.I. (Sale, London, Sotheby, Dec. 12, 1973); Thomas Agnew & Sons, London, 1973-1974

Exhibition: London, Royal Academy of Arts, *Old Masters,* 1881, no. 164, as *Geometry and Navigation* (with cross-staff) and no. 166 as *Astronomy* (with astrolabe)

Literature: Anon., *Athenaeum,* Jan. 8, 1881, p. 61; Sale catalog, *Important Old Master Paintings,* London, Sotheby, Dec. 12, 1973, no. 13 (pair) as *Astronomy* (with astrolabe) and *Patriarch* (with cross-staff), repr. opp. p. 16 and 25; T. Pignatti, *Paolo Veronese Catalogue raisonné,* Venice: Alfieri Edizioni (scheduled for 1975)

These two paintings will be published in the Veronese literature for the first time in Terisio Pignatti's forthcoming catalogue raisonné of Veronese. They were exhibited only once, in London in 1881, and remained unknown to Veronese scholars since they were in rather remote private collections. The pictures were lent to the London exhibition by the Hon. Robert Baillie-Hamilton, whose family seat was at Langton, near Duns, Berwickshire, Scotland. He presumably inherited them through his wife from John Campbell, 2nd Marquis of Breadalbane, who had acquired large numbers of paintings in Italy and other parts of the Continent in the early 1830s. After Baillie-Hamilton's death they apparently remained in the family until they were acquired through private sale by Robert Goelet of Newport, Rhode Island, who gave or bequeathed them to a private college in Newport. It was only after their cleaning by Mario Modestini in New York, following their public sale, that scholars of Venetian art became aware that beneath the layers of obscuring brown varnish were two major works of Veronese. Since the paintings changed hands so rarely, they were seldom moved or cleaned and are, consequently, in an unusually fine state of preservation.

The iconography of these works has not yet been adequately investigated. There seems to have been a tradition identifying them with astronomy, geometry, and navigation, for these are the titles used in the 1881 exhibition. In the sale of 1973, however, the older figure retained his title *Astronomy,* while the younger one, because of the resemblance of the instrument he carries to a patriarchal cross, was called *Patriarch.* Both figures seem, however, to be allegories of navigation. The older figure holds an astrolabe, an ancient Greek instrument for measuring the altitude of the sun and stars. The anchor behind him suggests the practical application of the instrument, used by mariners for centuries, until the invention of the sextant in the eighteenth century, to calculate latitude and time of day. Since the figure resting his arms on an ancient Corinthian capital is a vigorous old man with white beard and flowing robes, he might well be Hipparchus, the second century B.C. Greek astronomer who made the first known chart of the stars and who is credited with the invention, or at least the perfection, of the astrolabe. The younger man with dark beard and brightly colored modern costume, resting his hand on a fragment of less typically ancient frieze, carries an instrument which has been identified by Clovis Whitfield of Agnew's as a cross-staff. This instrument, a graduated pole with one or more sliding crosspieces, was a modern, more portable alternative to the astrolabe.

While the astrolabe was used for astronomical observations as well as navigation, the cross-staff seems to have been essentially a nautical instrument. Both astrolabe and cross-staff were used on the great voyages of discovery of the sixteenth century. Since the cross-staff was a Renaissance invention, it may eventually be possible to identify this figure as a known astronomer or navigator. A three-quarter-length replica of the painting of the figure with cross-staff is in the collection of the late Major Stephen Courtauld, Umtali, Southern Rhodesia, along with a similar replica of another image from the same series, a turbaned Arab holding a portable armillary sphere of which the full-scale version is still unknown (repr. G. Fiocco, *Paolo Veronese,* Rome, 1934, pl. LX a,b; R. Marini and G. Piovene, *L'Opera completa del Veronese,* Milan: Rizzoli, 1968, no. 403).

The Ahmanson Veroneses must have formed part of a grand decorative scheme of allegorical figures united by painted architecture. Pignatti wrote in a letter of October 19, 1974, "They may have been in a private palace of some fleet commander or in some official room at the 'Magistrato alle Acque' or even in the Arsenal. There is no mention of them in the known documents."

Because of the dearth of documents concerning Veronese's commissions, precise dates are difficult to establish. In the letter referred to above, Pignatti wrote of the Ahmanson pictures, "They remind me of the paintings of Veronese's most mature, most wonderful period, the series of the two Frick and the Metropolitan paintings with allegorical subjects. They ought to be dated, therefore, sometime around the 1570s, and indeed they are very similar also to the large figures in the San Sebastiano 'Martyrdoms' in the church of San Sebastiano in Venice." Without sacrificing either luxuriousness of color or the sense of atmospheric reality achieved by softening transitions and subtly modulating light, shadow, and color, Veronese has realized in these two paintings a strength of form and grandeur of design which do justify placing them among the most monumental of his works.

63

Il Morazzone (Pier Francesco Mazzuchelli)
Italian, 1571/3-1626
St. Francis' Vision of the Musical Angel
Oil on canvas
46½ x 62 in. (108.1 x 157.5 cm.)
Gift of The Ahmanson Foundation, 1973
M.73.6

Collection: Frederick Mont, New York

Literature: R. Longhi, "Codicilli alle 'Schede lombarde' di Marco Valsecchi," *Paragone,* no. 243 (May 1970), pp. 37-38, repr. pl. 31-33, color pl. V

Nothing is known of the history of the Ahmanson Morazzone before its acquisition in 1969 by Frederick Mont, at which time it was attributed to the Spanish painter Francesco Ribalta. Recognizing that the painting was not Spanish but Italian, Mr. Mont sent a transparency to Roberto Longhi who immediately identified it as a work of Morazzone and dated it about 1611 on the basis of its close stylistic affinity with the *Magdalene* installed in the Cappella della Maddalena in San Vittore in Varese on July 22, 1611 (repr. in exhib. cat., Milan, Palazzo Reale, *Il Seicento Lombardo,* 1973, vol. II, no. 103, pl. 118). This quite convincing comparison is based on a broad spectrum of stylistic considerations: concept, modeling, use of light, setting, and even details like the stems and leaves of the vines among the rocks which could be transferred from one to the other painting without any alteration.

Pier Francesco Mazzuchelli (1571/3-1626), called Morazzone from the town of his birth, was one of a group of artists who, under the inspiration of Carlo Borommeo (died 1584) and the patronage of his nephew Cardinal Federico Borommeo, Archbishop of Milan from 1594 to 1631, worked indefatigably to fill the churches and sanctuaries of Milan, Como, and the small Alpine villages to the north and west with altarpieces, frescoes, and the uniquely Lombard *tableaux vivants* of painting and sculpture, all expressing the new religious fervor of the Council of Trent.

Morazzone's Lombard colleagues, also from the Valsesia, were Cerano (1575/6-1632) and Tanzio da Varallo (1574/80-1635). All three were formed on Gaudenzio Ferrari (died 1546) but studied in Rome where they assimilated influences from Cesare d'Arpino, and in some instances from Caravaggio, which they combined with North Italian elements to create a distinctive Lombard style with aspects of Late Mannerism and Early Baroque. It was a deeply emotional art, typically depicting martyrdoms, penitential self-abnegation, miracles, and ecstasies. The Ahmanson Morazzone is characteristic in both content and style.

In the late sixteenth and early seventeenth centuries, St. Francis achieved a new popularity, not for the charming episodes from his life which delighted the age of Giotto but for his mystical experiences arising from his being consumed with love of God. Four themes became popular: the stigmatization in a new subjective interpretation, St. Francis supported by angels as a typological parallel to Christ, St. Francis adoring the crucifix, and St. Francis' vision of the musical angel.

The subject of the musical angel, which is often confused with other ecstasies of St. Francis or with his death, seems never to have been represented in painting until the end of the sixteenth century. According to the dates established by the Franciscan scholar Luke Wadding in the seventeenth century, the musical angel appeared to St. Francis at Rieti in 1225, a year after he had received the stigmata on Mount Alverna and a year before his death in 1226. Both

Thomas of Celano in his *Vita Secunda S. Francisci* of about 1247 and St. Bonaventura, whose *Legenda Maior* was the standard life of St. Francis from 1266 on, tell the story with some variations. The version adopted by the sixteenth- and seventeenth-century artists was from the *Fioretti di San Francesco,* popular since the mid-fourteenth century. At the end of the "Second Consideration on the Holy Stigmata," the author relates: "...St. Francis being much weakened in body through his great abstinence and his struggles with demons, wishing to comfort his body with spiritual food of the soul, began to think of the immeas- urable glory and joy of the blessed in eternal life, and thereupon began to pray God to grant him the grace of tasting a little of that joy. And while he was thus thinking, suddenly there appeared to him an angel with exceeding great splendor, that held a viol in his left hand and a bow in his right; and while St. Francis was all amazed at the sight of him, the angel drew the bow once upward across the viol; and immediately such sweetness of melody invaded St. Francis' soul and lifted him above all bodily sense, that, as he afterwards related to his companions, he doubted whether his soul would not have departed from his body if the angel had drawn the bow down again, because of the unbearable loveliness of the music."

According to Pamela Askew, who published an exhaustive study of "The Angelic Consolation of St. Francis of Assisi in Post-Tridentine Italian Painting" in the *Journal of the Warburg and Courtauld Institutes* (vol. 32 [1969], pp. 280- 306), the first painting of the subject was done by Annibale Carracci in 1586-1587 (London, Coll. Denis Mahon). In it St. Francis is seated in a rocky landscape, his head on his hand as if in reverie, filled with peace and joy by the music of the angel above. Agostino Carracci engraved a similar painting after Francesco Vanni with a somewhat more rapturous St. Francis. The subject spread rapidly with considerable variation. Morazzone's interpretation of the subject is a work of considerable originality in com- position and feeling. St. Francis, exhausted from a night of prayer on a mountain precipice, has fallen back as if in death; at the left the day begins to break on the little lake town which Longhi identifies as Varese. On the road toward town appear only Tobias and the Angel, whose icono- graphic role in this context has not yet been deciphered. On the right, the light barely picks out the falling water of a cascade. The light from the left does not completely dispel the darkness but gently gives form to the head, hands, and heavy tunic of Francis and the overturned skull in the foreground. The whole is a quiet harmony of browns and muted tones into which the incarnate Angel breaks. The contrast of the backward movement of Francis and the forward movement of the Angel, the moribund saint and the cherub brimming with life are characteristics of Morazzone. The closest parallel to Morazzone's *St. Francis* is not another picture of the same subject, but Caravaggio's *Stigmatization*

of *St. Francis* (Wadsworth Atheneum, Hartford) which Morazzone could have known during the years he worked in Rome, 1592-1598. While comparisons can be made of format, use of light, and nocturnal setting, the paintings are most closely related in their interpretation of the saint, metaphorically dead while living in Christ through the in- tensity of his love—an anticipation of the ecstatic experience which becomes one of the characteristic statements of High Baroque art.

64

Peter Paul Rubens
Flemish, 1577-1640
Young Woman with Curly Hair, ca. 1618-1620
Oil on panel
17 x 13⅛ in. (43.3 x 33.5 cm.), enlarged to
26⅜ x 20⅝ in. (67 x 52.4 cm.)
Promised gift of the Armand Hammer Foundation

Collections: Schamp d'Aveschoot, Ghent, recorded 1830; Duc d'Arenberg and descendants, Brussels and later south of France, purchased 1840 at Schamp sale; Edward Speelman, London, bought 1959 from present Duke; Jean Davray, Paris, by 1963; Armand Hammer, Los Angeles

Exhibitions: Memphis, Tennessee, Brooks Memorial Art Gallery, *The Armand Hammer Collection,* Oct. 2- Dec. 30, 1969, no. 2, repr. in color on cat. cover; Washington, D.C., Smithsonian Institution, *The Armand Hammer Collection,* Mar. 20-May 17, 1970, no. 2, repr. in color on cat. cover; Smithsonian Institution Traveling Exhibition Service, *The Armand Hammer Collection,* Kansas City, Missouri, William Rockhill Nelson Gallery of Art, June 30- Aug. 2, 1970; New Orleans, Isaac Delgado Museum of Art, Aug. 15-Sept. 20, 1970; Columbus Gallery of Fine Arts, Oct. 9-Nov. 1, 1970; Little Rock, Arkansas Art Center, Nov. 21, 1970-Jan. 12, 1971; San Francisco, California Palace of the Legion of Honor, *The Armand Hammer Collection,* Feb. 11-Mar. 14, 1971; Oklahoma City, Okla- homa Art Center, *The Armand Hammer Collection,* June 15- July 11, 1971; San Diego, Fine Arts Gallery of San Diego, *The Armand Hammer Collection,* July 23-Sept. 5, 1971; Los Angeles County Museum of Art, *The Armand Hammer Collection,* Dec. 21, 1971-Feb. 27, 1972, no. 2, repr. in color in cat.; traveled to London, Royal Academy, June 24- July 24, 1972; Dublin National Gallery of Ireland, Aug. 8-Oct. 1, 1972; Leningrad, State Hermitage Museum, Oct. 23-Dec. 2, 1972; Moscow, State Pushkin Museum of Fine Arts, Dec. 8, 1972-Feb. 11, 1973; Kiev, State Museum of Ukrainian Art, March 6-31, 1973; Minsk, Belorussian State Museum of Fine Arts, Apr. 26-May 26, 1973; Riga, State Museum of Latvian and Russian Art, June 8-July 8, 1973; Odessa, State Picture Gallery, July 25-Aug. 25, 1973

Literature: J. Smith, *Catalogue Raisonné of the Works of the Most Eminent Dutch, Flemish, and French Painters,* vol. II (Rubens), London: Smith & Son, 1830, pp. 260-261, no. 881, and vol. IX (supplement), 1842, p. 330, no. 317; Sale catalog, *Catalogue des tableaux…composant la galerie de M. Schamp d'Aveschoot, de Gand,* Sept. 14, 1840, p. 2; M. Rooses, *L'oeuvre de P. P. Rubens,* Antwerp, 1886-1892, vol. IV, pp. 138, 290, no. 1088; J. Nève, "Quelques Portraits de la Galerie d'Arenberg," *Annales de l'Académie Royale d'Archéologie de Belgique,* Antwerp, vol. V, 4th series, no. X (1897), pp. 275, 276; M. Rooses, "Oeuvres de Rubens —Addenda," *Bulletin Rubens,* Antwerp, vol. 5 (1909), pp. 83-84; R. Oldenbourg, *P. P. Rubens,* Munich/Berlin, 1922, p. 142; L. Burchard, "Portrait of a Young Woman with Curly Hair by Peter Paul Rubens," manuscript report on Arenberg-Hammer painting, ca. 1960; D. Cooper (ed.), *Great Private Collections,* New York: Macmillan, 1963, repr. p. 257; M. Jaffé, manuscript letter to Roland Balay, M. Knoedler & Co., New York, dated: Cambridge University, Feb. 3, 1967; M. Harvard, "Portrait of a Girl with Curly Hair by Rubens," manuscript report on the Arenberg-Hammer and Morris paintings, London, Mar., 1969; M. Jaffé, "The Girl with the Golden Hair," *Apollo,* vol. XC, no. 92 (Oct. 1969), pp. 310-313, repr. in color, p. 311

The portrait as Rubens painted it was only the head and shoulders of the young woman. A seventeenth-century copy in the museum in Cassel shows the portrait in its original size. Sometime in the seventeenth or early eighteenth century the beveled edge, about one inch all around, was trimmed off and the painting was set into a larger panel a little to the top and right of center. The new panel seems to have been an oval, to which wedges were then or later added to make the present rectangle.

The identity of the sitter is not known. Michael Jaffé believes that the painting is a study rather than a formal portrait. According to Burchard, Rubens made a second study of the same girl but in a more frontal pose (Munich, Alte Pinakothek, no. 793 in cat.; exhibited in Bamberg Museum in 1934). The Munich painting measures 18⅞ x 14½ in., approximately the same as the Hammer painting originally, and, in Burchard's opinion, was probably painted at the same sitting.

The Hammer picture must have been extraordinarily popular in the seventeenth and eighteenth centuries, for at least six early repetitions of it are known: the Cassel copy of the original before enlargement (canvas 17¼ x 13¾ in., no. 89 in cat. of 1888); four repetitions of the present enlarged image: Dresden Museum (panel 25¼ x 19½ in., no. 964A in cat. of 1908, repr. A. Rosenberg, *P. P. Rubens, des Meisters Gemälde,* Klassiker der Kunst, second edition, Stuttgart/Leipzig, 1906, p. 373); Leningrad, Hermitage (canvas said to have been transferred from panel 26 x 21¼ in., no. 577 in cat. of 1901, with additional drapery across chest and near shoulder); Althrop,

The Earl Spencer Collection (with two jeweled clasps holding bodice); Kiel, Prof. Götz Martins (panel 22⅞ x 16⅛ in.), similar to Spencer portrait; and a sixth painting still further enlarged in the collection of John C. Morris, Richmond, Surrey. The Morris painting (panel 28 x 23¼ in., repr. in R. Oldenbourg, *P. P. Rubens, des Meisters Gemälde,* Klassiker der Kunst, fourth edition, Berlin/Leipzig, 1921, p. 201) has a slightly lower neckline and extends the torso almost to the hips. Jaffé believes that all these repetitions of the enlarged picture were made after Rubens' death and that only the Hammer picture is an original by Rubens.

65

Peter Paul Rubens
Flemish, 1577-1640
The Israelites Gathering Manna in the Desert, 1625-1628
Oil on panel
25½ x 20¾ in. (64.8 x 52.7 cm.)
Frances and Armand Hammer Purchase Fund, 1969
M.69.20

Collections: Isabella Clara Eugenia, Archduchess of the Spanish Netherlands, Brussels; Philip IV and Charles II of Spain; Don Francisco Casimiro Pimentel, Count of Benavente, who in 1700, following the death of Charles II, received this and the other paintings from the Royal Collections kept in the Pieza de las Furias for himself and his successors; Dukes of Pastrana, Madrid, by inheritance from the Counts of Benavente; Emile Pacully, Paris (acquired from the Duke of Pastrana, Madrid, probably at sale of 1888); Baron Robert Gendebien, Brussels (acquired from A. Stein, dealer, Paris, ca. 1938); Rosenberg & Stiebel, New York, 1969

Exhibitions: Rotterdam, Boymans Museum, *Olieverfschelsen van Rubens,* Dec. 19, 1953-Feb. 14, 1954, no. 73, cat. by E. Haverkamp Begemann, pp. 85, 86, repr. pl. 63; Bordeaux, Centre de Tourisme, *Flandres, Espagne, Portugal du XVᵉ au XVIIᵉ Siècle,* May 19-July 31, 1954, no. 80, p. 83 in cat.; Brussels, Musées Royaux des Beaux-Arts de Belgique, *Le Siècle de Rubens,* Oct. 15-Dec. 12, 1965, no. 225, pp. 215, 216 in cat. by L. van Puyvelde, repr.; Memphis, Tennessee, Brooks Memorial Art Gallery, *The Armand Hammer Collection,* Oct. 2-Dec. 30, 1969, no. 3, repr. in cat.; Washington, D.C., Smithsonian Institution, *The Armand Hammer Collection,* Mar. 20-May 17, 1970, no. 3, repr. in color in cat.; Los Angeles County Museum of Art, *The Armand Hammer Collection,* Dec. 21, 1971- Feb. 27, 1972, no. 3, repr. in color in cat.; also traveled to London, Royal Academy, June 24-July 24, 1972; Dublin, National Gallery of Ireland, Aug. 8-Oct. 1, 1972; Leningrad, State Hermitage

Museum, Oct. 23-Dec. 2, 1972; Moscow, State Pushkin Museum of Fine Arts, Dec. 8, 1972-Feb. 11, 1973; Kiev, State Museum of Ukrainian Art, Mar. 6-31, 1973; Minsk, Belorussian State Museum of Fine Arts, Apr. 26-May 26, 1973; Riga, State Museum of Latvian and Russian Art, June 8-July 8, 1973; Odessa, State Picture Gallery, July 25-Aug. 25, 1973

Literature: M. Rooses, *L'Oeuvre de Pierre-Paul Rubens,* Antwerp, 1886-1892, vol. I, p. 73; idem, "De Verzameling Pacully te Paris," *Onze Kunst,* 1903, pp. 121-122; V. Josz, "La Collection Emile Pacully," *Les Arts,* year II, no. 16 (Apr. 1903), p. 35, repr. p. 36; Sale catalog, *Collection Emile Pacully,tableaux anciens et modernes,* Paris, Galerie Georges Petit, May 4, 1903, pp. 62-63, repr. with added garland; N. Sentenac y Cantanas, *La pintura en Madrid desde sus origenes hasta el siglo XIX,* Madrid, 1907, p. 78 (history and inventory of Pastrana collection); Sale catalog, *Tableaux…dépendant de la succession de Monsieur E. Pacully,* Paris, Hôtel Drouot, July 5, 1938, no. 28, repr. with added garland, as by Rubens and Jan Brueghel (This and several other pictures from the 1903 sale were apparently bought back by the owner and kept through his lifetime); E. Tormo, "Los Tapices: La Apotheosis Eucarística de Rubens," vol. II, pt. 2 of *En las Descalzas Reales de Madrid,* Madrid: Junta de Iconografía Nacional, 1945; L. von Puyvelde, *Les Esquisses de Rubens,* Basel: Holbein, 1940, p. 31, no. 7 (Engl. trans. London, 1947, p. 29); E. Haverkamp-Begemann, "Rubens Schetsen," *Bulletin Museum Boymans Rotterdam,* vol. V, no. 1 (Mar. 1954), p. 9, repr. p. 11; V. H. Elbern, "Die Rubensteppiche des Kölner Domes, ihre Geschichte und ihre Stellung im Zyklus Triumph der Eucharistie," *Kölner Domblatt,* vol. X, (1955), pp. 43-48, repr. pl. 29, vol. XIV/XV (1958), p. 121 ff.; vol. XXI/XXII (1963), pp. 77 ff.; J. Held, "Rubens' Triumph of the Eucharist and the *Modello* in Louisville," *J. B. Speed Art Museum Bulletin,* vol. XXVI, no. 3 (Feb. 1968). Tormo and Elbern are the most exhaustive studies of the series, Held the most concise study in English.

About 1625 the Archduchess Isabella Clara Eugenia, daughter of Philip II of Spain and ruler of the Spanish Netherlands, commissioned Rubens to produce eleven huge paintings and several smaller ones to be used as cartoons (full-size patterns) for a series of tapestries glorifying the Eucharist which she wished to present to the Convent of the Descalzas Reales (Franciscan Clarissa Nuns) in Madrid. The subjects were: four Old Testament prefigurations of the New Testament Eucharist, one of which was the Israelites gathering manna in the desert; two of the Evangelists and Eucharistic teachers and defenders; and five Eucharistic triumphs. The first series of tapestries made in Brussels was sent to the Convent in Madrid in July 1628. A second series is now in the Cathedral of Cologne. Other individual panels were woven as well.

In the preparation of the cartoons Rubens first painted rough sketches in grisaille, then full-color sketches *(modelli)* which were enlarged by the master and his shop to the desired size of the tapestry. The first sketch for *The Israelites Gathering Manna in the Desert* is a panel 5¾ x 4⅞ inches in the Musée Bonnat, Bayonne. In it Moses is in the background of a composition with a strong movement from left to right. In preparing the Los Angeles *modello* Rubens centralized the composition, confining it between Moses on the right and the woman with the child who turns towards center on the left. The woman is adapted from the woman with a jug in the Raphael *Fire in the Borgo* in the Vatican; other elements in both the grisaille and the *modello* are related to a Rubens drawing in the Louvre (Lugt no. 1038, fig. 52, also repr. in Elbern, 1958, fig. 12) after a Giulio Romano *Gathering of the Manna.* Employing Renaissance elements and classic compositional limits, Rubens has filled his stage with a dynamic movement and countermovement of form and light and has conceived his figures with a psychology of gesture not possible before the seventeenth century.

In 1648 Philip IV asked that the large cartoons and "other small paintings" for the Triumph of the Eucharist series be sent to Madrid. It is assumed by Rubens scholars that the sketches which were in the Royal Collections of Spain in the late seventeenth century, including the Los Angeles *modello,* were sent at that time. Presumably before 1648 the Los Angeles *modello* was set into a larger panel and surrounded by a garland of flowers and fruits. Max Rooses' (*Onze Kunst,* 1903) attribution of the garland, formerly called Jan Brueghel, to Pieter Bysels (1621-1690), would imply a date in the late forties. The *modello* with the garland is reproduced in the two Pacully sale catalogs and in *Les Arts,* 1903. The enlargement was removed and the painting restored to its original size after the sale of 1938.

The Los Angeles *modello* was separated from the other Triumph of the Eucharist *modelli* now in the Prado when it was inherited by the Count of Benavente. The Los Angeles *modello* had presumably been sold to Pacully before the Duchess of Pastrana presented a number of Rubens sketches for the Torre de la Parada from the same Benavente-Pastrana inheritance to the Prado on May 28, 1889 (Prado nos. 2038-2040).

The large cartoon (canvas, 192 x 163 in.) made from the Los Angeles *modello* was one of six cartoons sent in 1648 to Philip IV. He presented the six to Olivares, who placed them in his small family church at Loeches, near Madrid. They were removed by French troops during the Napoleonic invasions. Two became the property of the Louvre; four, including *The Israelites Gathering Manna in the Desert,* were sold in 1818 to the Duke of Westminster and in

1928 to John Ringling for the Ringling Museum in Sarasota, Florida (repr. William E. Suida, *A Catalogue of Paintings in the John and Mable Ringling Museum of Art,* Sarasota, 1949, pp. 178-183). A copy of the Los Angeles *modello* is in the Museum of Doornik (Tournai). A School of Rubens drawing of the composition is in the Louvre (Lugt. no. 1127).

66

Rembrandt van Rijn
Dutch, 1606-1669
Raising of Lazarus, ca. 1630
Oil on panel
37½ x 32½ in. (93.7 x 81.1 cm.)
Gift of H. F. Ahmanson & Co. in memory of
Howard F. Ahmanson, 1972
M.72.67.2

Collections: Gottfried II Winckler, Leipzig, until his death, 1795; Gottfried III Winckler, Leipzig, 1795; Jacob Duval, Geneva, before 1812 (Sale, London, May 12-13, 1846); Comte de Morny, Paris, 1846 (Sale, Paris, May 24, 1852); Jules Beer, Paris (Sale, Paris, May 29, 1913); Sedelmeyer, Paris, 1913-1921 or later; R. Langton Douglas, by 1932; Mme. Dübi-Müller, Schanzmühle, Solothurn, Switzerland, 1932-1959; Howard F. Ahmanson, 1959-his death, 1968

Exhibitions: Amsterdam, Rijksmuseum, *Rembrandt Tentoonstelling,* June 11-Sept. 14, 1932, no. 2, p. 35, in cat. (lent by Langton Douglas); Amsterdam, Rijksmuseum, on extended loan from Mme. Dübi-Müller, 1932-1959, no. 2024, A9; Amsterdam, Rijksmuseum, *Rembrandt Tentoonstelling ter Herdenking van de Geboorte van Rembrandt op 15 July 1606,* May 18-Aug. 5, 1956, no. 11, p. 23 in cat., repr. p. 22; traveled to Rotterdam, Museum Boymans, Aug. 8-Oct. 21, 1956 (lent by Rijksmuseum on loan from Mme. Dübi-Müller)

Literature: Sale catalog, *Catalogue de la Belle Collection de Tableaux...de M. Duval, de Genève...dans les Salles de M. Phillips,* London, May 12-13, 1846, no. 116; Sale catalog, *Catalogue d'une précieuse collection de Tableaux... formant le Cabinet de M. le Comte de M....(Morny),* Paris, May 24, 1852, no. 17; Sale catalog, *Catalogue des Tableaux ...de la Succession de M.x...(*Jules Beer), Paris, Galerie Georges Petit, May 29, 1913, no. 52, repr. opp. p. 52; Sedelmeyer Gallery, *Catalogue of the 12th Series of 100 Paintings by Old Masters,* Paris, 1913, p. 34, no. 20, repr. p. 20; C. Hofstede de Groot, *A Catalogue Raisonné of the Works of the Most Eminent Dutch Painters of the Seventeenth Century,* London: Macmillan, vol. VI (1916), p. 85, no. 107 A; W. R. Valentiner, *Rembrandt, Wiedergefundene Gemälde* (1910-1920) (Klassiker der Kunst), Stuttgart/Berlin, 1921, p.xvi, no. 17, repr. pl. 16 (Ch. Sedelmeyer, Paris); F. Saxl, "Rembrandt und Italien," *Oud Holland,* vol. XLI (1923-24), pp. 145-160; H. Schneider, *Jan Lievens,* Haarlem: Bohn, 1932, p. 38 A; A. Bredius,

The Paintings of Rembrandt, Vienna: Phaidon, 1936, repr. pl. 538, notes p. 23, no. 538; W. Teupser, *Kunst und ihre Sammlung in Leipzig,* Leipzig: Breitkopf u. Härtel, 1937, repr. of Wiegand watercolor pl. 1A; K. E. Schurman, *Carel Fabritius,* Amsterdam, 1947, pp. 20 ff.; S. Slive, *Rembrandt, Bible Paintings,* New York: Abrams, 1956, repr. in color pl. 13 (as in Rijksmuseum); J. Gantner, *Rembrandt und die Verwandlung Klassischer Formen,* Bern-Munich: Francke Verlag, 1964, pp. 15-19, repr. p. 17, fig. 3; K. Bauch, *Rembrandt Gemälde,* Berlin: de Gruyter, 1966, repr. pl. 51, note p. 4, no. 51 (Bauch reproduces the Los Angeles picture but locates it in Solothurn. Subsequent writers all consider Bauch 51 as the Los Angeles picture.); K. Bauch, "Zum Werk des Jan Lievens (II), *Pantheon,* vol. 25 (1967), pp. 160 ff.; H. Gerson, *Rembrandt Paintings,* New York; Reynal & Co., 1968, pp. 26, 182, 489, note 16, repr. p. 183, no. 16; A. Bredius, revised by H. Gerson, *Rembrandt, the Complete Edition of the Paintings,* London: Phaidon, 3rd edition, 1969, repr. p. 454, notes p. 604, no. 538 (Chicago painting repr. in appendix p. 543 as not by Rembrandt); B. Haak, *Rembrandt, His Life, His Work, His Time,* New York: Abrams, 1969, p. 63, repr. pl. 89; J. R. Judson, Catalogue of Paintings in *Rembrandt after Three Hundred Years,* Art Institute of Chicago, 1969, pp. 65-66 (Fabritius), 78-79 (Lievens); W. Stechow, "Rembrandt's Representations of the 'Raising of Lazarus'," *Los Angeles County Museum of Art Bulletin,* vol. XIX, no. 2 (1973), pp. 7 ff. repr. in color p. 6; B. Johnson, "Examination and Treatment of Rembrandt's 'Raising of Lazarus'," *Los Angeles County Museum of Art Bulletin,* vol. XX, no. 2 (1974), repr. with color detail (an extensive account of the condition and technique of the painting)

The history of the Ahmanson *Raising of Lazarus* before the Duval sale of 1846 has not yet been clarified. The inventory of Rembrandt's estate made at the time of his bankruptcy in 1656 records a *Raising of Lazarus* by his hand in the front parlor, unfortunately without any description or measurement. Since the Ahmanson *Raising of Lazarus,* the only Rembrandt painting of the subject known today, was most likely not a commissioned work and since the inventory lists a *Raising of Lazarus* by Rembrandt's friend from his youth, Jan Lievens, in the same room, it is tempting to conclude that Rembrandt had kept the painting most of his life. There are further references in the later seventeenth and early eighteenth centuries to a painting of the *Raising of Lazarus* by Rembrandt, but none complete enough to permit positive identification until the painting came into the collection of Gottfried II Winckler (1731-1795) in Leipzig. Here a local artist, Christian Friedrich Wiegand (1752-1832), made eight watercolors (Stadtgeschichtlichen Museum, Leipzig) of the walls of Winckler's Garden House Gallery, showing 218 paintings in place. In the lower left of the first watercolor (repr. in Teupser, 1937, pl. 1A) is the Ahmanson *Raising of Lazarus*. The painting was next reproduced in St. Petersburg, Russia, in 1812 in *Le Cabinet de M. Duval,* a folio of line engravings by Michailoff (probably Pavel Nicholaevich, 1786-1840) lightly retouched by his professor of graphic arts at the St. Petersburg Academy, Ignaz Sebastian Klauber (1773-1817). They were reprinted in the Duval sale catalog of 1846. The Rembrandt was one of a number of paintings acquired by Jacob Duval from the Winckler collection, more likely by private purchase than from public sale. There is some evidence that Winckler was in Russia in the early nineteenth century, e.g. Burton Fredericksen (letter, Malibu, Oct. 28, 1974) has found that he sold a painting to the Hermitage in 1805. The Rembrandt may well have been in St. Petersburg when it was engraved in 1812. Duval must have taken the pictures to Switzerland and established residence there before 1846, since he is referred to as "M. Duval de Genève" in the catalog of the sale of his collection in London in that year.

The early history of the Ahmanson painting is confused by the existence of an early copy (Yerkes, Brandus, Gates, Angell-Norris collections; since 1970, Art Institute of Chicago), once thought to be Rembrandt's, and by the attribution of paintings by his followers to Rembrandt himself.

A considerable body of literature has grown up over the past fifty years concerning the relationship of the Ahmanson Rembrandt to other representations of the subject in the Rembrandt circle: a drawing and two etchings by Rembrandt, an etching and a painting by Jan Lievens, and a painting by Carel Fabritius. (For summary and bibliography, see Judson, 1969.) Rembrandt's first concept of the subject is a red chalk drawing in the British Museum, boldly dated 1630. Within the interior of a cave, Lazarus, in a rectangular sarcophagus, is at the lower right. Far above him at the top of the tomb, as if on a podium, the figure of Christ stands isolated, facing forward, his hands folded before him, his head toward the heavens. At the left the two levels are united by mounded earth, a long upsweeping winding sheet, and the spectators. The direction of light is not indicated. Even though Rembrandt changed the drawing into a burial of Christ, the original subject is still easily discernible. This image is more faithfully preserved in an undated etching and a painting dated 1631 (Brighton Art Gallery), both by Rembrandt's collaborator in Leyden, Jan Lievens, than in any work of Rembrandt. The most distinguished Rembrandt scholars are therefore divided as to whether the invention was Lievens' or Rembrandt's. When Rembrandt adapted the drawing for the Ahmanson painting in 1630 or shortly thereafter, he made a number of changes consistent with his lifelong concern with representing the divine within the human Christ. In the drawing Christ is the intermediary looking up to his heavenly Father from whom comes the power to perform the miracle. In the Lievens

etching the light of Christ's divinity radiates from him to fill the cave. In the Ahmanson painting Rembrandt moved the figure of Christ from its isolated central position to the left to be part of the group of spectators and reduced the elevation of Christ above Lazarus to produce a single unified space. He replaced the light winding cloth by a darkly dressed woman seen from behind, who performs the same function of contributing to the spatial continuum from foreground to background. He enveloped most of the cave in darkness, permitting only a few highlights to be picked out by a sharp light from the left, a type of lighting ultimately from Caravaggio which Rembrandt could have known through his teacher, Pieter Lastmans, and the Utrecht Caravaggists. In this milieu Christ, partially enveloped in shadow and without any aura of divinity, raises his hand and by his very gesture brings the miracle to pass. Light, darkness, gestures, and facial expressions suggesting intense emotional involvement allow the spectator to participate in the unfolding drama.

In the highly finished etching of about 1632, Rembrandt used the same interpretation of the scene but altered the composition drastically to achieve greater spatial depth and grandeur of design. In doing this he sacrificed the directness of experience that the Ahmanson painting offers.

That the Ahmanson *Raising of Lazarus* was important in the Rembrandt studio for many years after it was painted is evident from its considerable influence on Carel Fabritius' *Raising of Lazarus* (Museum Narodowe, Warsaw), his first independent work after leaving Rembrandt about 1642.

By 1642 when Rembrandt again chose the *Raising of Lazarus* for an etching, his conception of Christ and the miracle had changed drastically. In Professor Stechow's words, "The magician has given way to the spiritual healer," who restores Lazarus to life with so little overt gesticulation that it is almost as if he had merely willed the miracle. The entire scene is extraordinarily quiet, without any violent emotions or sharp contrasts of light. The external drama of 1630 has given way to inward experience.

67

Rembrandt van Rijn
Dutch, 1606-1669
Portrait of a Man of the Raman Family, 1634
Oil on oval panel
25½ x 19⅞ in. (64.8 x 50.5 cm.), enlarged to rectangle
27⅛ x 20⅞ in. (68.8 x 53.2 cm.)
Signed and dated lower right: Rembrandt fe 1634
Inscribed lower left: AE:47
Frances and Armand Hammer Purchase Fund, 1969
M.69.16

Collections: The Raman Family, Amsterdam; August de Ridder, Schönberg near Cronberg, before 1909 (Sale, Paris, June 2, 1924); Ehrich Galleries, New York, 1930-1936; N. Katz, Basel, by 1948 (Sale, Paris, Apr. 25, 1951); Julius Weitzner Galleries, New York, by 1956; P. de Boer, Amsterdam, before 1966; H. Kohn, Wassenaar, Holland, by 1968; H. Shickman Gallery, New York, 1969

Exhibitions: Frankfurt-am-Main Städelsches Kunstinstitut, 1911-1913 (following death of de Ridder, May 13, 1911); New York, F. Kleinberger Galleries, *The Collection of Pictures of the late Herr A. de Ridder,* exhibition and private sale, Nov. 24-Dec. 15, 1913, no. 1, repr. in cat., p. 32; Detroit Institute of Arts, *Paintings by Rembrandt,* May 2-31, 1930, no. 22, repr. in cat. (lent by Ehrich Galleries, New York); The Hague, Mauritshuis, *Hervonnen Kunstbezit, Tentoonstelling van uit Duitsland teruggekeerde Nederlandsche kunstschatten,* Mar.-Apr. 1946, no. 49, p. 22 in cat.; Basel, Katz Galerie, *Rembrandt-Austellung,* July 24-Sept. 30, 1948, no. 13, repr. in cat.; Raleigh, North Carolina Museum of Art, *Rembrandt and His Pupils,* Nov. 16-Dec. 30, 1956, no. 9, repr. in cat. (lent by Julius Weitzner, New York); Memphis, Tennessee, Brooks Memorial Art Gallery, *The Armand Hammer Collection,* Oct. 2-Dec. 30, 1969, no. 4, repr. in cat.; The Art Institute of Chicago, *Rembrandt after Three Hundred Years,* Oct. 25-Dec. 7, 1969, no. 4, cat. p. 4, repr. p. 91; traveled to Minneapolis Institute of Art, Dec. 22, 1969-Feb. 1, 1970; Detroit Institute of Arts, Feb. 24-Apr. 5, 1970; Washington, D.C., Smithsonian Institution, Mar. 20-May 17, 1970, *The Armand Hammer Collection,* no. 4, repr. in cat. (painting shown in Memphis and Washington only on dates which did not conflict with Chicago and Detroit); Los Angeles County Museum of Art, *The Armand Hammer Collection,* Dec. 21, 1971-Feb. 27, 1972, no. 1, repr. in color in cat.; traveled to London, Royal Academy of Arts, June 24-July 24, 1972; Dublin, National Gallery of Ireland, Aug. 9-Oct. 1, 1972; Leningrad, State Hermitage Museum, Oct. 23-Dec. 2, 1972; Moscow, State Pushkin Museum of Fine Arts, Dec. 8, 1972-Feb. 11, 1973; Kiev, State Museum of Ukrainian Art, Mar. 6-31, 1973; Minsk, Belorussian State Museum of Fine Arts, Apr. 26-May 26, 1973; Riga, State Museum of Latvian and Russian Art, June 8-July 8, 1973; Odessa, State Picture Gallery, July 25-Aug. 26, 1973

Literature: W. R. Valentiner, *Rembrandt, des Meisters Gemälde* (Klassiker der Kunst), 3rd edition, Stuttgart/ Berlin: 1909, repr. p. 193 as "Portrait of a Man"; W. Bode, *Die Gemäldegalerie des Herr A. de Ridder,* Berlin: Julius Bard, 1910, pp. 4, 35, repr. pl. 1 as "Portrait of a Man of the Raman Family"; idem, *The Collection of Pictures of the late Herr A. de Ridder* (trans. H. Virgin), Berlin: Julius Bard, 1913, no. 1, repr. pl. 1; C. Hofstede de Groot, *A Catalogue Raisonné of the Works of the Most Eminent Dutch Painters of the Seventeenth Century,* London:

Macmillan, 1916, vol. VI, p. 347, no. 739 as "A Man in a Large Slouch Hat, said to be a member of the Raman family"; Sale catalog, *Catalogue des tableaux anciens... composant la Galerie de feu M. A. de Ridder,* Paris, Galerie Georges Petit, June 2, 1924, no. 55, repr.; A. Bredius, *Rembrandt Gemälde,* Vienna: Phaidon, 1935, no. 194; idem, *The Paintings of Rembrandt,* Vienna: Phaidon, 1937, no. 194; J. Rosenberg, *Rembrandt,* Cambridge: Harvard University Press, 1948, vol. 1, p. 243 (concordance); Sale catalog, *Catalogue des Importants Tableaux Anciens provenant de la Succession N.K.* (N. Katz), Paris, Galerie Charpentier, Apr. 25, 1951, no. 6, repr. pl. XXXIX; K. Bauch, *Rembrandt Gemälde,* Berlin: de Gruyter, 1966, p. 19 (notes), no. 374, repr.; H. Gerson, *Rembrandt Paintings,* Amsterdam and New York: Reynal & Co., 1968, p. 495, no. 168, repr. p. 289; H. Gerson (ed.), *Rembrandt, The Complete Edition of the Paintings of Rembrandt by A. Bredius,* London: Phaidon, 1969, p. 564, no. 194, repr. p. 158

The sitter has been called a member of the Raman family since, according to Bode, 1910, the painting came "directly from the old Amsterdam patrician family, Raman," to the de Ridder collection. It had presumably been in that family from the time it was painted. The name Raman, however, is not recorded in J. E. Elias *De vroedschap von Amsterdam, 1578-1795* (Haarlem: V. Loosjes, 1903-05), the most extensive book on Amsterdam families of the seventeenth century. Neither does it appear in the Amsterdam archives of that period, according to an oral communication from Dr. I. H. van Eeghen to Professor E. Haverkamp-Begemann. If the painting did pass to the Raman family by direct descent, it must have been through marriage. The name of the sitter would, therefore, not have been Raman, but it may be discovered by a genealogical investigation of the Raman family.

The picture did not appear in the Rembrandt literature until Valentiner included it in the third edition of the Klassiker der Kunst *Rembrandt* in 1909. By that time it had already been enlarged from its original shape to a rectangle. In subsequent literature (Hofstede de Groot, 1916; Bauch, 1966; Gerson, 1968; Gerson-Bredius, 1969) the statement is made that the painting was originally ten-sided. If that were true, the enlargement would follow a simple decagonal pattern. X-rays show, however, a quite irregular twelve-sided pattern which suggests that the painting was originally an oval, approximately the same as that shown in the present frame. Cleaning has also shown the original to be oval rather than decagonal. Bode, 1910, noted the extraordinarily fine state of preservation of the picture, and this has been attested in a recent cleaning at the Los Angeles County Museum of Art.

The Raman portrait has much in common with
Rembrandt's other commissioned portraits of the 1630s in
pose, dress, composition, and oval format. Less common
but not unique elements are the uneven thickness of paint
application in the background, allowing the panel to show
through in places, the transparent painting of the ruff,
and the warm dense shadows cast on it, all suggesting an
atmospheric space around the figure. It is in the face that the
Raman portrait achieves its distinction. Here short, uneven
brushstrokes break up the surface and wiry ones depict
the bristle of hair and beard. The degree of idealization
produced in many of the portraits of the early thirties by the
use of subtly graduated light to model form, is here self-
consciously avoided to achieve an unmitigated naturalism,
rare in Rembrandt's work. It is a provocative face, which,
like Rembrandt's self-portraits, implies a wealth of
human experience.

The assumption often found in Rembrandt literature
that *The Portrait of a Lady in a Broad Ruff,* 1636, in the
collection of Lord Kinnaird, Rossie Priority, Perthshire
(Bredius no. 354), is a companion to the Hammer portrait,
has been supported by recent technical investigations of
Herbert Lank, London, who reported (letter, October 9, 1974)
that the additions that make the panels rectangular
are identical.

68

Frans Hals
Dutch, 1580-1666
Portrait of Pieter Tjarck (?)
Oil on canvas
33½ x 27½ in. (85 x 70 cm.)
Gift of The Ahmanson Foundation, 1974
M.74.31

Collections: Comte d'Oultremont (Sale, June 27, 1889);
Arnold & Tripp, Paris; Sir William Cuthbert Quilter,
London and Bawdsey Manor Suffolk, 1889/1890-his
death, 1911; The Dowager Lady Quilter, Bawdsey Manor,
Suffolk, 1911-her death, 1927; Sir William Eley Cuthbert
Quilter, Bawdsey Manor, Suffolk, 1927-1937; Sir Harry
Oakes, Nassau, Bahamas, 1937-his death, 1943 (acquired
through Knoedler & Co., New York); Eunice, Lady Oakes,
Nassau, Bahamas, 1943-1974 (sold through Colnaghi,
London)

Exhibitions: Brussels, 1882, no. 86; Paris, *Exposition
Universelle Internationale,* 1889; London, Royal Academy
of Arts, Exhibition of Works by the Old Masters, Jan. 5-
Mar. 14, 1891, no. 69 in cat.; The Hague, Cercle Artistique,
Exposition de Portraits Anciens, July 1-Sept. 1, 1903,
no. 36 in cat.; London, Royal Academy of Arts, *Exhibition*

of Dutch Art 1450-1900, Jan.-Mar. 1929, no. 51 in cat.;
Haarlem, Frans Halsmuseum, *Frans Hals Tentoonstelling,*
July 1-Sept. 30, 1937, no. 75, repr. in cat., pl. 76; New York,
World's Fair, *Masterpieces of Art,* May-Oct. 1939, no. 182
in cat.; New York, Duveen Galleries, *Paintings by the
Great Dutch Masters of the Seventeenth Century,* Oct. 8-
Nov. 7, 1942, no. 22, repr. in cat., p. 114; Art Institute of
Chicago, *Paintings by the Great Dutch Masters of the
Seventeenth Century,* Nov. 18-Dec. 16, 1942, no. 17, repr.
in cat., p. 85; New York, M. Knoedler & Co., *Twenty-four
Masterpieces to Commemorate the Hundredth Anniversary
of the Knoedler Gallery,* Nov. 4-23, 1946, no. 10, repr.
in cat.; Los Angeles County Museum, *Loan Exhibition of
Paintings of Frans Hals and Rembrandt,* Nov. 18-Dec. 31,
1947, no. 13, repr. in cat.; Raleigh, North Carolina Museum
of Art, *Masterpieces of Art in Memory of William R.
Valentiner, 1880-1958,* Oct. 6-May 17, 1959, no. 61, repr.
in cat., p. 109; Richmond, Virginia Museum of Fine Arts,
Treasures in America, 25th Anniversary Exhibition,
Jan. 13-Mar. 5, 1961, repr. in cat., p. 62

Literature: Sale catalog, *Catalogue de Douze Tableaux
importants...de la collection d'Oultrement,* Paris, Hôtel
Drouot, June 27, 1889, p. 11, no. 3, repr.; F. G. Stephens,
"The Collection of Mr. W. Cuthbert Quilter, M.P.,"
Magazine of Art, XX (1897), p. 316 ff., repr. p. 321;
G. S. Davies, *Frans Hals,* London: G. Bell, 1902, p. 137,
repr. pl. 43 b; W. Martin, "L'Exposition des portraits
anciens à La Haye," *Les Arts,* Dec. 1903, p. 21 ff., repr. on
cover; C. Hofstede de Groot, *Meisterwerke der Porträt-
malerei auf der Austellung im Haag,* Munich: F. Brinckmann,
1903; p. 14, no. 36, repr. pl. 23; E. W. Moes, *Iconographia
Batavia,* Amsterdam: F. Muller, 1897-1905, vol. II (1905),
p. 469, nos. 7993-1 (incorrectly dated 1608) and 7993-2;
E. W. Moes, *Frans Hals, sa vie et son oeuvre,* Brussels:
G. van Oest, 1909, p. 104, no. 77; C. Hofstede de Groot,
*A Catalogue Raisonné of the Works of the Most Eminent
Dutch Painters of the Seventeenth Century,* vol. III,
London: Macmillan, 1910, p. 69, no. 231, English translation
of original German edition, Esslinger A.N., 1910, no. 231;
J. Peladan, *Frans Hals,* Paris: Goupil, 1912, p. 122, repr.;
W. von Bode and M. J. Binder, *Frans Hals Sein Leben und
Seine Werke,* Berlin: Photographische Gesellschaft, 1914,
vol. II, p. 57, no. 178, repr. pl. 110; W. R. Valentiner,
Frans Hals, des Meisters Gemälde (Klassiker der Kunst),
Stuttgart/Berlin, 1921, repr. p. 160; 2nd revised edition
1923, repr. p. 172; *Commemorative Catalogue of the
Exhibition of Dutch Art Held in the Galleries of Royal
Academy, Burlington House, London, January-March 1929,*
London: Milford, 1930, p. 46; F. Dülberg, *Frans Hals,*
Stuttgart: P. Neff, 1930, p. 148, repr. p. 150, fig. 61; Anon.,
"A Great Frans Hals Goes to the West Indies," *Art News,*
XXXV, 31, sec. II (May 1, 1937), p. 17, repr. on cover,
detail, p. 17; Anon., *Magazine of Art,* XXX, 8 (Aug. 1937),
repr. p. 511; F. van Thienen, "Die Hals-Austellung in

Haarlem," *Pantheon,* XX, 9 (Aug. 1937), p. 261 ff., repr. p. 268; M. Salinger, "Old Masters in America," *American Collector,* XV (Nov. 1946), p. 8 ff., repr. p. 9; N. S. Trivas, *The Paintings of Frans Hals,* Oxford: Phaidon, 1941, p. 46, no. 65, repr. pl. 88; S. Slive, *Frans Hals,* Oxford: Phaidon, 1970-74, vol. I, p. 122, vol. II, repr. pl. 176-177, vol. III, p. 59-60, no. 108; C. Grimm, *Frans Hals,* Berlin: Geb. Mann, 1972, p. 35, cat. no. 81, repr. fig. 110; Sale catalog, *Highly Important Pictures by Old Masters,* London, Christie's, June 29, 1973, p. 100-101, no. 104, repr. in color (bought in); M. Boot, "Uber Willem van Heythuysen, Seinen Nachlass und die symbolische Bedentung des Porträts von Frans Hals in München," *Pantheon,* XXXI, 4 (Oct.-Dec. 1973), pp. 420-424, repr., p. 422 fig. 4

The first documented appearance of the Ahmanson portrait is in the Oultremont sale of 1889 where it is listed in the catalog as "Portrait de Messire Pierre Tiarck" without any cited evidence for the identification. In examining the picture on its arrival in Los Angeles in September 1974, Ben Johnson, Head of Conservation, noted many layers of paper adhered to the back of the stretcher bars. By removing and separating them carefully he discovered a pen and ink label in what appears to be an eighteenth-century script: "Messire Pierre Tiarck/fils de Théodore et de/mademoiselle Gertrude/Worp." The label is apparently by the same hand as that on the *Portrait of a Woman* in the National Gallery in London (no. 6413), which reads: "Mademoiselle Marie Larp fille/de Nicolas Larp et de/Mademoiselle de/ Wanemburg." These pictures were nos. 3 and 4 in the Oultremont sale. Since they are of relatively similar dimensions (the male portrait is 1.6 cm. taller and 1.9 cm. wider) and are both in simulated oval frames, the portraits have usually been considered to be a pair. Jaap Temminck, Deputy Archivist of Haarlem, searched the archives for Seymour Slive (vol. III, p. 60) and found that a marriage between a Pieter Dircksz. and a Maria Claesdr. is recorded on February 11, 1634 (R. A. 96[1], f. 62[v]); that Maritgen Claesdr. Larp is mentioned in 1645 as the widow of Pieter Dircksz. whose occupation was "verwer," dyer of silk and cloth (R.A. 76[65], 161), and again in 1646 as the widow of Pieter Dircksz. Tjarck (R.A. 76[65], 28[v]). The couple had only one child, Nicolaes Pietersz. Tjerck (sic) (R.A. 76[82], 221). Since Dirck in French is Thierry or Théodoric, the translation as Théodore is understandable, especially if the eighteenth-century label were copied from a still earlier inscription. There are, however, differences between the two paintings which can be rationalized only if we assume that for Hals the presence of a simulated oval and the incidence of light were adequate to relate the paintings. The newly discovered label does give added credence to the tradition of this relationship and to the identity of the Ahmanson sitter as Pieter Tjarck.

It is tempting to think of this painting as a wedding portrait, since the sitter dangles a rose. From antiquity the rose, colored by the blood of Venus when she accidentally stepped on a thorn, was an emblem of earthly love, especially popular in seventeenth-century Holland. Hals, himself, represented this device in an unambiguous manner in his pair of portraits of Isabella Coymans (Paris, Coll. de Rothschild) extending a rose to Stephanus Geraerdts (Antwerp, Museum of Fine Art) who reaches out to receive it. The same rose which symbolizes love between two human beings was also used in Hals' time as a reminder of the brevity of love and life. The human skull was the traditional emblem of human vanity which Hals used in some early works, but like his Dutch contemporaries he preferred more commonplace objects, timepieces, books, and roses. There are numerous poems and engraved emblems of the time comparing life to a rose. Perhaps the image closest to the Ahmanson portrait is Heinrich Goltzius' engraving of 1582 (Boot. p. 424) which shows an elegantly dressed young man holding two flowers, one already dropping its petals, encircled by the inscription: *sic transit gloria mundi.*

In the entire history of art, few artists have been able to equal Frans Hals in capturing a transient moment of life in portraiture with such brilliant and spontaneous brushwork. There is, however, considerable variation in style and objective during his long career. His early portraits bubble with the gaiety, optimism, and self-assurance of the new Dutch Republic. Poses are nonchalant, colors are bright, and the light is sparkling. Paint is applied in rapid, visible brushstrokes which give an independent pictorial interest to the surface. Hals' late portraits on the contrary are sober and sometimes melancholy, with penetrating characterizations of his sitters. Colors are dark, their harmonies subtle, with an increasing predominance of black.

The Ahmanson portrait, dated 1638 in most of the Hals literature, has been placed slightly earlier in recent publications: 1636 by Klaus Grimm and 1635-38 by Seymour Slive, just at the midpoint of Hals' career. In the 1630 s the style of life changed in Holland. Deportment became more reserved. The sober black costume replaced the more highly decorated one of the preceding decades. In keeping with the new spirit, the Ahmanson portrait is more restrained than early portraits. The vitality is still there but it is more concentrated in the sitter. The brushwork is no less brilliant but less obvious because of the darkness of the colors. The position of the sitter with his arm resting on the back of a chair, used by Hals to suggest the momentary, is here less transitory. The oval simulated frame was used by Hals in both early and middle works to heighten the illusion of space. It is the artist's concern with form, however, that distinguishes the painting and makes it one of the most classic in Hals' oeuvre. The torso, enveloped for the most part in a black cloak, acts as a strong pyramidal support for the head, the focal center of the painting. The black hat stabilizes the figure by counteracting the strong upward movement given emphasis by the collar. The face is firmly modeled and reflects the seriousness of the 1630s; only the moustache recalls the playfulness of earlier decades.

Seymour Slive (III, 1974) has recorded the following copies and variants: a weak copy without the painted oval on the New York art market in 1929; a three-quarter-length variant by another hand with the model standing, his arm resting on the corner of a draped table, in the museum at Liège, cat. 1926, no. 646; and a feeble version of the Liège painting on the European market in the late 1920s.

69

Jusepe de Ribera
Spanish, 1591-1652
Ancient Greek Philosopher
Oil on canvas
49 x 39 in. (124.3 x 99.1 cm.)
Signed and dated at left center:
Jusepe de Ribera español F. 1637
Promised gift of R. Stanton Avery

Collections: Liechtenstein Collection, Vienna and Vaduz, before 1767-1957; Newhouse Galleries, New York, 1957; private collection, New York, 1957-1973; Newhouse Galleries, New York, 1973; Mr. and Mrs. R. Stanton Avery, Pasadena, 1973

Literature: V. Fanti, *Descrizione completa di tutto ciò che ritrovarsi nella Galleria di pittura e scultura di sua altezza Giuseppe Wenceslas del S.R.I. principe regnante della casa di Liechtenstein,* Vienna: de Trattnern, 1767, p. 105, nos. 531-536; *Description des tableaux et des pièces de sculpture que renferme La Gallerie de Son Altesse François Joseph chef et Prince Regnant de la Maison de Liechtenstein...,* Vienna: de Trattnern, 1780, p. 160, nos. 550-553, p. 169, nos. 573, 574; A. Kronfeld, *Führer durch die Fürstlich Liechtensteinsche Gemäldegalerie in Wien,* Vienna: Wolfrum, 1922, p. 80, no. A372, 3rd ed. 1931, p. 84, no. A372 (as "unknown philosopher, old man with gaze directed upwards"). The A(= Alt) signifies that the description was taken from H. O. Miethke's catalog of 1873; A. L. Mayer, *Jusepe de Ribera,* Leipzig, 1923, p. 197; G. A. Gaya Nuño, *La Pintura Española fuera de España,* Madrid: Espasa-Calpe, 1958, p. 280, no. 2327; E. H. Turner, "Ribera's Philosophers," *Wadsworth Atheneum Bulletin,* Ser. IV, no. 1 (Spring 1958), pp. 5-14, repr. p. 10

In the *School of Athens* in the Vatican, Raphael at the peak of the High Renaissance painted an assemblage of ancient and modern philosophers with such idealism of concept and perfection of form that they can be seen only as immortals in an ideal temple of learning presided over by Plato and Aristotle. Only a little more than a century later, the Spaniard José de Ribera, working in Naples, gave many of these same philosophers mortality with a full measure of human weaknesses, defects, and virtues. The humanization and individualization of apostles, saints, prophets, and eventually ancient philosophers and writers began, but not without violent opposition, when Caravaggio about 1590 painted his first St. Matthew for S. Luigi dei Francesi in Rome. Caravaggio, his detractors said, violated all the principles of art by merely calling into his studio a man from the market place and painting him, rough and simple as he was with poor clothes and dirty feet, in the act of writing the gospel, and compounded his disregard for tradition by using a new kind of light which fell sharply on only part of the picture leaving the rest in darkness. The church rejected the picture, but many of the younger artists and collectors responded so favorably that Caravaggio's style and outlook quickly spread through Europe as a major component of Early Baroque painting.

José de Ribera, as a Valencian artist of his early twenties, spent several years in Rome with possible side trips to Emilia and the Veneto, before he settled in 1616 in Naples, a Spanish possession since 1443. In Rome the major works of Caravaggio were easily available for study; in Naples Caravaggism flourished as nowhere else in Italy. Ribera assimilated concepts of style and interpretation from Caravaggio and lesser influences from the Carracci tradition which he modified with a more atmospheric use of a viscous paint, a more somber tonality, and the Spanish predilection for realistic details to form his personal style.

It is in this style that he painted a number of half-length tattered philosophers between 1630 (*Democritus,* Prado) and 1638 (*Anaxagoras,* Worcester), some individual, some in series to be hung together. The impetus for this reincarnation of ancient sages as ordinary impoverished contemporaries is unclear. It may have come from Velásquez who visited Naples in 1629 and who had made several such pictures in the preceding decade, or more likely from the new Spanish Viceroy, Fernando Enríquez y Afán de Ribera, Duke of Alcalá, a humanist with an extensive library and a collection of coins, medals, and paintings. Dr. Delphine Fitz Darby in her exhaustive study of "Ribera and the Wise Men" (*Art Bulletin,* vol. LIV [1962], pp. 279-305) states that Alcalá not only commissioned the first series of philosophers but devised the iconography for a number of ragged sages. Like the saints, each philosopher is given an attribute: the lamp of Diogenes, the skull cap of "Dr. Aristotle," the constant smile of Democritus, the tears of Heraclitus, or, more difficult to recognize today, an attitude, expression, or posture. For the artist and his patron, each painting was a challenge in finding a model on the streets of Naples who resembled most closely the ancient literary descriptions or sculptural representation of the philosopher or who seemed to express best his philosophic attitude as it was interpreted in the seventeenth century. Ribera's ancient savants, as is evident in the Avery *Philosopher,* are men of dignity who are not impoverished by lack of ability but because they have put aside their concern for material things to devote themselves entirely to learning and teaching. Hanging together, a series of philosophers was most likely the source of learned conversation and even a test of wits.

The Avery *Philosopher* was part of a series of six ancient wise men which remained together for more than three hundred years, most of that time in the collection of the Princes of Liechtenstein. The canvases are identical in size, all are signed, four are dated 1637, one 1636, and one not dated is stylistically consistent with the others. They are first recorded in the Liechtenstein catalog of 1767 as six philosophers by Jusepe Ribera numbered 531-536: Aristotle, Plato, Crates of Thebes, Anaxagoras, Diogenes, and Protagoras. There is no indication of the time or place they were acquired; no documents or earlier references exist. The catalog was prepared by Vincenzio Fanti, painter, Master of Design to the Family, Commissioner of the Imperial Academy of Arts and Sciences, and Inspector of the Gallery. He was the son of Gaetano Fanti, a Bolognese architect, former member of the Accademia Clementina and Inspector and Director of the Liechtenstein Gallery. It seems likely, therefore, that with this type academic background, the author would have retained the identifications traditionally associated with the philosophers. In the 1690 catalog following rehanging of the collection, the same names of the philosophers are kept but the numbers are changed to 550-553, 573-574. In the catalogs of the late nineteenth and twentieth centuries, only the names Diogenes and Anaxagoras are retained, the name Archimedes is added and the remaining four are called only "unknown philosopher." An entirely new numbering system is introduced, A 55-57 and A 372-377, so it is not possible to trace the original identifications through them. Only two of the pictures remain in the Liechtenstein collection, the Anaxagoras and "an unknown philosopher with book and a roll of paper." The Diogenes is in a private collection in Europe, the Archimedes, which Dr. Darby prefers to reinstate as Aristotle, is at the Indianapolis Museum of Art. Another "unknown philosopher" has been acquired by the Wadsworth Atheneum in Hartford; the sixth is the Avery *Philosopher.* If the 1767 list is correct, the Avery sage should be Plato, Crates, or Protagoras. Without the advantage of a seventeenth-century written source of interpretation, it is still tempting to speculate that the intense visionary upward gaze of the Avery *Philosopher,* the ruffled hair and errant forelock might be those of the enthusiastic, mystical idealist, Plato.

70

Rembrandt van Rijn
Dutch, 1606-1669
Clement de Jonghe, 1651
Etching and drypoint
Watermark: Crowned shield
8¼ x 6¼ in. (21.0 x 15.9 cm.)
Gift of the Graphic Arts Council, 1967
M.67.4

Collections: Hibbert, London (Lugt 2849); Utterson, London (Lugt 909); Craddock & Barnard, London

Literature: A. Bartsch, *Le peintre graveur,* Leipzig: J. A. Barth, 1876, vol. 7, no. 272; A. M. Hind, *A Catalogue of Rembrandt's Etchings,* New York: Charles Scribner's Sons, 1923, 251; G. Biörklund, *Rembrandt's Etchings True and False,* Stockholm, New York, London: Biörklund, 1968, 51c

At least six states of the portrait of Clement de Jonghe are recorded, but only four of these are generally considered Rembrandt's work. The first state is in pure etched line, before the addition of drypoint and some burin in the second state, subtly changing the expression of the face and bringing tonal accents to the cloak and chair.

In the third state, the blank background is defined by the beginning of an arch drawn in drypoint. The transparent shadows on the face are increased, veiling the right eye and endowing the expression with an enigmatic, far-off look which has given the sitter a mysterious quality, quite possibly at variance with his personality as a print-seller and man of business. At this stage Rembrandt also evened the contours of the hat and allowed for the appearance of a band on it. In the fourth and quite possibly final state, the folds of the garments are considerably darkened, adding new definition to the form, while the arch is given a surer outline. Later states show alterations which detract from the quality of the work. But in its early states, the representation of *Clement de Jonghe* ranks unequivocally with the greatest of Rembrandt's etched portraits in terms of solid form, equipoise, and subtle characterization.

71

Giovanni Battista Foggini
Italian, 1652-1725
Time Ravishing Beauty
Bronze, dark brown varnish over red brown natural patina
h: 21⅜ in. (54.3 cm.)
Gift of the Michael J. Connell Foundation, 1974
M.74.8

Collection: Michael Hall, New York City

Exhibitions: New York, The Metropolitan Museum of Art,
Florentine Baroque Art from American Collections,
Apr. 16-June 15, 1969, no. 80, repr. in cat. fig. 41; Detroit
Institute of Arts, *The Twilight of the Medici,* Mar. 27-June 2,
1974, no. 30, repr. in cat. p. 67, in collaboration with
Florence, Palazzo Pitti, June 28-Sept. 30, 1974

Literature: "Nota de' quadri...nella villa Imperiale della
Ser. ma," 17th-century MS, *Arte e Storia,* II, 1883, p. 8;
MS Inventory of Palazzo Pitti, 1761, Guardaroba App. 94,
c. 480 v., Archivio di Stato, Florence; B. Bonsi, *Il trionfo
delle bell'arti...in occasione, che gli Accademici del
Disegno...fanno le solenne mostra delle opere antiche di
più eccellenti artefici nella propria cappella, e nel chiostro
secondo de' PP. della Nunziata in Firenze l'anno 1767,*
Florence, p. 15; MS Inventory of Doccia factory models,
fil. 37, no. 22 bis: 21, Archivio Ginori-Lisci, Florence;
E. Roma, *La porcellana di Capodimonte,* Naples, 1959,
fig. 36; L. Ginori-Lisci, *La porcellana di Doccia,* Milan,
1963, p. 64, pl. XXXVIII

Florentine Baroque sculpture is a late Baroque art—
courtly, often self-consciously refined, and essentially
pictorial. It was not the result of a natural evolution out of
the tradition of Giambologna, which persisted in Florence
long into the seventeenth century, but was the creation of
its chief patron, the Grand Duke of Tuscany, Cosimo
de'Medici (1642-1670-1723). Early in his career Cosimo
recognized that "the fine arts of sculpture and statuary are
declining in Florence." He therefore established a Florentine
Academy in Rome in 1673 and sent the most gifted young
Florentines, Foggini among them, there to study design with
Ciro Ferri and sculpture with Ercole Ferrata. Foggini had
three years of exposure to the whole range of Baroque
sculpture, but seems to have been most greatly influenced
by his teachers who represented the classical Baroque of
Algardi, which avoided the psychological drama and intense
emotional impact of Bernini for "a more measured and
distant art, graceful, possessed of a linear elegance...and
dedicated to the search for formal beauty" (Detroit catalog,
p. 26). In 1676, Foggini returned to Florence with a vivid
memory of the great masters, Bernini and Algardi, and with
a classic Baroque training to which he could adapt elements
of the Florentine tradition. He also brought a predilection
for sculpture in high relief, which in its tangibility satisfied
the Late Baroque taste for eliminating the boundaries
between illusion and reality. By 1687 Foggini had achieved
the highest artistic position in Florence, "Primo Scultore
della Casa Serenissima" and was assigned the studio and
foundry of Giambologna, the center of Florentine bronze
production. In 1694-1695 he was appointed also to the
second most important position, "Primo Architetto," in
charge of all construction and head of the grand ducal workshops with more than a hundred artists and artisans. His
personal sculptural production included large pictorial marble
reliefs, busts of the grand ducal family, and small bronze
groups often intended as royal presents.

From the early fifteenth century Florence was a center
for the production of small bronzes. Those of the Early
Renaissance were to be handled and enjoyed for their formal
balance. In the late sixteenth and early seventeenth centuries,
the bronzes of Giambologna with their twisting and intertwining figures were to be viewed, but viewed from every
point around the sculpture. The Late Baroque bronzes of
Foggini and his contemporaries, often with a complexity of
pictorial details, were usually to be seen two-dimensionally
as small *tableaux vivants.*

In the Connell bronze Foggini departs from his usual
frontal construction to achieve a more dynamic movement
and greater freedom of space, blending Roman Baroque
and Giambolognesque stylistic elements. From Rome he
took the forceful forward movement, the lavish draperies,
and the fusion of drapery, wings, and bodies into a cohesive
design; from his Florentine predecessor he seems to have
taken the countermovement to Time's advance effected by
the figure of Beauty, the turn of the body of Time, and the
relationship between the two bodies, reminiscent of two
figures in a relief on the base of Giambologna's *Rape of the
Sabines.* On the basis of style, the distinguished British
scholar Jennifer Montagu suggests a late date for the
Connell bronze.

The most recent research on this Foggini was done by
Dr. Montagu for the Detroit exhibition catalog from which
the following specific information was taken with inter-
polations. Although only the Connell cast is known today,
at least two must have been made. One was included in
two exhibitions in SS. Annunziata sponsored by the
Accademia del Disegno. In the first, in 1727, the bronze
was lent by Foggini's sons (*Nota de'quadri,* p. 8). In the
second, in 1767, it was shown without the name of the artist
from the collection of Giuseppe Borri (Bonsi, p. 15); since
Borri seems to have had a number of bronzes from Foggini's
heirs, it is probable that the cast shown in 1727 and 1767
are the same object. In 1761, however, the inventory of the
Palazzo Pitti lists "a bronze group, maximum height
⅚ braccia (ca. 48 cm.), representing an old man with wings
who bears a woman on his shoulders in the act of carrying

her off, with a putto at his feet, and the base similarly of bronze" (ASF Guardaroba App. 94, c 480v).

In 1735 Marchese Carlo Ginori founded a ceramic factory at Doccia, Sesto Fiorentino. As models for porcelains, he acquired wax casts of bronzes, the inventory of which is extraordinarily accurate in its attributions. A wax cast of *Time Ravishing Beauty* listed in the inventory as Foggini (AGL, fil. 37, no. 22bis:21) was used in 1756 to make a porcelain cast to serve as the centerpiece of a *Tempietto*, dedicated to the glory of Tuscany (Ginori-Lisci, 1963). The *Tempietto*, made to celebrate the appointment of Carlo Ginori as "Lucomone" or head of the Accademia Etrusca of Cortona, was an elaborate structure adorned with a number of figures mainly from models by Foggini and medals of the rulers of Tuscany. Dr. Montagu believes that *Time Ravishing Beauty* was selected for formal not iconographic reasons. A different porcelain copy of the group, made in the Capodimonte factory, is in the Ambrosiana in Milan (Romano, 1959).

The subject, Time ravishing Beauty and breaking Cupid's bow as he does so, is not to be confused with Boreas abducting Orithyia or the more philosophical Time revealing Truth, all of which have some iconographic similarities.

72

Jan van Huysum
Dutch, 1682-1749
Flowers
Oil on panel
31½ x 23½ in. (80 x 59.5 cm.)
Signed lower right: Jan van Huysum fecit 1724
Promised gift of Mr. and Mrs. Edward W. Carter

Collections: Johan Diedrik Pompe van Meerdervoort, Dordrecht or Jan van Huysum, Amsterdam (Sale, Oct. 14, 1749); Gerret Braamcamp, Amsterdam (Sale, July 31, 1771); Jan Gildemeester, Jz., Amsterdam (Sale, June 11, 1800); Pieter de Smeth van Alphen, Amsterdam (Sale, Aug. 1, 1810); Herr Six von Hillegom, Amsterdam (ref. Smith, 1835); Prof. Jan Six, Amsterdam (Sale, Amsterdam, Oct. 16, 1928, no. 15a not included in cat.); A. Staal (dealer), Amsterdam; Esther Surrey (dealer), The Hague; Dr. Gopel, Amsterdam; Arthur Hartog, The Hague and New York; Newhouse Galleries, New York, 1974; Mr. and Mrs. Edward W. Carter, Los Angeles, 1974

Exhibitions: Amsterdam, Stedelijk Museum, *Tentoonstelling der verzameling Schilderyen en familie-portretten van de Herren Jhr. P.H. Six van Vromade, Jhr. Dr. J. Six en Jhr. W. Six,* 1900, no. 48 in cat.; Amsterdam, Rijksmuseum, *Tentoonstelling van Oude Kunst door de Vereeniging von Handelaren in Oude Kunst in Nederland,* July-Aug. 1929,

no. 76, repr. in cat. (Lender A. Stall, Amsterdam); The Hague, Gemeentemuseum, *Oude Kunst uit Haagsch Bezit,* Dec. 12, 1936-Jan. 31, 1937, no. 104 in cat. (Lender A.H.); The Hague, Mauritshuis, *Herwonnen Kunstbezit Tentoonstelling van uit Duitsland teruggekeerde Nederlandsche Kunstschatten,* Mar.-May 1946, no. 28, p. 15 in cat. (Works removed from Holland during war and returned Oct. 1945)

Literature: Sale catalog, *Catalogus van Schilderyen van den Wel Ed Heer Johan Diedrik Pompe van Meerdervoort, Burgermeester te Dordrecht; en van den beroemden Bloemschilder Jan van Huysum, verkocht den 14 October 1749 in Amsterdam,* no. 8, reprinted in G. Hoet, *Infra,* vol. 2, p. 268, no. 8; G. Hoet, "Catalogus van Schilderyen in het Kabinet van den Heere Gerard Braamcamp in Amsterdam" in *Catalogus of Naamlyst van Schilderyen, mit derzelver pryzen,* s'Gravenhage, van Baalen, 1752, vol. 2, p. 503 "Een dito (Huysum) 2 v. 8½ d. x 2 v. 1½ d. P."; J. F. de Bastide, *Le Temple des Arts ou le Cabinet de Monsieur Braamcamp,* Amsterdam, 1766 (Description of 228 pictures in Braamcamp collection; Huysum in Salon overlooking garden.) See Bille, 1961; Sale catalog, *Catalogus van het uitmutend Kabinet Schilderyen, Tekeningen, Prenten, Beelden enz. door geheel Europa beroemd, en in veele Jaaren by eenverzemld door den Heere Gerret Braamcamp,* Amsterdam, Logement *Het Wapen van Amsterdam,* July 31, 1771, p. 35, no. 90; Sale catalog, *Catalogus van het Kabinet van Schilderijen nagelaaten door den Kunstnaar Jan Gildermeester Jansz. Agent en Consul General van Portugal, by de Bataassche Republik,* Amsterdam, Huis C. S. Ross, June 11, 1800, p. 43, no. 89; Sale catalog, *Catalogus van het Kabinet Schilderijen nagelaaten door...Heer Mr. Pieter de Smeth van Alphen,* Amsterdam, Oude Zijds Heeren Logement, Aug. 1-2, 1810, p. 19, no. 47; J. Smith, *Catalogue Raisonné of the Works of the Most Eminent Dutch, Flemish and French Painters,* London, Smith & Sons, 1835, VI, p. 476, no. 55 (In coll. Six van Hillegom); C. Hofstede de Groot, *Beschreibendes und kritisches Verzeichnis der herrvorragendsten holländischen Maler des 17. Jahrhunderts,* vol. X, Esslingen, A.N., 1928, p. 346, no. 43; M. H. Grant, *Jan van Huysum 1682-1749,* including a *Catalogue Raisonné of the Artist's Fruit and Flower Paintings,* Leigh-on-Sea: F. Lewis, 1954, p. 17, no. 4; C. Bille, *De Temple der Kunst of het Kabinet den Heer Braamcamp,* Amsterdam: de Bussy, 1961, 2 vols., vol. I, pp. 81, 226, repr. fig. 90, vol. II, p. 21, no. 90, p. 100, no. 90. Indispensable for information concerning Braamcamp and the works of art he collected.

The esteem in which this painting was held in the eighteenth century may indeed be responsible for the completeness of its history. It is not certain who its earliest owner was since it is first documented in a joint auction in 1749 of the collections of Johan Diedrik Pompe van Meerdervoort, Burgomaster of Dordrecht, and of the artist himself, both recently deceased. The catalog does not clearly separate the two collections. Since, however, this work was offered at the beginning of the sale, it has been assumed that the owner was Pompe van Meerdervoort. (There is still the possibility that the painting was retained by the artist for his personal collection.) The Carter painting brought the highest price in the sale. It was bought by the renowned collector Gerret Braamcamp who eventually placed it with four other van Huysum flower still lifes in the Grand Salon which he added to his house at 462 Heerengracht. The Salon, overlooking the garden and filled with costly French furniture, was reserved for festive occasions. In 1751 the poet Dirk Smits celebrated the collector and his 172 paintings in verse, citing specifically the Huysums. On May 18, 1762, M. d'Argenson (probably Marc-René Merkies d'Argenson) is recorded in a letter as having offered Braamcamp whatever price he might ask for the Huysums, but the offer was not considered (Bille, pp. 39, 64). It is not surprising, therefore, that after Braamcamp's death in 1771 the painting should have passed to a number of equally distinguished collectors and has been consistently one of the best-known and most admired of van Huysum's works.

When Jan van Huysum wrote to a client in a letter of July 17, 1742 (*Oud Holland,* XVIII [1900] p. 141) that he had not finished a flower piece the previous year because he could not obtain a yellow rose, he expressed an ideal of fidelity to nature which he shared with his predecessors Ambrosius Boschaert the Elder and Jan Davidsz. de Heem. Together these three artists exemplify the history of flower painting in seventeenth- and eighteenth-century Holland. Ambrosius Boschaert the Elder (1573-1621) was the founder of a dynasty of flower painters who dominated the early seventeenth century. His typical composition is a glass of flowers in an open niche before a blue sky and gentle landscape. The flowers painted with a miniaturist's precision of detail and lucidity of color are arranged in an open, symmetrical bouquet. L. J. Bol, the leading specialist on the Boschaerts, wrote that Ambrosius' flowers are "like individual portraits placed beside and above each other, each being given its pound of recognizability." Jan Davidsz. de Heem (1606-1683/4) brought the Flemish Baroque taste to Dutch still life painting with abundant masses of flowers, fruit, and other objects. In his vases of flowers of the second half of the century the individual blossoms form part of a more compact mass before a black background. His compositions are still symmetrical with only a small displacement of equilibrium; bold modeling and deep colors give a greater solidarity to forms than in either Boschaert or van Huysum.

Jan van Huysum, a painter of extraordinary virtuosity, adapted the same ideal of fidelity to nature to the eighteenth-century taste for an ordered casualness, delicacy, and

elegance. In the Carter painting, the flowers in dense array are intricately related. The arrangement seems casual: some flowers have dropped onto the table, others stray from the vase, and in the center of the bouquet, a tulip with broken stem falls forward. All of this masks careful pictorial organization. A strong diagonal extends from lower left to upper right, crossed by three shorter diagonals and overlaid with a large S-curve from the fruit blossoms at top through the light flowers in the center to the red peony on the marble ledge. Huysum has brought his bouquet back into the land-scape, now a gray green stage drop. Before it, he created a lively play of complementary colors, predominantly red-green and orange-blue, with wide ranges of value and intensity. While there is light from above and left, many of the flowers seem to glow from within, their petals thinned at times for transparency and textural variations. Huysum, who was a splendid draftsman and made many drawings from nature, has recorded a myriad of precise details for the careful observer. Rewarding seen individually, they contribute in concert to the experience of light and atmosphere, the rhythm of line and modulation of color.

73

Dresses for Ecclesiastic Lay Figures
Italy (Venice), ca. 1725
Brocaded silk and metallic threads
Los Angeles County Funds, 1965
65.1

These two gowns were probably utilized in religious pageants and festivals to clothe effigies and statues of the Madonna and Child. Certainly the sumptuous fabric of the gowns would have greatly enhanced the majestic pomp of ecclesiastical functions. Both are made of silk with red, green, and silver brocading that forms designs on the gold ground. The fabric is designed in the style of the lace-pattern silks that were popular at the beginning of the eighteenth century. Such brocades have a floral pattern composed symmetrically about a vertical axis of a lace pattern; large floral motifs are surrounded by small floral forms, giving a very full, rich appearance to the textile.

While the fabric is baroque in nature, the cut of the Madonna's dress reflects adaptations from earlier historical periods. The use of separate upper and lower sleeves is an Italian style that allows the linen to show between the sleeves. The gathering of the upper sleeve at the elbow is a stylistic feature of the eighteenth century. However, the tucks are inverted and turned down, whereas in contemporary gowns the sleeve tucks turn up to form a cuff. Reminiscent of Renaissance fashions, the lower sleeve side opening is closed with large brass hooks and eyes. Round braided silver thread buttons decorate the side closure and anchor the sleeve drape. Both the outer metallic fabric and the green brocade lining are constructed of piecings. The sleeve cap has large hooks to join it to the bodice.

The bodice, lined with coarse linen, is heavily boned to the waist; the front is also boned and interlined with light padding over the area of the stomacher. In assembly of the bodice, the front and back units were constructed and lined separately, then seamed together at the sides and right shoulder; hooks and eyes provide the closures for the left shoulder. Careful placement of the dominant floral motif in the center front of the bodice and deliberate use of gold braid and ribbon function as a decorative stomacher. The shallow point of the stomacher and the placement of short tabs around the waistline of the bodice are more typical of the seventeenth century. There are four front tabs and four at the back, each narrowly bound with yellow silk. A narrow band over the shoulder covers the placement of eyes for attaching the oversleeve. The bodice has eyelets for closure.

The skirt has been reconstructed and there is evidence of a red silk lining at the waist where the skirt has been pleated onto a coarse cotton waistband. For ease in draping statues, the center back of the skirt has been left open. Seven panels of fabric make up the skirt; the two center back panels are slightly shaped while the rest are straight lengths of fabric.

The Child's gown, simple in cut, is similar to the alb, a traditional ecclesiastical vestment; the back is closed with hooks and eyes. The same silver buttons as those on the sleeves of the Madonna's dress are used as decorative accents on the Child's gown. The simplicity of the garment is contrasted with the intricate meandering of the floral composition of the fabric. The use of rich gold brocade is in keeping with the baroque pageantry of this period.

Literature: P. A. S. Phillips, *Paul de Lamerie, Citizen and Goldsmith of London—A Study of His Life and Work,* London: B. T. Batsford Ltd. under the patronage of The Worshipful Company of Goldsmiths of the City of London, 1935, p. 81, one sconce ill. pl. XXXVII

Paul de Lamerie is acknowledged as England's greatest silversmith by the company of his peers, The Worshipful Company of Goldsmiths, London.

With the 1935 publication of Philip A. S. Phillips' definitive study of de Lamerie's life and work, an understanding of his development of rococo style became possible. Throughout his career, de Lamerie, though born of Hugenot parents in Holland, practiced the simple "English Style" of silversmithing. This plain style relies on simplicity of line and proportions for its beauty. At the same time de Lamerie developed the new rococo style to the degree that his name is synonymous with it in silversmithing today.

An unusual juncture in the development of de Lamerie's silver work is evident in the pair of Gilbert wall sconces of about 1725. The back plates are an elaboration of a decorative vocabulary both traditional to the silversmith and unique to de Lamerie. The strapwork patterning on the lower one-third of the back plate follows the French tradition of decoration while the tripartite composition of the back plate and the exotic "turband" masques which serve as focal points of the scene are inventions of de Lamerie.

These are believed the only ones of their kind by de Lamerie's hand. Because of the increasing popularity of candelbra in England, silver wall sconces were rarely made there after 1725.

74

Paul de Lamerie
English, 1688-1751
Pair of Wall Sconces, ca. 1725
Silver gilt
h: 22 in. (55.8 cm.); comb. wt.: 228 oz. 12 dwts.
Maker's first mark only, on backs and drip-pans
Arms of Thomas, 1st Baron Foley of Kidderminster,
co. Worcester
Promised gift of Mr. and Mrs. Arthur Gilbert

Collections: The Barons Foley of Kidderminster; The Goldsmith and Silversmiths Co. Ltd., London; J. A. Mango, Esq.; Florence, Lady Trent, Nottingham; The Hon. Mrs. A. M. Holman; Madame J. Farago; Mr. and Mrs. Arthur Gilbert, Beverly Hills

Exhibition: Cambridge, The Fitzwilliam Museum, *Silver Exhibition,* 1969

75

Paul de Lamerie
English, 1688-1751
Sideboard Dish and Ewer, 1742
Silver
d: 29 in. (73.6 cm.), dish; h: 18½ in. (47 cm.), ewer;
comb. wt. 442 oz. 10 dwts.
Maker's third mark, script "PL," Leopard's head for London
"g" letter date for the year 1742
Arms applied below the lip of the ewer are
those of Coote impaling Newport for Algernon,
6th Earl of Montrath (1689-1744)
Promised gift of Mr. and Mrs. Arthur Gilbert

Collections: Messrs. Christie, Manson and Wood, Ltd.; J. H. Bourdon-Smith, Ltd., London; Mr. and Mrs. Arthur Gilbert, Beverly Hills

Literature: R. Edwards & L. G. G. Ramsey, eds., *The Connoisseur's Complete Period Guide to the House, Decoration, Furniture and Chattels of the Classic Periods,* vol. III, London: The Connoisseur, 1956, repr. pl. 41; pp. 607, 642, 644; A. Grimwade, *Rococo Silver, 1727-1765,* London: Faber & Faber, 1974, p. 48, ewer ill. pl. 54B

With the acceptance of the fork for table use in the late seventeenth century, the historically and hygienically functional form of the rosewater ewer and dish became redundant. By the eighteenth century it had gradually assumed a new and most important role as purely decorative plate.

Paul de Lamerie's imaginative decorative designs and expert craftsmanship won him numerous commissions for decorative plates. The best known of these is the silver gilt ewer and sideboard dish he devised as plate for The Worshipful Company of Goldsmiths, London. When first seen, de Lamerie's new rococo style was said to be "performed in a very curious and beautiful manner," and must have inspired the commission of the Gilbert ewer and sideboard dish. Such lavish designs for plate were not exclusively for livery companies or the highest royalty, as our ewer and dish were commissioned by Algernon, 6th Earl of Montrath (1689-1744) who has been referred to as "a peer of little political importance."

The Gilbert dish is as successful as that designed for The Worshipful Company of Goldsmiths, but the ewer surpasses in design that in the Company's set. The recurved female figure handle gives a more complete silhouette to the helmet-shaped ewer than does its male counterpart on the earlier ewer, and the surface decorations break with vestiges of earlier French style (i.e., banding as seen on the Goldsmiths' ewer and on the ewer of 1736 in the collection of the Victoria and Albert Museum) and become a totally rococo design.

76

Jacques Angot
French, maître 1753, active through 1788
Commode sans traverse, Louis XV style, 1745-1749
Oak with tulipwood and mahogany; marquetry of kingwood, satinwood, rosewood, greenwood, and others
Fitted with chased gilt bronze mounts
Rouge royal marble top
h: 34½ in. (87.6 cm.); w. 50½ in. (128.2 cm.);
d: 23½ in. (59.7 cm.)
Stamped: I. Angot for Jacques Angot
Gift of Mr. and Mrs. Jerome K. Ohrbach, 1967
M.67.57

Collection: Mr. and Mrs. Jerome K. Ohrbach, Beverly Hills

This two-drawered commode of serpentine plan and subtle bombé elevation is designated *Commode sans traverse* to indicate that there is no visible lateral member between the two drawers. This design refinement permitted a more unified line in veneer over the compound curves of the front of the commode.

The entire front of the piece is composed as one panel with quartered and re-quartered tulipwood veneering. The cornucopias and floral sprays to either side of the central

cartouche relate this commode to a similar one in the Wrightsman Collection (F. J. B. Watson, *The Wrightsman Collection, vol.* I, *Furniture,* New York, The Metropolitan Museum of Art, 1966, p. 164, no. 97) and may be the work of the same marqueteur who moved from the workshop of one *maître eboniste* to another.

The fine chased gilt bronze mounts give a vital clue to the dating of this commode in the stamped crowned "c" which they bear. This stamp indicates the metalworker's tax on metals imposed in France between March 5, 1745, and February 4, 1749. The "c" stands for *cuivre* or the copper content of the bronze. Struck on top of the left-front stile, under the marble top, is the maker's mark, I. Angot.

This commode is a pleasantly proportioned example of a very popular mid-eighteenth-century style and is one of the rare examples of Jacques Angot's artistry still extant.

77

Woman's Gown
England, 1775-1785
Brocaded silk taffeta
Gift of Mrs. Delmar Lawrence Daves, 1964
M.64.66.1

Exhibition: Los Angeles County Museum,
Rococo, Eighteenth Century Costumes and Textiles,
Nov. 15, 1960-Feb. 12, 1961

The richness of this eighteenth-century gown is characteristic of the later rococo style in its cut and decoration of delicate flowers and meandering vines. The striped silk taffeta intimates the early neoclassical style and did not become prominent until the 1770s. It is woven with white and blue gray stripes in a yellow ground with a small multicolored floral design produced by extra warp threads woven into the stripes.

Surface decoration of gown and petticoat is of chenille flower garlands that curve in the familiar rococo S-curve on the front panels of the petticoat. The artificial flowers are imitative of decoration used in architecture for stucco walls of this period.

The gown is constructed in the *robe à la française* fashion. The petticoat, worn over small side hip pads or paniers, is of the same fabric as the overgown. By the close of the eighteenth century the elliptical skirt shape had decreased greatly from the extreme widths of earlier paniers and after 1770, the petticoat length became shorter as well.

Robe à la française, also termed a "sack gown" in England, refers to an overgown with the back fullness forming box pleats and falling freely to the floor. For control, underpleats are stitched inside to a complete bodice which functions as both lining and reinforcement. The side front skirt of the robe is pleated onto a fitted bodice lined with linen and stiffened with whalebone in the back.

The sleeves are instrumental in dating this gown. Fitted elbow-length sleeves, cut to allow the stripes to circle the arm and trimmed with flounces, were fashionable from 1770 to 1785. *Engageants,* two or three graded lace flounces, were worn under the three shaped flounces.

The skirt of the robe has inner loops and covered buttons attached to the back sections to enable the skirt to be worn looped up through the tapes and secured to the buttons in the polonaise style.

An interesting feature of this robe is the low rounded neckline with its small casing at the edge for a drawstring to aid bodice fit. The fabric pattern is evenly matched down the center front, and there is no evidence of a decorative stomacher over the bodice. Except for the drawstring tie, the bodice lacks closures or any evidence of them. A crease line suggests that the center edges of the bodice were folded under at one time. All of this indicates that this gown may have been worn open as was the *robe à la française* in the late eighteenth century. The front section was filled in with a soft muslin fichu around the shoulders with the ends crossed in front and tied behind under the robe. A soft decorative stomacher, referred to as a "zone" or a false waistcoat, was worn under the bodice. Zones varied in design but were always in the shape of an inverted stomacher. A predominately English style, this manner of dress was not prevalent throughout European fashion. The Snowshill Collection of gowns contains a robe of this period which also has no evidence of any method of closure except for the bodice drawstring.

78

Royal Gates
Church of the Nativity of the Mother of God
Kiev, Ukraine, 1784
Silver and silver gilt
91½ x 40½ in (232.3 x 102.8 cm.); wt.: 74 lbs. 9 oz.
Promised gift of Mr. and Mrs. Arthur Gilbert

Cyrillic inscription, extreme lower zone:
"These Gates in the Church of the Nativity of the Mother of God were made during the reign of the very Orthodox Sovereign Empress Ekaterina Alexeievna and her Heir the Orthodox Sovereign Tsesarevich, Grand Duke Pavel Petrovich, and his spouse the Orthodox Lady Grand Duchess Maria Fedorovna and the Orthodox Lords and Grand Dukes Alexander Pavlovich and Konstantin Pavlovich and the Orthodox Lady the Grand Duchess Alexandra Pavlovna, with the blessings of the Lord Archimandrite Father Zosim Valkevich of the Kievo Pecherskaia Lavra, and with the dedicated devotion of the Keeper of the same Pechera the Elder of the Church Brother Vitali. The year 1784, 31st day of March. The weight in silver is 2 pouds, 6 lots. Thirty-five foreign chervonets were used for gilding."

Collections: William Randolph Hearst; S. J. Phillips, London; Francis Stonor, London, 1962; S. J. Phillips, London, 1972; Mr. and Mrs. Arthur Gilbert, Beverly Hills

Literature: "Cathedral Gates in Silver Gilt," *The Antique Collector,* Apr. 1961, pp. 66, 67, repr.; M. Z. Petrenko, *Ukrainske Zolotarstvo* XVI-XVIII *st.,* Kiev: Naukova Doumka, 1969 (in Ukrainian), p. 193

The Church of the Nativity of the Mother of God (1696) stands on the territory of the Far Caves of the Pecherskaia Lavra (Monastery) in Kiev (see cat. no. 79), a site of extraordinary architectural and artistic monuments dating from the eleventh century. Throughout numerous invasions, the monastery sustained a high level of religious and cultural activity, creating workshop centers which supplied the rich religious community with expert woodcarvers, builders, silversmiths, printers, engravers, etc. The present *Royal Gates* are the product of such a workshop. They are attributed to Master Gregory Chizhevski (active in the last decades of the eighteenth century), who received large commissions from the Fathers of the Monastery and who made—as is documented in the State Central Historical Archives in Kiev—"in 1784 for the Church of the Nativity of the Kievo-Pecherskaia Lavra Royal Gates of silver and silver gilt." There are no known hallmarks of the Master.

In the early twenties the government of the U.S.S.R. secularized and nationalized monasteries, and in subsequent art sales many ecclesiastical objects were sold to foreign collectors.

Royal Gates, or Holy Gates, always double doors, are the dramatic focal point of an *iconostasis.* A continuous wall-like screen to conceal the altar at the eastern end of a church, the *iconostasis* is formed by horizontal rows of individual icons mounted in prescribed iconographical patterns. The prototype of the *iconostasis* goes back to the time of Emperor Justinian (527-565). The Royal Gates, the largest of three entrances in an *iconostasis,* are the most important central architectural element in the interior of an Orthodox Church. They not only isolate from the congregation the Sanctuary where the sacrament of Eucharist is celebrated, but are symbolically significant and have a specific liturgical function. While usually closed, the Royal Gates are opened at certain moments during the service when the Holy Eucharist is brought forward by the priest. Traditionally the Royal Gates symbolize the entrance into the Kingdom of God and show five scenes: the Annunciation in the two top panels, and in the four panels below, the Evangelists, heralds of the Heavenly Kingdom. The Gilbert Gates differ only slightly from the prescribed traditional iconographical pattern. There are six icons in bas-relief, framed in ornamental cartouches, placed symmetrically on both leaves of the gates. On the left Mary and the Angel are brought into a single representation of the Annunciation, the Day of Incarnation of the Son of God; a pendant on the right is the Entry into Jerusalem, the beginning of Christ's Passion; in the middle medallions are St. Matthew with his angel on the left and St. John with his eagle on the right; in the two lower medallions are St. Mark with the lion at his feet and St. Luke with the ox. At the bottom of each leaf immediately above the inscription is a basket of flowers and leaves enclosed in a medallion. In the visual center of the gates, on the vertical projecting molding, a small engraved oval icon depicts Christ Pantocrator, the Redeemer, with one hand blessing and the other holding the Gospel, presiding over the destiny of mankind.

The lavish splendor and elegance of these monumental gates is enhanced by interlaced garlands of flowers and foliage. They are cast in deep relief, chiseled, and chased to create a dramatic play of light and dark. The use of rocaille-inspired scrolls, curves, and countercurves adds gracefulness to the design. The pierced work renders the entire surface lighter and modifies the massive luxuriousness of the "Ukrainian Baroque," the prevailing style of the time.

The gates represent a dramatic and exceptionally striking combination of regional carving tradition with motifs of the more "modern" or "western" style then influencing the artists of Kiev.

79

Royal Gates
Church of the Elevation of the Holy Cross
Kiev, Ukraine, 1784
Silver gilt
106 x 49½ in. (269.2 x 125.1 cm.); wt. 88 lbs. 8 oz.
Promised gift of Mr. and Mrs. Arthur Gilbert
Marked AH 12

Cyrillic inscriptions, extreme lower zone:
"These Gates in the Church of the Elevation of the Holy Cross were made during the reign of the very Orthodox Sovereign Empress Ekaterina Alexeievna and her Heir the Orthodox Sovereign Tsesarevich, Grand Duke Pavel Petrovich, and his spouse the Orthodox Lady Grand Duchess Maria Feodorovna and the Orthodox Lords and Grand Dukes Alexander Pavlovich and Konstantin Pavlovich and the Orthodox Lady the Grand Duchess Alexandra Pavlovna, with the blessings of the Lord Archimandrite Father Zosim Valkevich of the Kievo Pecherskaia Lavra. In the year 1784, ninth day of the month of June, the weight in silver is 2 pouds, 17 founts, 2 lots. Ninety-five foreign chervonets were used for gilding. At the expense of the good-hearted donors, under (in the presence of) the Keeper of the Pechera the Elder of the Church Brother Markian."

Collections: William Randolph Hearst; S. J. Phillips, London; Peter Moores, Parbold Hall, Lancashire, 1961; S. J. Phillips, London, 1972; Mr. and Mrs. Arthur Gilbert, Beverly Hills

Literature: "Cathedral Gates in Silver Gilt," *The Antique Collector,* Apr. 1961, pp. 66, 67, repr.; M. Z. Petrenko, *Ukrainske Zolotarstvo* XVI-XVIII *st.,* Kiev: Naukova Doumka, 1969 (in Ukrainian), pp. 139, 161

The Monastery complex of Pechersk stretches over sixty-nine wooded acres on the right bank of the river Dnieper. The Upper Lavra (Monastery) and the Far Caves are on two hills; in a hollow between them are the Near Caves. The caves are underground cells which for centuries have been occupied by monks and hermits.

The stone structure of the Church of the Elevation of the Holy Cross (1700, Near Caves) dates from the period of revived architectural activity in Kiev that followed the War of Liberation (1648-1654). At this time great emphasis was placed on the decoration of church interiors, especially of the *iconostasis,* which during the seventeenth and eighteenth centuries became a complex three-dimensional background for icons. The Gilbert Royal Gates formed part of such a decoration. They are attributed to Alexis Timothy Ishchenko (active 1780-died 1811), successful author of numerous ecclesiastical objects who, according to documents in the State Central Historical Archives in Kiev, made in "1784 for the Church of the Elevation in the Near Caves, Royal Gates of gilded silver." His mark was АИ which appears as AH on the object. The hallmark 12 specifies that the silver content falls approximately between thirty-four and fifty-seven per cent.

The iconography of the Royal Gates deviates from traditional subjects. A crucifixion in the upper center symbolizes the triumph and glorification of God incarnate indicating the relation and reconciliation between God and man, heaven and earth. Three main themes—the Incarnation, the Passion, and Christ's divinity—are represented in the medallions below.

The Annunciation (upper left)—One of four Feasts devoted to the Mother of God, it shows the promise of salvation fulfilled through the Incarnation of Christ, when the Son of God became Son of the Virgin.

Christ's Entry into Jerusalem (upper right)—This prologue to Christ's Passion also signifies his triumph as Saviour and King and his ultimate victory in the Resurrection.

The Presentation of Christ in the Temple (center left)—One of the twelve principal Feasts of the Orthodox Church, it represents the consecration of the first born and alludes to Christ's sacrificial death.

The Presentation of the Virgin in the Temple (center right)—As one of the four Feasts celebrating an event in the life of Mary, it occupies a particularly important place in the Marian cult of the Orthodox Church. The Virgin consecrates herself into the service of God as Mother of the eternal divine Logos.

The Transfiguration (lower left)—An event in the course of Christ's ministry when his divinity was revealed to his disciples, it also manifests Christ's future Passion as well as the anticipation of his second coming.

The Raising of Lazarus (lower right)—A prefiguration of the Resurrection, it is the revelation of Christ's divine power, immediately preceding his entry into Jerusalem.

Three additional scenes are depicted on the central vertical molding. The first small oval medallion has two images, a Deësis above, and below an angel lifting and supporting a cross for the Church of the Elevation of the Cross. The second medallion pictures the Adoration of the Shepherds, a scene recalling the Feast of the Nativity. The last medallion represents the Uspenski Cathedral of the Pechersk Monastery framed by the two founders of the monastery: St. Anthony and St. Theodosius.

Christ's ancestors are represented on the extreme lower field of the gates: on the left, David as king with crown and harp, and on the right, Jesse, father of David. The figures express the fulfillment of messianic prophecy and characterize Christ's true humanity.

The elaborate monumental framework of the cast, embossed, and chased *Royal Gates* belongs to a style called "Kievan" or "Ukrainian" Baroque, derived in concept and execution from the tradition of the Ukrainian woodcarver. Their rich decorativeness combines various rocaille motifs in endless ornamental complexity. The C- and S- scrolls, shells, grooves, and slender decorative elements arranged in unpredictable asymmetry but without repetitious details produce a harmonious whole. The low relief gives the gates a two-dimensional appearance, while the *à jour* treatment of the entire pattern creates an effect of unity and lightness.

80

Giovanni Battista Tiepolo
Italian, 1696-1770
The Holy Family with St. John
Brown ink and wash over black lead drawing
11¾ x 8½ in. (29.8 x 21.6 cm.)
Gift of Cary Grant, 1969
M.69.14.2

Collections: Richard Owen, London; Barbara Hutton; Cary Grant, Beverly Hills

Literature: *Drawings in the Collection of the Los Angeles County Museum of Art,* Los Angeles, 1970; T. Pignatti, *Venetian Drawings from American Collections,* Washington, 1974, p. 40, no. 80

One of the largest series of drawings by Giovanni Battista Tiepolo was based on the theme of the Holy Family. These brilliant studies were originally given by Tiepolo himself to the library of the Sommasco Convent of S. Maria della Salute, Venice, where his son, Giuseppe Maria, was a priest of the order. Later, many of the drawings came into the possession of a nineteenth-century English collector, Edward Cheney. Cheney's Tiepolo albums eventually formed

the basis for the Tiepolo drawing collection of the Victoria and Albert Museum as well as of other leading European and American museums.

The two drawings of the Holy Family in the Museum's collection are closely related to two studies acquired from Edward Cheney in the thirties for the Gentili Collection, Paris. *The Holy Family* is similar to the Gentili sketch for a *Holy Family with Three Figures* (published in *Old Master Drawings,* Sept. 1933, pl. 18); while the Museum's *Holy Family with St. John* seems almost a reverse image of the Gentili sketch for an *Adoration of the Magi* (ibid., pl. 22). Although these various drawings have not been directly linked to any paintings, the Museum's two studies coincide in the arched motif of the backgrounds with an oil sketch by Tiepolo (The Metropolitan Museum of Art) which is connected with an altarpiece dated about 1753 for the Benedictine Abbey in Franconia. All these related Holy Family drawings have been dated by Vigni around 1753 to 1757, while George Knox gives them a larger span of time, 1750 to 1760.

81

Giovanni Domenico Tiepolo
Italian, 1727-1804
Centaur Arrested in Flight, a Female Faun on His Back
Bister
7⅝ x 10⅞ in. (19.3 x 27.6 cm.)
Signed lower left, no. 40 upper left
Museum Purchase, 1965
65.15

Collections: Rudolf, London; Drey Gallery, New York

Literature: J. B. Shaw, *Drawings of Domenico Tiepolo,* 1962, p. 42, no. 2; J. Cailleux,"Centaurs, Fauns... among the drawings of Domenico Tiepolo," *The Burlington Magazine,* July 1974, no. 53, repr. fig. 48

According to Jean Cailleux, Domenico Tiepolo executed at least one hundred drawings of centaurs, fauns, and satyrs. Among these works the most important group of approximately thirty-two drawings is related to the seduction or abduction of a female faun. Of these studies, the Museum's drawing belongs to the nine scenes in the series of flirtations between the centaur and female faun.

Although there is no absolute certainty regarding the dating of these drawings, Cailleux suggests they were made between 1753, the time of Domenico's return from his work in Wurzburg, and 1762, when he departed with his father for Madrid. However, Cailleux's conjectural dating does not exclude the possibility of Tiepolo's further development of these faun drawings during his sojourn in Spain.

Along with two other drawings (one in The Metropolitan Museum of Art, the other in the National Gallery of Victoria, Melbourne), the Museum's *Centaur Arrested in*

Flight, a Female Faun on His Back is directly related
to a fresco in the Camerino dei Centauri of the Tiepolo villa
at Zianigo. The question, however, of whether these
drawings were executed for the fresco or drawn after it as
individual works remains as yet unanswered.

82

Selection of Mosaic Boxes
(clockwise from upper left)
Faustulus Discovering Romulus and Remus
Late 18th century
Mosaic
d: 2¾ in. (7.1 cm.)
Profile of Bacchus
1804
Gold and enamel with mosaic
h: ¾ in. (2.0 cm.); d: 3¼ in. (8.2 cm.)
Signed in mosaic: c. civli Romano, 1804
View of the "Basilica" at Paestum
Ca. 1830
Gold and tortoise shell with mosaic
h: 1⅞ in. (4.9 cm.); 2⅜ x 3⅛ in. (5.9 x 8.1 cm.)
View of Berchtesgaden
Mid-19th century
Gold with mosaic
h: 1⅞ in. (4.9 cm.); 2⅜ x 3⅞ in. (5.9 x 9.9 cm.)
Promised gift of Mr. and Mrs. Arthur Gilbert

Collection: Mr. and Mrs. Arthur Gilbert, Beverly Hills

Literature: Plaque: Anthony C. Sherman, *The Gilbert
Mosaic Collection,* West Haven: Pendulum Press, 1971,
repr. pp. 18-19

After the fall of Byzantium the ancient art of mosaics
was reborn in the classicism of the Renaissance. Few
changes were made in historic techniques until the late
eighteenth century when the taste for brilliantly decorated
gold boxes, like those in the Gilbert Collection, produced
micro-mosaics made with tiny tesserae. The micro-mosaic
tesserae are made of stone, paste, and glass to produce
a wide color palette and, with their small size, the possibility
of delicate shading.

The earliest of the group, *The Discovery by Faustulus
of Romulus and Remus,* like its counterpart in the
Hermitage, still employs baroque pictorial imagery.
The Profile of Bacchus illustrates the progression of the
neoclassical style toward more natural imagery. In this
example, delicate variations of color revivify the sculptural
representation of the god of wine. The mosaic of
"The Basilica" at Paestum, probably based on an engraving
done during the excavations of 1830, exemplifies the
transformation of the tortoise shell box which it adorns into
a "souvenir" in the true sense.

The passing of the fad for snuff or beauty patches
removed the need for boxes in personal equipage, but the
box form persisted as a presentation piece. The mosaic
atop the latest box depicts a contemporary scene, the resort
Berchtesgaden in Bavaria. Only vestiges of the neoclassical
spirit are retained in the gold work.

83

Circular Table
19th century
Gilt bronze with marble mosaic top, mirrored base
d: 31¼ in. (79.4 cm.), top; h: 36½ in. (92.7 cm.)
Promised gift of Mr. and Mrs. Arthur Gilbert

Collection: Mr. and Mrs. Arthur Gilbert, Beverly Hills

This gilt bronze table is conceived architecturally with
cornice molding and frieze of overlapping triangular
scalelike petals supported on eight pairs of reeded engaged
columns with composite capitols and raised polygon base.
It is markedly formal in design, relaxed in part by the charm
of the central figure of the mosaic top and by the illusion
of extension created by opposed mirrors in the base.
The table was intended as a center table, literally one placed
commandingly in the center of a room or vestibule.
Early in the nineteenth century other furniture in the same
room, if any, would have been clustered at the perimeters of
the room permitting free circulation about this focal piece.

The design of the mosaic table top is characteristic of
the first third of the nineteenth century. Its black background follows a tradition in mosaics from fourth-century
Greece that continued through the nineteenth century.
But in style and execution the colored band and ivy-wreath
borders show neoclassical taste in a purer form than one
sees in later examples. The central figure of a cupid driving
a Roman-style chariot pulled by paired tigers derives its
inspiration from classical sources as well. A similar mosaic
top is in the collection of the Hermitage Museum, Leningrad.

84

Théodore Géricault
French, 1791-1824
Portrait of a Gentleman
Oil on canvas
25⅝ x 21¼ in. (65.1 x 54.0 cm.)
Signed lower left: T.G.
Promised gift of the Armand Hammer Foundation

Collections: Christi, Paris, 1879; Le Bohélec, Paris (Sale,
Paris, Galerie Charpentier, June 16, 1955); Drs. Fritz and
Peter Nathan, Zurich; Armand Hammer, Los Angeles

Exhibitions: Winterthur, Kunstmuseum, 1953,
Théodore Géricault, Aug.-Nov. 1953, no. 92; Los Angeles
County Museum of Art, Oct. 12-Dec. 12, 1971, *Géricault,*
pp. 36, 176, repr. in cat. no. 3, notes by L. Eitner;

traveled to the Detroit Institute of Arts, Jan. 23-Mar. 7, 1971, and Philadelphia Museum of Art, Mar. 30-May 14, 1972; Los Angeles County Museum of Art, *The Armand Hammer Collection,* Dec. 21, 1971-Feb. 27, 1972, repr. in color in cat., no. 3; traveled to London, Royal Academy, June 24-July 24, 1972; Dublin, The National Gallery of Ireland, Aug. 8-Oct. 1, 1972; Leningrad, The State Hermitage Museum, Oct. 23-Dec. 2, 1972; Moscow, The State Pushkin Museum of Fine Arts, Dec. 8, 1972-Feb. 11, 1973; Kiev, State Museum of Ukrainian Art, March 6-31, 1973; Minsk, Belorussian State Museum of Fine Arts, Apr. 26-May 26, 1973; Riga, State Museum of Latvian and Russian Art, June 8-July 8, 1973; Odessa, State Picture Gallery, July 25-Aug. 25, 1973

Literature: C. Clément, *Géricault, étude biographique et critique,* Paris, 1867, 3rd ed., enlarged, 1879, p. 307, no. 121; *Sale catalog, Additif à la vente du 16 Juin 1955,* Paris, Galerie Charpentier, repr.; F. H. Lem, "Géricault portraitiste," *L'Arte,* Jan.-June, 1963, p. 68

Signed "T.G." at the lower left, this picture was traditionally supposed to be a portrait of the composer F. A. Boïeldieu (1775-1834) although it does not bear any very pronounced resemblance to his known portraits. Of unusually tight and careful finish, the portrait is to be considered one of Géricault's master copies, executed probably about 1810-1812, after a slightly earlier work by a portraitist in the vicinity of Boilly or the elder Isabey. Other copies by him are known (e.g., that after H. Rigaud's *Portrait of the Mother of the Artist,* private collection, Paris).

85

Jean Auguste Dominique Ingres
French, 1780-1867
Portrait of Thomas Church, 1816
Graphite
7⅜ x 6¼ in. (18.9 x 15.9 cm.)
Signed and dated, lower left: Ingres Del Rom 1816
Loula D. Lasker Estate Fund, 1967
M.67.62

Collections: Church Family, London; John Longe, Spixworth Park; David C. Wilson, Sheffield, and the Reverend Michael Wilson of Ndola, Northern Rhodesia; Marianne Feilchenfeldt, Zurich

Literature: Sale 1912, B. Ford, "Ingres' Portrait Drawings of English People at Rome, 1806-1820," *The Burlington Magazine,* July 1939, p. 9, pl. D, III; E. Feinblatt, "An Ingres Drawing for Los Angeles," *The Connoisseur,* Apr. 1969, pp. 262-265

One of the outstanding studies of an Englishman by the master draftsman Jean Auguste Dominique Ingres is the pencil *Portrait of Thomas Church.* The downfall of Napoleon's dynasty brought many visiting Englishmen to Italy where the artist worked from 1806 to 1820. Thomas Church (1758-1821), a surgeon and a bachelor, and his brother, the Reverend Joseph, Rector of Frettenham, Norfolk, were among those who sat for Ingres.

Ingres' Roman period was the most brilliant in the history of his drawing. Influenced by Raphael and John Flaxman, as well as by classical gems, he achieved a perfect mastery of line and form. To this he added an unerring ability to represent the likeness, individuality, and character of his sitters, even to pose and gesture. In this period Ingres used a finely sharpened pencil for his portraits, creating variation in the width and strength of the line by carefully manipulating the pressures and angles of the point. This explains the difference in the treatment between the head and body of Thomas Church. In general, Ingres, despite his close study of nature, leaned towards idealizing his sitters, particularly in the case of his countrymen, whose age or lineaments he would some- times soften. The knotted, intense face of Thomas Church, however, is one of the most realistically characterized of all the Ingres pencil portraits. Of the thirty-odd portraits of Englishmen by Ingres in existence, there are only about a half-dozen in the United States.

86

Claude Monet
French, 1840-1926
The Beach at Honfleur, 1867
Oil on canvas
23½ x 32 in. (59.7 x 81.3 cm.)
Signed lower right: Claude Monet
Gift of Mrs. Reese Hale Taylor, 1964
Life Tenancy
64.4

Collections: Collection Frédéric Mallet, Paris; Wildenstein Co., New York; Mrs. Reese Hale Taylor, Pasadena, 1957

Exhibitions: Zurich, Kunsthaus, *Claude Monet,* May 10-June 15, 1952, no. 7 in cat.; Paris, Galerie des Beaux-Arts, *Claude Monet,* June 19-July 17, 1952, no. 7 in cat.; The Hague, Gemeentemuseum, *Claude Monet,* July 24-Sept. 22, 1952, no. 8 in cat.; New York, The Museum of Modern Art, *Claude Monet: Seasons and Moments,* Mar. 9-May 15, 1960, no. 4, p. 60 in cat. by W. C. Seitz; traveled to Los Angeles County Museum, June 14-Aug. 7, 1960

In the middle 1860s Monet spent several months each year in his home town of St. Andresse and the neighboring village of Honfleur on the Normandy coast. In 1862, during one of these visits, he met two older seascape painters, Boudin and Jongkind, whose influence dictated the choice and arrangement of subject in *The Beach at Honfleur.* The painting is one of several from this period where Monet used the scene as an opportunity to explore his concern with shape and light. He simplified solid natural forms into flat, dark shapes and created strong visual accents, as in the boats on the left. The whole picture is organized in terms of these value contrasts: bright sky, sparkling beach, and a progression of spiky or angular dark shapes—boats, lighthouse, rocks, and cliffs—arrayed across the canvas. In using this approach, Monet probably followed Manet's example, which he had seen in a Paris exhibition in 1863. The result of this technical method in *The Beach at Honfleur* is a striking painting that resounds with the confident energy characteristic of the best of Monet's oeuvre.

87

Henri Fantin-Latour
French, 1836-1904
Peonies in a Blue and White Vase
Oil on canvas
23⅞ x 19⅝ in. (60.8 x 49.9 cm.)
Signed and dated upper right: Fantin 1872
Promised gift of the Armand Hammer Foundation

Collections: Dr. J. van Alphen-Carp, The Netherlands; E. J. van Wisselingh & Co., Amsterdam; M. L. de Boer, Amsterdam; Armand Hammer, Los Angeles

Exhibitions: New York, Hammer Galleries, *40th Anniversary Loan Exhibition, 1928-1968,* Nov. 7-Dec. 7, 1968, repr. in color in cat., p. 28; Memphis, Tennessee, Brooks Memorial Art Gallery, *The Armand Hammer Collection,* Oct. 2-Dec. 30, 1969, no. 34, repr. in cat.; Washington, D.C., Smithsonian Institution, *The Armand Hammer Collection,* Mar. 20-May 17, 1970, no. 36, repr. in color in cat.; Smithsonian Institution Traveling Exhibition Service, *The Armand Hammer Collection,* Kansas City, Missouri, William Rockhill Nelson Gallery of Art, June 30-Aug. 2, 1970; New Orleans, Isaac Delgado Museum of Art, Aug. 15-Sept. 20, 1970; Columbus, Ohio, Columbus Gallery of Fine Arts, Oct. 9-Nov. 1, 1970; Little Rock, Arkansas Art Center, Nov. 21, 1970-Jan. 12, 1971; San Francisco, California Palace of the Legion of Honor, *The Armand Hammer Collection,* Feb. 11-Mar. 14, 1971; Oklahoma City, Oklahoma Art Center, *The Armand Hammer Collection,* June 15-July 11, 1971; San Diego, Fine Arts Gallery of San Diego, *The Armand Hammer Collection,* July 23-Sept. 5, 1971; Los Angeles County Museum of Art, *The Armand Hammer Collection,* Dec. 21, 1971-Feb. 27, 1972, repr. in color in cat., no. 24; traveled to London, Royal Academy, June 24-July 24, 1972; Dublin, National Gallery of Ireland, Aug. 8-Oct. 1, 1972; Leningrad, State Hermitage Museum, Oct. 23-Dec. 2, 1972; Moscow, State Pushkin Museum of Fine Arts, Dec. 8, 1972-Feb. 11, 1973; Kiev, State Museum of Ukrainian Art, March 6-31, 1973; Minsk, Belorussian State Museum

of Fine Arts, Apr. 26-May 26, 1973; Riga, State Museum of Latvian and Russian Art, June 8-July 8, 1973; Odessa, State Picture Gallery, July 25-Aug. 25, 1973

Literature: Mme. Fantin-Latour, *Catalogue de l'oeuvre complet de Fantin-Latour,* Paris: H. Floury, 1911, p. 72, no. 616; *Art Journal,* Fall 1968, p. LIV, repr.; *Connoisseur,* Nov. 1968, p. 11, repr.; F. Daulte, "Hammer en dix chefs-d'oeuvre," *Connaissance des Arts,* Sept. 1970, p. 83, repr.

Fantin is most widely known for his flower pictures, in the best of which white predominates against a cool-hued background. Seen in isolation, the flowers in these paintings project in astonishing relief and tactility. This heightened sense of reality is partly due to the apparent lack of atmosphere in the flower pieces. Perhaps none of these paintings illustrates as well as this one Jacques-Emile Blanche's observation that "Fantin studied each flower, each petal, its grain, its tissue as if it were a human face.... It is an individual flower and not simply one of a type.... Some canvases are worthy of Chardin."

88

Gustave Moreau
French, 1826-1898
Salome Dancing Before Herod, 1876
Oil on canvas
56⅝ x 41⅛ in. (143.8 x 104.2 cm.)
Promised gift of the Armand Hammer Foundation

Collections: Louis Mante, Marseilles (Sale, Paris, Galerie Charpentier, Nov. 28, 1956); Robert Lebel, Paris; Julius Weitzner, London, 1958; Huntington Hartford (Sale, New York, Sotheby Parke-Bernet Galleries, Mar. 10, 1971); Armand Hammer, Los Angeles, 1971

Exhibitions: Paris, *Salon of 1876,* no. 1506, p. 187 in cat.; Paris, *Exposition Universelle Internationale,* 1878, vol. I, sect. I of cat., no. 657, p. 51; Paris, Galerie Georges Petit, *Gustave Moreau, Exposition au Profit des Oeuvres du Travail et des Pauvres Honteux,* 1906, no. 76 (lent by Louis Mante); Paris, Musée du Louvre, *Gustave Moreau,* June 21-July 13, 1961, p. 32, no. 22 in cat., repr. pl. 11 (Coll. Huntington Hartford); New York, Museum of Modern Art, Dec. 4, 1961-Feb. 4, 1962, and Art Institute of Chicago, Mar. 2-Apr. 15, 1962, *Odilon Redon—Gustave Moreau—Rodolphe Bresdin,* p. 179, no. 177, repr. p. 116 (lent by Huntington Hartford); New York, Gallery of Modern Art, Permanent Collection, 1964-1969; Oklahoma City, Oklahoma Art Center, *The Armand Hammer Collection,* June 15-July 11, 1971; traveled to San Diego, Fine Arts Gallery of San Diego, July 23-Sept. 5, 1971; Los Angeles County Museum of Art, *The Armand Hammer Collection,* Dec. 21, 1971-Feb. 27, 1972, repr. in cat. no. 29; traveled to London, Royal Academy, June 24-July 24, 1972; Dublin, National Gallery of Ireland, Aug. 8-Oct. 1, 1972; Leningrad, State Hermitage Museum, Oct. 23-Dec. 2, 1972; Moscow, State Pushkin Museum of Fine Arts, Dec. 8, 1972-Feb. 11, 1973; Kiev, State Museum of Ukrainian Art, March 6-31, 1973; Minsk, Belorussian State Museum of Fine Arts, Apr. 26-May 26, 1973; Riga, State Museum of Latvian and Russian Art, June 8-July 8, 1973; Odessa, State Picture Gallery, July 25-Aug. 25, 1973; Los Angeles County Museum of Art, *Gustave Moreau,* July 23-Sept. 1, 1974, no. 42, p. 34 ff., 132, repr. in color in cat., pl. 42

Literature: T. Gautier, "Le Salon II," *Le Rappel,* May 6, 1876; A. Darcel, *Journal de Rouen,* May 6, 1876; E. Drumont, *La Gazette,* May 7, 1876; E. Chesneau, *La Gazette,* May 8, 1876; L. Gonse, *La Nouvelliste de Rouen,* May 8, 1876; G. Guillemot, "Salon de 1876," *Le Soleil,* May 10, 1876; A. Wolff, "Quatrième Promenade au Salon," *Le Figaro,* May 12, 1876; E. Bergerat, "Salon de 1876," *Journal Officiel,* May 12, 1876; G. Lafenestre, *Le Moniteur Universel,* May 12, 1876; Ch. Clément, "Exposition de 1876," *Journal des Débats,* May 13, 1876; J. Clarerie, *La Presse,* May 16, 1876; Artiste, *L'Indépendance Belge,* May 18, 1876; E. Bergerat, *Journal du Loiret,* Orléans, May 19, 1876; P. de Saint-Victor, "Salon de 1876," *La Liberté,* May 19, 1876; A. Castagnary, *Le Siècle,* May 20, 1876; A. Pothey, *Le Corsaire,* May 20, 1876; P. Mantz, *Le Temps,* May 21, 1876; Ch. Darcours, *Journal Illustré,* May 21, 1876; L. Pichat, *Le Phare de la Loire,* Nantes, May 22, 1876; M. Vachon, *La France,* May 24, 1876; E. Boysse, *La Patrie,* May 25, 1876; *Le Monde Illustré,* May 27, 1876; E. About, *Le 19e Siècle,* May 28, 1876; Von Heym, *La Défense,* May 30, 1876; V. Cherbuliez, "Le Salon de 1876," *Revue des Deux Mondes,* June 1, 1876, pp. 521-522; Ch. Yriarte, "Le Salon de 1876," *Gazette des Beaux-Arts,* XIII (June 1, 1876), pp. 705-708, repr. p. 698 (sketch for Salomé); *La Gazette de France,* June 15, 1876; P.H., *L'Avenir de la Sarthe,* Le Mans, June 17, 1876; E. Blavet, *Le Gaulois,* June 21, 1876; Zig Zags, *Salon de 1876, Gustave Moreau,* June 25, 1876, no. 9, p. 2; S***, "Salon de 1876," *L'Electeur du Finistère,* Brest, June 28, 1876; G. Dufour, "Le Grand Art et le Petit Art du Salon de 1876," *L'Artiste,* Amiens: Typographic Delattre-Lenoel, pp. 24, 25; P. de Savarus, "Le Salon de 1876," *A vol d'Oiseau,* Paris: Chez Dentu, 1876, pp. 43-44; V. De Swarte, *Lettres sur le Salon de 1876,* St. Omer: Imprimerie Fleury-Le Maire, 1876, p. 79; E. Bergerat, *Les Chefs-d'Oeuvre d'Art à l'Exposition Universelle 1878,* Paris: L. Baschet, 1878, p. 156, repr. pl. 20; Ch. L. Duval, *Les Beaux-Arts à l'Exposition de 1878 Impression et Notes d'Artistes,* Meaux: Librairie Ch. Cochet, 1878, p. 127 (from Le Publicateur, Arron-dissement de Meaux); *Exposition Universelle de Paris,* *1878, Le Livre d'Or des Exposants,* Section 1 (Beaux-Arts), Paris: André Sagnier, 1878, p. 10; H. Gautier and A. Desprez, *"Curiosités de l'Exposition de 1878,* Paris: Libraire Ch. Delagrave, 1878, p. 87; P. Mantz, "Paris Exposition Universelle, La Peinture Française," *Gazette des Beaux-Arts,* 1 (Dec. 1, 1878), p. 47; M. Proth, *Les Artistes Français à l'Exposition Universelle de 1878,* Paris: Décaux, ed., 1878, p. 56; P. Mantz, "L'Art Moderne à l'Exposition de 1878," *Gazette des Beaux-Arts,* 1879, pp. 31, 33; P. de Savarus, *Dix Années d'Art (Souvenir des Expositions),* Paris, 1879, pp. 89-91; D. de Pesquidoux, *L'Art dans les Deux Mondes—Peinture et Sculpture, L'Art au XIXeme Siècle,* Paris: E. Plon et Cie., 1881, I, 4, p. 82; J. K. Huysman, *A Rebours,* Paris, 1884, pp. 71-76; P. Leprieur, *L'Artiste,* 1889, Mar.: pp. 175, 177, 180, May: pp. 339, 350, 351, June: pp. 444, 449, 450, 452; *Moreau's Autograph Writings,* Notebooks III, pp. 49, 63, IV: pp. 55, 67, transcriptions from his original notes by H. Rupp and J. Paladilhe, Moreau Museum, Paris, 1890; A. Castagnary, *Salons,* Paris, 1892, II, pp. 227-228; G. Larroumet, *Etudes de Littérature et d'Art,* Paris: 1896, pp. 227-278; L. Thévenin, *L'Esthétique de Gustave Moreau,* Paris: Vanier, 1897, pp. 9, 12-13; G. White, "The Pictures of Gustave Moreau," *The Pageant,* London, 1897, p. 11; L. Bénédite, "Deux Idéalistes, Gustave Moreau et E. Burne-Jones," *La Revue de l'Art Ancien et Moderne,* Apr. 1899, pp. 265-290, p. 273 repr.; A. Renan, "Gustave Moreau," *Gazette des Beaux-Arts,* 1900, pp. 62, 63, repr.; G. Geffroy, *La Vie Artistique,* 6th series, chap. XVI, Paris: H. Floury, 1900, pp. 143-147; H. Frantz, "The New Gustave Moreau Gallery," *Magazine of Art,* 1900, pp. 99-104; G. Larroumet, Institut de France, Académie des Beaux-Arts, *Notice Historique sur la Vie et les Oeuvres de M. Gustave Moreau,* Paris: Firmin-Didot et Cie., 1901, pp. 21, 22, 29, 30, repr. p. 36; F. H., "Gustave Moreau," *Kunst für Alle,* 1902, repr. p. 268; Musée National Gustave Moreau, *Principales Oeuvres du Maître dans les Musées et Collections Particu-lières* (intro. G. Desvallières), Paris: J. E. Bulloz, 1906, no. 9 (Mante coll.); G. Geffroy, *L'Oeuvre de Gustave Moreau,* Paris: L. Lambert, 1906, pp. 5, 9, 26, 27; A. Symons, *Studies in Seven Arts,* London: A. Constable & Co., 1906, pp. 73-77; H. Daffner, *Salome: Ihre Gestalt in Geschichte und Kunst,* Munich: H. Schmidt, 1912, pp. 289, 290; A. Loisel, "L'inspiration chrétienne du peintre Gustave Moreau," *Notes d'Art et d'Archéologie,* XXIV (1912), p. 52; L. Deshairs and J. Laran, *L'Art de Notre Temps, Gustave Moreau,* Paris: Librairie Centrale des Beaux-Arts, 1913, pl. XXVIII, pp. 71, 72, repr. opp.; Musée National Gustave Moreau, *L'Oeuvre de Gustave Moreau* (intro. G. Des-vallières), Paris: Bulloz, 1913, no. 9, repr.; Anonymous, *Gustave Moreau (Les Peintres Illustrés, no. 55),* Paris: Lafitte, 1914, pp. 69-70; G. Coquiot, *Des Gloires Deboulonnées,* Paris: Delpeuch, 1924, pp. 115-116; G.

Rouault and A. Suarès, "Gustave Moreau," *L'Art et Les Artistes,* vol. XIII, no. 66 (Apr. 1926), p. 223 repr.; M. Praz, *The Romantic Agony,* London: Oxford Press, 1933, 3rd ed., New York, 1956, pp. 291-293; G. Duthuit, "Vuillard and the Poets of Decadence," *Art News* 53 (1954), repr. p. 31; Sale catalog, *Catalogue de la Vente Collection Louis Mante,* Paris, Galerie Charpentier, Nov. 28, 1956, no. 10, pl. III; J. K. Huysmans, *Against Nature* (translation of *A Rebours,* 1884, by R. Baldick), Baltimore: Penguin, 1959, pp. 63-67; R. von Holten; "Oedipe et le Sphinx, Gustave Moreau's Genombrottsverk," *Symbolisher 3,* Tidskrift för Kunst-vetenskap, 23 (1957), repr. 48; idem, *L'Art Fantastique de Gustave Moreau,* Paris: Pauvert, 1960, pp. 19, 20, pl. III, p. 27, repr. in color; idem, "Le développe-ment du personnage de Salomé à travers les dessins de Gustave Moreau," *L'Oeil,* Aug. 1961, pp. 44-51, 72; J. Simon, "The Torments of Imagination," *Arts,* Feb. 1962, pp. 20-27, repr.; D. Grojnowski, "Les Mystères Gustave Moreau," *Revue Générale des Publications Françaises et Etrangères,* XIX, 190 (Mar. 1963), pp. 225-238, p. 237, sketch; *Catalogue of Paintings from the Huntington Hart-ford Collection in the Gallery of Modern Art,* New York: The Foundation for Modern Art, Inc., 1964, no. 14, repr. in color; R. von Holten, *Gustave Moreau Symbolist,* Stockholm: Natur och Kultur, 1965, pp. 48-65, repr. p. 49; M. Gérard, *Dali,* New York: Harry N. Abrams, 1968, no. 169, detail repr. in color; J. Kaplan, "Gustave Moreau's Jupiter and Semele," *Art Quarterly,* XXXIII (1970), pp. 393-414; Sale catalog, *Important Impressionist and Modern Paintings and Drawings,* New York: Parke-Bernet Galleries, Mar. 10, 1971, no. 29, p. 52, repr. in color; H. O. Borowitz, "Visions of Salome," *Criticism,* Detroit, XIV, 1 (Winter 1972), pp. 14-15, repr.; M. L. Frongia, "Finito' e 'Non Finito' Nell' Opera di Gustave Moreau," *Commentari,* 1972, pp. 146-147, repr. no. 4; idem, "Su alcuni recenti interpretazioni dell' opera di Gustave Moreau," *Annali delle Facoltà di Lettere Filosofia e Magistero,* Università Degli Studi Di Cagliari, Gallizzi, 1973, pp. 397, 399-400, repr. no. 3; *Mizue,* 1973, repr. p. 39; J. Meyers, "Huysmans and Gustave Moreau," *Apollo,* Jan. 1974, pp. 39-41, repr. no. 3, pl. VI

The best-known version of the artist's most-known subject, *Salome* fully realizes the tendency toward accumu-lation in Moreau's art, as well as representing the apotheosis of one of the most notable and hermetic themes in late nineteenth-century French art and literature. Holten believes the subject to have been inspired by Flaubert's *Salammbô,* while Duthuit traces it to Mallarmé's *Herodiade,* but perhaps no specific source is needed for this theme of the *belle dame sans merci* (cf. Mario Praz, *The Romantic Agony)* so common to the *fin de siècle.* For Moreau, Salome was at once mysterious and fatal, "a woman in search of a vague, sensual, and unhealthy ideal, who destroys men, be they geniuses or saints." Daffner *(Salome,* Munich, 1912, p. 289)

has pointed out that Moreau's interpretation of the Orpheus myth, the poet's severed head lying on a lyre, is closely related to the Salome theme.

The painting is tantalizing in part because it seems to represent an exclusively personal interpretation of a scene, yet to possess a degree of historical accuracy. An eclectic combination of precisely identifiable details from many different sources, *Salome* is nonetheless not an archaeological reconstruction. Moreau was interested in the decorative elements he borrowed from his sources because they helped him create an imaginary setting which suited his thematic content. His fusion of them was purely personal, without historical precedent. But he did rely on research and his knowledge of other art to provide an *aura* of authenticity to his setting.

Salome marks a strong stylistic change in Moreau's oeuvre; it was the first time he chose to fill a large and extremely complicated space with a number of small figures. As his thinking about the conception of the picture as a whole became more rigorous, he executed a series of drawings and oil sketches to serve as experimental compositions. (The figure of Salome herself was studied in a wooden figure covered with clay and dressed in cloth, one of his dozen or so surviving sculptures.) At this time also he began using complex plays of light and dark and gleaming color to create a sense of opulence within the firm, clear structure of the painting. This new treatment of light and dark contributed greatly to the painting's atmospheric and spatial effects and added to the general mysteriousness of the work. Yet the emphasis on value relationships never caused Moreau to abandon fully his concern for the precise definition of objects—an obsession he shared with nineteenth-century academic art. He continued to draw in certain details with a very hard and strong line, marking each as clearly as possible. In *Salome* these two different techniques co-exist, creating a sense of oscillation between precise and amor-phous elements. Indeed, this oscillation, which fights the stasis of the figures, is the visual basis for the evocative, mysterious power of the painting.

89

Paul Cézanne
French, 1839-1906
Still Life with Cherries and Peaches, ca. 1883-1887
Oil on canvas
19¾ x 24 in. (50.4 x 61 cm.)
Gift of The Adele R. Levy Fund, Inc. and
Mr. and Mrs. Armand S. Deutsch, 1961
M.61.1

Collections: Charles A. Loeser, Florence; Mrs. M. Loeser Calnan, Florence; Dr. and Mrs. David M. Levy, New York; The Adele Rosenwald Levy Fund, New York

Exhibitions: Venice, *XII^a Esposizionale d'Arte della città di Venezia,* 1920, no. 28; New York, Museum of Modern Art, *Art in Our Time,* May 10-Sept. 30, 1939, no. 57, repr. in cat.; New York, Wildenstein Gallery, *Cézanne,* Nov. 5-Dec. 5, 1959, no. 27, repr. in cat.; New York, Museum of Modern Art, *The Mrs. Adele R. Levy Collection,* June 9-July 16, 1961, p. 19, repr. in cat.; Claremont, Pomona College Gallery, *Muse or Ego, Salon and Independent Artists of the 1880's,* Apr. 17-May 12, 1963, no. 19; Washington, D.C., Phillips Collection, *Cézanne,* Feb. 27-Mar. 28, 1971, no. 13, repr. in color in cat.; traveled to Chicago, the Art Institute of Chicago, Apr. 17-May 16, 1971, and Boston, Museum of Fine Arts, June 1-July 3, 1971; Tokyo, National Museum of Western Art, *Exposition Cézanne,* Mar. 30-May 19, 1974, no. 36, repr. in color in cat.; traveled to Kyoto, Municipal Museum, June 1-July 12, 1974, and Fukuoka Cultural Center, July 24-Aug. 18, 1974, pp. 16, 53, repr. in cat. p. 52 and in color no. 13

Literature: Venturi, *Cézanne,* Paris: Paul Rosenberg, 1936, vol. I, p. 172, no. 498, vol. II, plate 154, no. 498; D. Brian, "Art in the Modern Museum's Time," *Art News,* May 20, 1939, repr. p. 8 (lent anonymously); "Accessions of American and Canadian Museums," Jan.-Mar. 1961, *The Art Quarterly,* Summer 1961, p. 207, repr. no. 2; "La Chronique des Arts," Supplement à la *Gazette des Beaux-Arts,* Feb. 1962, vol. 59, p. 46, repr.; Los Angeles County Museum of Art, *Illustrated Handbook,* 1965, p. 90, repr. in color, p. 91; A. Frankfurter, "Los Angeles: The New Museum," *Art News,* Mar. 1965, p. 31, repr. in color no. 5; J. Elderfield, "Drawing in Cézanne," *Art Forum,* June 1971, vol. 9, p. 51; S. Orienti, *The Complete Paintings of Cézanne,* New York: Abrams, 1972, p. 109, no. 472, repr. p. 108

For Paul Cézanne an unrelenting study of nature was indispensable to art. While his investigations of the visual world led logically to analytical Cubism, Cézanne himself came to theory late in life, exhorting those few younger painters who sought him out to work and to avoid theorization. "One must make a vision for oneself...an optic, one must see nature as no one has seen it before," he told Emile Bernard. By nature he meant both the artist's nature and nature itself. And art he conceived as "a personal apperception situated in sensation and organized by intelligence into a work." Sensations were both retinal and felt; but foremost for Cézanne were the visual sensations. His painting is an ordered whole, constructed from the reference points of a multiplicity of probed sensations.

In *Still Life with Cherries and Peaches,* a radically tipped table top offers a triangular arrangement of objects seen from separate vantage points and reinforced by the reverse triangle of the chair in a spatially ambiguous background. Spherical forms of fruit and curving ovals of plates and the jug opening continue an intricate coiling movement initiated by the undulating cloth and stopped emphatically by an isolated peach. Unsupported, the cloth projects well over the table edge without falling. Cloth, wood, fruit, and ceramic are all fabricated of the same firm substance, woven by Cézanne's color modulations into a new solid geometry. The sense of natural structure is heightened by a flattening of curves and a slight curving of all straight lines.

Color for Cézanne was the supreme element in painting, and he regretted that the rich intensity of natural color was unattainable. Color also represented light, as light could not be reproduced. And with color he drew form: "nature for us men is more depth than surface, whence the need for introducing into our light vibrations, represented by reds, and yellows, a sufficient amount of blue to give the impression of air." Against a table painted in subtle grays that move from mauve to orange brown, red cherries complement a green jug, and yellow orange peaches pull toward the blue background; whites of the plates and cloth are modulated by pale yellow, blue, lavender, and a few rapid accents of deep blue and intense green.

90

Paul Gauguin
French, 1848-1903
Thatched Cottages at Pont-Aven
Oil on canvas
23⅜ x 36¼ in. (72.0 x 92.0 cm.)
Signed and dated lower right: P. Gauguin '86
Promised gift of Mr. and Mrs. Hal B. Wallis

Collections: Georges-Daniel de Monfreid, Paris; Mme. Agnes Huc de Monfreid, Béziers; Wildenstein & Co., New York; Mr. and Mrs. Hal B. Wallis, Los Angeles

Exhibitions: Paris, Boussod et Valadon, *Gauguin,* Jan. 1888; Paris, Galerie Dru, *Gauguin,* Apr. 16-May 11, 1923, no. 8; Paris, Le Portique, *Gauguin,* 1931, no. 27; Paris, Gazette des Beaux-Arts, *La Vie ardente de Gauguin,* 1936, no. 11; Paris, Galerie Charpentier, *Georges-Daniel de Monfreid et son ami Paul Gauguin,* Oct. 19-31, 1938, p. 25, no. 150; Paris, Musée National d'Art Moderne, *Collection G. D. de Monfreid,* Apr. 25-May 27, 1951, no. 1; New York, Wildenstein, *Olympia's Progeny,* Oct. 28-Nov. 27, 1965, no. 46, repr.

Literature: F. Fénéon, *La Revue Indépendante, calendrier,* Jan. 15, 1888, p. 170; Ch. Chassé, *Gauguin et le groupe de Pont-Aven,* Paris: H. Floury, 1921, p. 39, repr. p. 45, as "Landscape at Pont-Aven"; R. Rey, *Gauguin,* Paris, F. Rieder et Cie, 1923, repr. pl. 4 as "Cour de ferme en Bretagne"; J. Rewald, *Gauguin,* Paris: Hyperion Press, 1938, p. 166, repr. p. 62 as "Thatched Cottages at Pont-Aven";

M. Malingue, *Gauguin,* Paris, 1944, no. 49, repr. p. 49; idem, *Gauguin, le peintre et son oeuvre,* Paris: Les presses de la cité, 1948, no. 105, repr. p. 105 as "Chaumière à Pont-Aven," 1886; L. Van Dovski, *Paul Gauguin Paintings,* Basel: Amerbach, 1950, p. 341, no. 77; G. Wildenstein, "Gauguin en Bretagne, Pont-Aven, Dans le Champ Derout-Lollichon, 1886-1888," *Gazette des Beaux-Arts,* Jan.-Apr. 1956, vol. 47, pp. 83-87, repr. fig. 3, as "Cour de ferme en Bretagne"; idem, *Gauguin,* Paris: Les Beaux-Arts, 1964, p. 74, no. 200, repr. p. 74 (Coll. H. Wallis); W. Jaworska, *Paul Gauguin et l'Ecole de Pont-Aven,* Neuchatel, Ides et Calendes, 1971, repr. in color, p. 21; G. M. Sugana, *L'opera completa di Gauguin,* Milan, 1972, p. 89, no. 47, repr. p. 89

Gauguin first went to Pont-Aven in Brittany in 1886 because, as he said, it was an inexpensive place to live and he needed time to paint. Since his style at that time was Impressionist, the Breton countryside offered a wealth of subject matter for his pictures. Gauguin reproduced the landscape with such accuracy that the subject of this painting has been identified as a field called Derout-Lollichon (Wildenstein, 1956). Once the subject was chosen, Gauguin proceeded to explore it as an Impressionist would—with small, often curving strokes of unmixed pigment to capture accurately its infinite variety of shape and color. While *Thatched Cottages at Pont-Aven* is by and large an example of Gauguin's Impressionist phase, it does hint at the new direction his art would take within the next two years. His emphasis on the large geometric shapes of the cottages and the sharp edge of the shadow falling on the wall of the house in the foreground reveals the impetus toward simplification which characterizes his mature, symbolist style.

91

Paul Gauguin
French, 1848-1903
Bonjour M. Gauguin, 1889
Oil on canvas mounted on panel
29½ x 21½ in. (74.9 x 54.6 cm.)
Inscribed lower left: Bonjour M. Gauguin
Promised gift of the Armand Hammer Foundation

Collections: Mme. Marie Henry, Le Pouldu; Galerie Barbazanges, Paris; Meyer Goodfriend, New York (Sale, New York, American Art Galleries, Jan. 4-5, 1923, no. 107); B. M. Alexander, New York; Howard Young Galleries, New York; Carlton Mitchell, Annapolis; Count Ivan Podgoursky, San Antonio; Mrs. Mary Ermolaev, Princeton (Sale, Geneva, Christie, Manson & Woods, Nov. 6, 1969, no. 169, repr.)

Exhibitions: Paris, Galerie Barbazanges, *Exposition d'Oeuvres Inconnues,* Oct. 10-30, 1919, no. 2; New York, Wildenstein & Co., Inc., *A Retrospective Loan Exhibition for the Benefit of Les Amies de Paul Gauguin and the Penn Normal Industrial and Agricultural School,* Mar. 2-Apr. 18, 1936, no. 14; Montreal Museum of Fine Arts, *Manet to Matisse,* May-June, 1949, no. 14; Paris, Galerie Loize, *Les Amitiés de Montfreid et ses reliques de Gauguin,* May 11, 1951, no. 108 (inaugurated by Georges Salles, Director of the Museums of France); Houston, Museum of Fine Arts, *Paul Gauguin, His Place in the Meeting of East and West,* Mar. 27-Apr. 25, 1954, no. 15; Wichita Falls, The Museum Association of Midwestern Universities, Sept.-Oct. 1955, no. 16; Tulsa, Philbrook Art Center, *Four Centuries of European Art,* Oct. 1956, no. 34; Oklahoma City, Oklahoma Art Center, *Four Centuries of European Art,* Nov. 1957, no. 23; Little Rock, Arkansas, Museum of Fine Arts, Dec. 1958, no. 30; Phoenix Art Museum, *One Hundred Years of French Painting, 1860-1960,* Feb. 1-26, 1961, no. 42 (lent by Count Ivan Podgoursky, San Antonio, Texas); Oakland, California, Art Museum, *One Hundred Years of French Painting, 1860-1960,* Mar. 5-31, 1961, no. 42; New York, Christie, Manson & Woods (U.S.A.) Ltd., *Van Gogh, Gauguin and Their Circle,* Nov. 1968, no. 9; Memphis, Tennessee, Brooks Memorial Art Gallery, *The Armand Hammer Collection,* Dec. 19, 1969-Jan. 18, 1970; Washington, D.C., Smithsonian Institution, *The Armand Hammer Collection,* Mar. 20-May 17, 1970, no. 57 (repr. in cat. in color); traveled to Kansas City, Missouri, William Rockhill Nelson Gallery of Art, June 30-Aug. 2, 1970; New Orleans, Louisiana, Isaac Delgado Museum of Art, Aug. 15- Sept. 20, 1970; Columbus, Ohio, Columbus Gallery of Fine Arts, Oct. 9-Nov. 1, 1970; Little Rock, Arkansas, Arkansas Art Center, Nov. 21, 1970-Jan. 12, 1971; San Francisco, California Palace of the Legion of Honor, *The Armand Hammer Collection,* Feb. 11-Mar. 14, 1971; Oklahoma City, Oklahoma, Oklahoma Art Center, *The Armand Hammer Collection,* June 15-July 11, 1971; San Diego, California, Fine Arts Gallery of San Diego, *The Armand Hammer Collection,* July 23-Sept. 5, 1971; Los Angeles County Museum of Art, *The Armand Hammer Collecion,* Dec. 21, 1971-Feb. 27, 1972, repr. in cat. no. 33; traveled to London, Royal Academy, June 24-July 24, 1972; Dublin, National Gallery of Ireland, Aug. 8-Oct. 1, 1972; Leningrad, State Hermitage Museum, Oct. 23-Dec. 2, 1972; Moscow, State Pushkin Museum of Fine Arts, Dec. 8, 1972-Feb. 11, 1973; Kiev, State Museum of Ukrainian Art, Mar. 6-31, 1973; Minsk, Belorussian State Museum of Fine Arts, Apr. 26-May 26, 1973; Riga, State Museum of Latvian and Russian Art, June 8-July 8, 1973; Odessa, State Picture Gallery, July 25-Aug. 25, 1973

Literature: C. Chassé, *Gauguin et le Groupe de Pont-Aven,*
Paris: H. Floury, 1921, pp. 48-50; American Art Journal,
1923-24, vol. 20, p. 275; J. de Rontonchamp, *Gauguin,* Paris:
Les Editions G. Crès et Cie., 1925, p. 70; Canadian Art,
Summer 1949, vol. VI, no. 4, p. 176 repr.; J. Loize, *Les Amitiés
du peintre Georges-Daniel de Monfreid et ses reliques de
Gauguin,* 1951, no. 108, pp. 86-87; C. Chassé, *Gauguin et
son Temps,* 1955, pp. 70, 79; M. Malingue, "Du Nouveau
sur Gauguin," *L'Oeil,* July-Aug. 1959, p. 38; J. Rewald,
Le Post-Impressionisme, Paris: Albin Michel, 1961, p. 176;
G. Baudaille, *Gauguin,* London: 1964, pp. 89, 130, repr.
in color; G. Wildenstein, *Gauguin Oeuvre Catalogue,* Paris:
1964, no. 321, pp. 121-122; Art in America, Sept. 1969,
p. 15, repr.; Art News, Sept. 1969, p. 26, repr.; Apollo,
Oct. 1969, p. IX, repr.; Connaissance des Arts, Oct. 1969,
p. 67, repr.; Apollo, Feb. 1970, p. 170, repr.; Connoisseur,
Feb. 1970, p. 116, repr.; F. Davis, "A Royal Record of
Portraiture," Country Life, Feb. 5, 1970, pp. 302-303, repr.

In 1889 Gauguin and the painters working with him
transferred their Breton activities from Pont-Aven to
Le Pouldu, which they found more primitive. In October of
that year they moved to an inn kept by Marie Henry and
soon thereafter began decorating its walls with paintings
and sculpture. Gauguin's *Bonjour M. Gauguin* occupied
the upper panel of a door in the inn. There are two
existing versions of the composition, the other at the
Národní Galerie in Prague. Both Wildenstein and Sutton
are agreed that the Hammer picture is the one originally
fastened to the door at Le Pouldu while the Prague version
precedes it or is a later replica. In any case, the two pictures
cannot have been created more than a few weeks apart.
This picture is distinguished from the Prague version by a
somewhat more unified composition and more consistent
brushwork. The subject was almost certainly inspired by
Courbet's *Bonjour Monsieur Courbet* which Gauguin and
van Gogh had seen on a visit to Montpellier in December
1888. A related watercolor on silk (Rewald, *Gauguin
Drawings,* no. 18) is apparently a study for the right-hand
figure in the Prague version.

92

Vincent van Gogh
Dutch, 1853-1890
Hospital at Saint-Rémy, 1889
Oil on canvas
35½ x 28 in. (90.2 x 71.1 cm.)
Promised gift of the Armand Hammer Foundation

Collections: A. Schuffenecker, Paris; Galerie Druet, Paris,
1907; Dr. J. Keller, Paris, 1908-10; Galerie Druet, Paris,
1910; Paul von Mendelssohn-Bartholdy, Berlin, 1911; Paul
Rosenberg & Co., New York; Norton Simon, Los Angeles,
1964 (Sale, New York, Parke-Bernet Galleries,
May 5, 1971); Armand Hammer, Los Angeles

Exhibitions: Paris, Galerie Druet, *Vincent van Gogh,*
Jan. 6-18, 1908, no. 16; Berlin, Galerie Paul Cassirer,
Vincent van Gogh, May-June, 1914, no. 65; Amsterdam,
Stedelijk Museum, *Vincent van Gogh en Zijn Tijdgenooten,*
Sept. 6-Nov. 2, 1930, no. 92, repr. in cat. p. 18; Frankfurt,
Städelsches Kunstinstitut, *Vom Abbild zum Sinnbild,*
June 3-July 3, 1931, no. 69, repr. in cat. p. 26; Oklahoma
City, Oklahoma Art Center, *The Armand Hammer
Collection,* June 15-July 11, 1971; San Diego, Fine Arts
Gallery of San Diego; *The Armand Hammer Collection,*
July 23-Sept. 5, 1971; Los Angeles County Museum of
Art, *The Armand Hammer Collection,* Dec. 21, 1971-
Feb. 27, 1972. repr. in color in cat., no. 37; traveled to
London, Royal Academy, June 24-July 24, 1972; Dublin,
National Gallery of Ireland, Aug. 8-Oct. 1, 1972;
Leningrad, State Hermitage Museum, Oct. 23-Dec. 2, 1972;
Moscow, State Pushkin Museum of Fine Arts, Dec. 8,
1972-Feb. 11, 1973; Kiev, State Museum of Ukrainian Art,
Mar. 6-31, 1973; Minsk, Belorussian State Museum of
Fine Arts, Apr. 26-May 26, 1973; Riga, State Museum
of Latvian and Russian Art, June 8-July 8, 1973; Odessa,
State Picture Gallery, July 25-Aug. 25, 1973

Literature: *Aesculape,* XIIIth Year, II (Nov., 1923, p. 250);
L. Piérard, *La Vie Tragique de Vincent van Gogh,* Paris:
Les Editions G. Crès et Cie., 1924, p. 184, repr.; R. Grey,
Vincent van Gogh, Rome: Edition de Valori Plastici,
R. Garroni, repr.; *Aesculape,* XVIth Year, VI (June, 1926)
p. 158; F. Fels, *Vincent van Gogh,* Paris: H. Floury, 1928,
p. 171, repr.; J. B. Faille, *L'oeuvre de Vincent
van Gogh, catalogue raisonné,* Paris and Brussels: Editions
G. van Oest, 1928, no. 643, vol. II, pl. CLXXIX; V. Doiteau
and E. Leroy, *La folie de van Gogh* (preface P. Gachet),
Paris: Editions Aesculape, 1928, p. 64 repr. opp.; *The
Letters of Vincent van Gogh to His Brother,* Memoir by
J. van Gogh-Bonger, London: Constable & Co., Boston
and New York: Houghton Mifflin Co., 1929, vol. III,
letter 610, p. 400; J. Rewald, "Van Gogh en Provence,"
l'Amour de l'Art, VIII (Oct. 1936), p. 297, repr.; W. Scherjon
and W. Jos. de Gruyter, *Vincent van Gogh's Great Period,*
Amsterdam: "De Spieghel," Ltd., 1937, p. 205, repr.;
J. B. de la Faille, *Vincent van Gogh* (preface C. Terrasse),
Paris, London, and New York: Editions Hyperion, 1939,
no. 648, repr. p. 446; Dr. F. J. Beer, *Du démon de
van Gogh* (after *Van Gogh à l'Asile,* by Dr. E. Leroy), Nice:
Imprimerie Nouvelles Réunis, 1945, p. 75; J. B. de la Faille,
*The Works of Vincent van Gogh, His Paintings and
Drawings,* Amsterdam: Meulenhoff International, New
York: Reynal & Co. with W. Morrow & Co., Inc., 1970,
no. F643, pp. 256, 636, repr. p. 257; Sale catalog, *Highly
Important 19th and 20th Century Paintings, Drawings,
and Sculpture, from the Private Collection of Norton Simon,*
New York, Parke-Bernet Galleries, Inc., May 5, 1971,
no. 48, repr. in color p. 92

Van Gogh stayed at the hospital at St. Rémy for almost exactly one year, from May 1889 until May 1890, and took its gardens and surroundings as the subject for many of his pictures. In the fall of 1889 he wrote to his brother Theo that he had "two views of the park and the asylum," one of which was undoubtedly this work. Only one other painting (de la Faille 653) shows a substantial portion of the façade of the hospital. One sees in this picture the remnants of an older style in the squared rendering of the building, while the flamelike brushwork of the trees, which Vincent saw as "warped as in old wood," announces the style for which he has become best known. Few of van Gogh's pictures show as well as this the tendency of his brushstrokes to cling to the surface of the canvas or the increasing density and intensity of his paint application during the last three years of his life.

93

Auguste Rodin
French, 1840-1917
Head of Iris, no. 4, 1890-1891
Bronze
24 x 13 x 13 in. (61 x 33 x 33 cm.)
Signed in cast: Rodin; stamped in cast at right rear: Copyright Musée Rodin 1967; stamped in cast at left side: Georges Rudier Fondeur, Paris
Gift of the B. G. Cantor Art Foundation, 1969
M.69.52

Collection: B. Gerald Cantor, Beverly Hills

Exhibitions: Los Angeles County Museum of Art, *Homage to Rodin,* Collection of B. Gerald Cantor, Nov. 14, 1967-Jan. 7, 1968, p. 79, no. 51 in cat., repr. p. 90; traveled to Houston, The Museum of Fine Arts, Jan. 31-Mar. 3, 1968; The Brooklyn Museum, May 13-Aug. 25, 1968; Richmond, Virginia Museum of Fine Arts, Sept. 16-Oct. 20, 1968; San Francisco, California Palace of the Legion of Honor, Nov. 21, 1968-Jan. 5, 1969; Berkeley, University of California Art Museum, *Excellence: Art from the University Community,* Nov. 6, 1970-Jan. 9, 1971, no. 293 in cat.

Literature: R. Alley, *The Foreign Paintings, Drawings and Sculpture,* London: Tate Gallery, 1959, p. 217; D. Sutton, *Triumphant Satyr: The World of Auguste Rodin,* New York: Hawthorne Books, 1966, repr. fig. 72, p. 87; A. E. Elsen, *Rodin,* New York: Museum of Modern Art, 1967, repr. p. 117, pp. 116, 119; The Hayward Gallery, *Rodin: Sculpture and Drawings,* an exhibition organized by the Arts Council of Great Britain and the Association Française d'Auction Artistique, London, Jan. 24-Apr. 5, 1970, pp. 69, 75, repr. in cat., no. 74

This consummate sculpture of a woman's head represents Iris, Goddess of the Rainbow and swift messenger of Olympians Hera and Zeus. It was developed from a smaller sculpture, which in turn was based on a portrait head incorporated in the monumental *Gates of Hell.*

A sensual nature and an inquiring eye made Rodin a contemplative and perpetual observer of women, whose physical and psychological qualities he explored with intense fascination. In the *Head of Iris* he departs from the idealized refinement of conventional female portraits to create a work which is astonishingly precocious in its defiance of literal observation—the neck is impossibly massive, the mouth and chin are marred, unformed. Even more extraordinary than the shape of the asymmetrical head is the treatment of flesh and features. They seem wrought of a viscous substance, inert as scar tissue, yet imbued with a living, almost vulnerable quality. To strengthen the psychological impact, Rodin offsets the deformed, almost grotesque face of Iris with the gentle manipulation of light and shadow upon the surface, thus revealing the endless variety and expressive possibilities of a human head.

This enigmatic *Head of Iris,* serene in its ugliness, devoid of erotic undertones, remains one of the most haunting, psychologically powerful sculptures of the last decade of the nineteenth century.

94

Auguste Rodin
French, 1840-1917
Study of Nude for Balzac C, no. 4, 1893
Bronze, Rudier cast
50¼ x 20½ x 24¾ in. (127.6 x 52 x 62.8 cm.)
Signed right on the base: A. Rodin; stamped to the right: Copyright by Musée Rodin 1967
Gift of the B. G. Cantor Art Foundation, 1967
M.67.59

Collection: B. Gerald Cantor, Beverly Hills

Exhibitions: Los Angeles County Museum of Art, *Homage to Rodin,* Collection of B. Gerald Cantor, Nov. 14, 1967-Jan. 7, 1968, p. 91, no. 58, repr. p. 90; also traveled to Houston, The Museum of Fine Arts, Jan. 31-Mar. 3, 1968; New York, The Brooklyn Museum, May 13-Aug. 25, 1968; Richmond, Virginia Museum of Fine Arts, Sept. 16-Oct. 20, 1968; San Francisco, California Palace of the Legion of Honor, Nov. 21, 1968-Jan. 5, 1969; Berkeley, University of California, University Art Museum, *Excellence: Art from the University Community,* Nov. 6, 1970-Jan. 9, 1971, cat. no. 291; Stanford University Museum of Art, *Rodin and Balzac: Rodin's Sculptural Studies for the Monument to Balzac from the Cantor, Fitzgerald Coll.,* May 2-Aug. 2, 1973, pp. 38, 69, no. 26; traveled to Boise, Idaho, Boise Gallery of Art, Sept. 3-Oct. 28, 1973; The Denver Art Museum, Feb. 10-Mar. 20, 1974; Athens, The University

of Georgia, Georgia Museum of Art, Apr. 7-May 5, 1974;
Shreveport, Louisiana, The R. W. Norton Art Gallery,
May 26-June 30, 1974; Cincinnati Art Museum, July 15-
Aug. 23, 1974; Northampton, Smith College Museum
of Art, Sept. 20-Oct. 28, 1974; New York City, New York
Cultural Center, Nov. 9-Dec. 15, 1974

For literature and descriptive text, see 95.

95

Auguste Rodin
French, 1840-1917
Monument to Balzac, 1897
Bronze
117 x 47¼ x 47¼ in. (297.1 x 120.0 x 120.0 cm.)
Signed right front: Rodin; stamped right rear in base:
Susse Fondeur. Paris; stamped right side in base: Copyright
by Musée Rodin 1967
Promised gift of the B. G. Cantor Art Foundation

Collection: B. Gerald Cantor, Beverly Hills

Exhibition: Los Angeles County Museum of Art,
extended loan, Mar. 1973

Literature: E. Werdet, *Portrait intime de Balzac,* Paris,
1859; A. de Lamartine, *Balzac et ses oeuvres,* Paris, 1866;
Le Temps, July 18, 1891; *Le Matin,* Jan. 11, 1892; R. Marx,
"Balzac et Rodin," *Le Voltaire,* Feb. 23, 1892; G. Geffroy,
"L'Imaginaire," *Le Figaro,* Aug. 29, 1893; Ch. Chincholle,
"Balzac et Rodin," *Le Figaro,* Nov. 25, 1894; Sévérine,
Le Journal, Nov. 27, 1894; G. Stiegler, *L'Echo de Paris,*
Nov. 12, 1894; *Le Matin,* Aug. 19, 1896; *L'Art Moderne,*
July 25, 1897; *Le Journal,* Apr. 17, 1897; A. Alexandre,
Le Balzac de Rodin, Paris, 1898; L. Bénédite, "Les Salons de
1898," *La Gazette des Beaux-Arts,* series 3, xx, Aug. 1,
1898, p. 129 ff.; Ch. Chincholle, "La Statue de Balzac,"
Le Figaro, May 12, 1898; T. Gautier Fils, "Le Balzac
d'Auguste Rodin," *Le Figaro Illustré,* June 1898; F. Harris,
"A Masterpiece of Modern Art," *Saturday Review,* LXXXVI,
1898; *Le Journal,* May 12, 1898 (article signed "X.");
L'Echo de Paris, May 27, 1898; *Le Figaro,* May 11, 1898;
J. Rameau, "La victoire de M. Rodin," *Le Gaulois,* May 3,
1898; G. Rodenbach, "Une Statue," *Le Figaro,* May 17,
1898; G. Ferry, "La statue de Balzac," *Le Monde Moderne,*
x, 1899; Ch. Morice, "L'Oeuvre de Rodin," *L'Art Moderne,*
May 21, 1899; H. Frantz, "Le Balzac de Rodin," *Rodin et
son oeuvre (Numéro spécial de La Plume),* Paris, 1900;
Ch. Blanc, *Grammaire des arts du dessin,* Paris, 1903;
F. Lawton, *The Life and Works of Auguste Rodin,* London:
T. Fisher Unwinn, 1906; *La Revue,* Nov. 1, 1907, unsigned
article; *Le Matin,* July 13, 1908, interview by unnamed
reporter; Ch. du Bousquet, "Chapu, lettres, pages d'album
et croquis inédits," *Revue de l'Art Ancien et Moderne,* XXX,

1911-1912; M. Ciolkowska, *Rodin,* London: Methuen,
1912; P. Gsell, "Chez Rodin," *L'Art et les Artistes,* 1907,
p. 393 ff., reprinted ibid., 1914; G. Coquiot, *Rodin à
l'Hôtel Biron et à Meudon,* Paris: Ollendorf, 1917;
A. Ludovici, *Personal Reminiscences of Auguste Rodin,*
London: Murray, 1926, pp. 28-32, 41, 148; E. Zola,
Correspondance, 1872-1902, Paris, 1929; M. Morhardt,
"La bataille du Balzac," *Mercure de France,* Dec. 15,
1934; A. Fontainas, "Le 'Balzac' de Rodin est offert à Paris,"
Mercure de France, CCLXXXV, Dec. 15, 1938; V. Frisch
and J. T. Shipley, *Auguste Rodin, a Biography,* New York:
Stokes, 1939; J. Cladel, *Rodin, sa vie glorieuse, sa vie
inconnue,* definitive edition, Paris: Grasset, 1950, pp. 181-
228; Musée Rodin, Paris, *Balzac et Rodin,* Paris, 1950;
C. Goldscheider, "La genèse d'une oeuvre: Le Balzac de
Rodin," *Revue des Arts,* II, Mar. 1952, pp. 37-44; E. and J.
de Goncourt, *Journal mémoires de la vie littéraire,* XXI,
Monaco, 1956-58; R. Alley, *The Tate, Foreign Paintings,
Drawings and Sculpture,* London, 1959; C. Eisler, "The
Athlete of Virtue: The Iconography of Asceticism,"
De Artibus Opiscula, XI, *Essays in Honor of Erwin Panofsky,*
New York, 1961; J. A. Ducourneau, *Album Balzac,* Paris,
1962; J. Lethève, "Les Portraits de Balzac: Essai de répertoire
iconographique," *L'Année balzacienne,* Paris, 1963;
J. de Caso, "Rodin and the Cult of Balzac," *The Burlington
Magazine,* CVI, 1964, p. 279 ff.; A. Maurois, *Prometheus:
The Life of Balzac,* London, 1965; J. de Caso, "Balzac and
Rodin in Rhode Island," *Bulletin of the Rhode Island
School of Design,* vol. LII, no. 4, May 1966, pp. 1-21; A. E.
Elsen, "Rodin's Portrait of Baudelaire," 25 *(Festschrift
for Henry Hope),* Bloomington, Indiana, 1966; D. Sutton,
Triumphant Satyr: The World of Auguste Rodin, New
York: Hawthorne Books, 1966; B. Champigneulle, *Rodin,*
New York: H. N. Abrams, 1967, p. 175 ff.; R. Descharnes
and J. F. Chabrun, *Auguste Rodin,* Lausanne: Edita,
1967; A. E. Elsen, "Rodin's Naked Balzac," *The Burlington
Magazine,* CIX, Nov. 1967, pp. 606-616; idem, *Rodin,*
New York: Museum of Modern Art, 1967; I. Jianou and
C. Goldscheider, *Rodin,* Paris, 1967; A. Spear, *Rodin
Sculpture in the Cleveland Museum of Art,* Cleveland, 1967;
Maison de Balzac, Paris, *Les Portraits de Balzac, connus et
inconnus,* Paris, 1971; Ph. Fehl, *The Classical Monument,*
New York, 1972

In 1891 the Société des Gens de Lettres in Paris entrusted
Auguste Rodin with creating a monument to commemorate Honoré de Balzac. The project, originally to have been
accomplished within a few months, lasted for seven years.

Rodin, confronted with the problem of synthesizing the
extraordinary spiritual and physical forces of Balzac, studied
all available literary and visual sources with painstaking
and conscious care. A series of documentary *maquettes* and
studies of heads, nude and clothed figures of the novelist,
reflect Rodin's various visions and the progressively
simplified conception of the sculpture.

Studies of the nude figure culminated in the masterful *Naked Balzac with Folded Arms* of 1893. In it an older Balzac emerged, in an astonishing and daringly unconventional composition: the image of the novelist, in a posture of an orator, with widespread stance and heavy arms crossed above a bulging abdomen, betrayed the sculptor's concentration in presenting a psychological portrait devoid of unnecessary attributes.

Elsen remarks in *Rodin and Balzac* (p. 44) that "Rodin's decision to position his figure thus was a genuinely inspired one, not suggested by the visual iconography or written descriptions of the man. Paintings, drawings, prints and sculptures do not show this pose, nor do such biographers as Lamartine and Werdet specifically describe this wide open stance as being natural or instinctive to him....
The pose of the *Naked Balzac with Folded Arms* satisfies different demands. It imparts suggestions of strong character and a self-assured attitude toward the world. Secondly, it was the brilliant artistic solution to the problem of achieving an imposing sculpture of a short obese subject. In the present-day absence of rhetorical sculpture we have forgotten how important were figure composition and symbolism before and during Rodin's lifetime. (We have even forgotten of what single-figure composition consists and that since antiquity the naked body was used metaphorically.) Rodin's sculpture reminds us that good figure composition included minimizing and harmonizing physical disparities. Better than any alchemist, Rodin was able to transform the lead of Balzac's physical liabilities into artistic gold." The Société, however, found the figure unsatisfactory.

Rodin continued to work intermittently on successive studies for the final monument. Yielding to the pressures of the Société he exhibited the *Monument to Balzac* in plaster at the Salon National des Beaux-Arts in May 1898. The peculiarly tilted figure of Balzac, fully wrapped in a floor-length robe, produced a scandal with the press and public; the work was found unacceptable and the city of Paris refused to install it in front of the Palais Royal. Not until 1937 was the sculpture finally cast in bronze and placed on a pedestal at the Boulevard Raspail and Montparnasse in Paris.

"After so many fragmented and incomplete interpretations of Balzac," Elsen wrote in *Rodin and Balzac* (pp. 56-58), "Rodin had met the challenge for a psychological and formal wholeness and achieved a stricter unity of form and subject that today we recognize as belonging more to this century than the last. The concessions to his vision of sculptural form, which demanded subordination of detail to the contours, were not made at the expense of Balzac's character. The final silhouettes presuppose the reconstitutions of a naked body, just as the explosive head is the summation of the writer's life and Rodin's chronicling of temperament and aging. As a mountain from a distance reveals its physiognomy, the ridges, caves and crevices of Balzac's features mock the efforts of light and space to erase their identity....From the front, it represents Rodin's effort to revitalize monumental commemorative sculpture and to be modern through exaggeration of the features....From the back, Rodin's *Balzac* is as astonishing as from the front. Seen against the sky, it is an abstract sculpture and was compared by his contemporaries to a pre-historic menhir."

For Auguste Rodin, the monument was his most important achievement. In crystallizing his personal image of the novelist in this bold and dramatic conception, he revitalized the sculptural portrait and delivered a vigorous blow to the prescribed institutionalized academism.

96

Aubrey Beardsley
English, 1872-1898
Enter Herodias, 1893
Pen, black ink, and wash on Whatman paper
8¾ x 6⅜ in. (22.3 x 16.3 cm.)
Gift of the Graphic Arts Council, 1973
M.73.49

Collections: John Lane, London; Bailey Gallery, London

The Museum's *Enter Herodias* by Aubrey Beardsley is the expurgated version of the drawing for plate five of the illustrations to Oscar Wilde's play, *Salomé*. The play was refused performance in England but was published in France in 1893 by Matthews and Lane. Two versions of *Enter Herodias* exist. In the first, the androgynous figure at the right appeared completely nude, and the artist was forced to make a new drawing with a fig leaf. Other changes that appear in the second version of the drawing are slight alterations of the faces and a greater regularity in the "dotting" both for modeling and decorative purposes.

Beardsley's *Salomé* drawings were made when the artist was only twenty-one. Notorious in their time for their frank sensuality, they are unparalleled in the history of illustration for their aesthetic originality and individuality. These drawings confounded the Victorian world, sounding a note of modernity which transformed the art of the future by influencing such artists as Matisse, Klee, and Picasso.

Enter Herodias is a drawing composed chiefly of voids. Expressive of the artist's love for "fantastic impressions treated in the finest outline with patches of black blots," its daring new patterning reflected little that had been seen before. Even Whistler's peacock patterning was more detailed, and Japanese prints with their curving, rhythmic, organic lines were scarcely echoed in Beardsley's purposely hard, cold, artificial lineality, while the "decadence" of his jeweled decorativeness and sardonic exposure of the "poisons of the flesh" were new and unsettling experiences for Victorian society. A character by D. H. Lawrence, when confronted with the *Salomé* illustrations said, "I sat and looked, and my soul leaped out upon the new thing. I was bewildered, wondering, grudging, fascinated...."

Dominating in her monolithic massiveness, and invested with all the viciousness described by Wilde, the columnar figure of Herodias is flanked by two equally decadent figures—the monstrous eunuch who lifts her drapery at the left, and the nude with powder box and mask at the right. Below the "wing" or curtain at the right is the caricature of Wilde who wears a curious cap with bells and an owl crown. He holds his play and a caduceus and points to the middle candle, his hand crossing the flame of the first taper. The irregular line which passes from behind the arm of the nude onto Herodias' body and down to the left taper divides the space in what may seem an arbitrary manner, yet creates a plane of an ambiguous abstract character.

Enter Herodias is one of the strongest of the *Salomé* drawings. The reduction of forms to their barest outlines and the vivid contrasts of flat blacks against the large voids of the composition make Beardsley's style the most vital single influence upon Art Nouveau.

97

Jean Worth
French, 1856-1926
Afternoon Dress, 1896
Printed silk taffeta
Gift of Mrs. Murray Ward, 1971
M.71.36

The House of Worth (1858-1946), established by Charles Frederick Worth, dominated European fashion design in its period of greatest productivity, 1858 to 1910. Their clientele was comprised of aristocracy and nobility who delighted in the innovations of the Worths. Eighteen ninety-six, the beginning of "la Belle Epoque," was a period of extravagance, gaiety, and excitement before World War I. As women gained more independence, fashion moved toward more comfortable, practical clothing. The afternoon dress, designed during this transitional period, embodies the elegance of luxurious materials with the new simplicity of line and detailing. Following the ideal silhouette of the period this gown has a smooth skirt in front constructed of five gored sections. Extra fullness is gathered at the back in inverted and cartridge pleats; back tapes attached to the skirt lining maintain the back fullness, preventing the fabric from falling to front or sides. Tan silk taffeta lining gives the outer fabric of the skirt extra body.

The trimmings on the skirt are minimal, with bodice decoration dominating. From just above the knee to the hem, three rows of narrow taffeta bands (called frou-frou because of their rustling sound) are arranged in a deep zigzag pattern. Only the top points of the zigzag are sewn to the skirt, creating a geometric petallike effect over the scalloped hem of the skirt which is edged with red and blue braid above a narrow ruffle of lace.

The bodice is cut in the traditional manner with a center back seam, two narrow side back seams originating from the armscye, underarm seams, two front darts for each side, and a front closure of hooks and eyes. Each piece is mounted on a firm lining with all seams and darts boned for support. The bodice detail continues the emphasis on a slim silhouette. Narrow ribbons of the skirt fabric are appliqued in vertical lines onto the short, basqued blue silk of the bodice. The tapering revers optically decrease the size of the waist and increase the width of the shoulders. White silk chiffon covers a high standing satin collar and also provides a decorative jabot. The gown shows the transition from the extreme gigot to the softer shaped sleeve as it begins to lose stiffness and fullness. The voluminous effect of the three-quarter-length sleeve, mounted on a two-piece foundation sleeve, is softened by dividing the puff into two sections with bands of blue velvet ribbon and by gathering the fullness to the back, thus diminishing the sleeve width. The shoulder width is accented by a narrow lace oversleeve around the sleeve cap, and a lace fall hangs from a second velvet band at the bottom of the sleeve.

Reported to have been made for President McKinley's inauguration on March 4, 1897, this afternoon gown reflects a patriotic theme. The fabric chosen is printed with a red and blue cross-stitch embroidery pattern on an ivory silk taffeta ground. The cross-stitch motifs resemble the tulip design (also called Virginia Lily or North Carolina Lily) used in samplers and patchwork quilts of the early nineteenth century. Worth's reference to American historical costume can also be seen in the jabot and lace sleeve falls that resemble those worn at the time of the Revolution.

98

Edvard Munch
German, 1863-1944
Seascape, 1899
Color woodcut, hand-colored with yellow and white gouache
14¾ x 22¼ in. (37.4 x 56.5 cm.)
Signed lower right on Bristol board mount: Edv. Munch
Gift of Mr. and Mrs. Felix Juda, 1966
M.66.87

Collection: Mr. and Mrs. Felix Juda, Los Angeles

Exhibition: Los Angeles County Museum of Art, *Edvard Munch,* Jan. 28-Mar. 9, 1969, no. 42, repr. in color in cat. p. 53

Literature: G. Schiefler, *Verzeichnes des Graphischen Werks Edvard Munch bis 1906,* Berlin: Bruno Cassirer, 1907

With its flat, simplifying forms and subtle, muted colors, this woodcut suggests the essence of a seascape, stopping short of pure abstraction. In doing his own printing, Munch was able to alter the application of color from impression to impression so that each print from a so-called edition varied enough from the others to be considered "unique." The number of impressions of this woodcut, as is the case with many of Munch's prints, is still uncertain but in all probability is quite small.

The Museum's woodcut closely resembles the description of the same print Schiefler mentioned as in his own collection. Another rare multi-colored impression, not recorded by Schiefler, is in the Fogg Museum.

99

Pierre Bonnard
French, 1867-1947
Bridge in Paris, ca. 1903
Oil on canvas
28⅛ x 39⅜ in. (71.5 x 100.0 cm.)
Signed lower left: Bonnard
Gift of Mr. and Mrs. Sidney F. Brody, 1967
M.67.3

Collections: Ambroise Vollard, Paris; Henkel Collection, Weisbaden; Mr. and Mrs. Sidney F. Brody, Los Angeles

Exhibitions: New York, Museum of Modern Art, *Bonnard and His Environment,* Oct. 7-Nov. 29, 1964, no. 17, repr. in cat., p. 69; in collaboration with the Art Institute of Chicago, Jan. 8-Feb. 28, 1965, and the Los Angeles County Museum of Art, Mar. 31-May 30, 1965; The American Federation of Arts, *Exposition Bonnard au Japon,* 1968, no. 24, repr. in cat., pl. 49; traveled to Tokyo, National Museum of Western Art, Mar. 9-Apr. 21, 1968, and Kyoto, National Museum of Modern Art, Apr. 27-June 9, 1968

Literature: M. Benedikt, "Continuity of Pierre Bonnard," *Art News,* Oct. 1964, vol. 63, pp. 20-23 ff, repr. p. 22; "Key to the Pattern; Exhibition at the Museum of Modern Art in New York," *Apollo,* Feb. 1965, vol. 81, pp. 84-86, repr., p. 86; J. and H. Dauberville, *Bonnard: catalogue raisonné de l'oeuvre peint,* vol. 1 (1885-1905), Paris, 1966, no. 289, p. 273; *Los Angeles County Museum of Art, Annual Report 1965-1967,* Bulletin XVIII, no. 1-2, p. 10, repr. p. 11

Pierre Bonnard came to artistic maturity in Paris in the 1890s. His position in modern French art is a singular one: he resides chronologically between Impressionism and the Fauvist movement, unattached to either. Stylistically Bonnard's only true parallel is in the work of Edouard Vuillard. Bonnard was for a time affiliated with the symbolist Nabi group in Paris, but he remained uncommitted to their rather dogmatic theories and indeed insistently heeded his own very personal vision throughout his prolific career.

Bonnard's particular genius has to do with seeing in the ordinary—in passing street scenes or everyday household activities—the extraordinary. He is never bombastic or morally pretentious, and yet in his best work Bonnard achieves at the highest level a painterly synthesis of abstract values and evocative representation of subject. The chief irony of Bonnard's approach is that despite the mundane character of his subject matter he seldom recorded events or scenes; unlike the Impressionists, he painted from memory or from small sketches and brief color notations.

The first decade of the twentieth century was a time in Bonnard's stylistic evolution when his work was relatively close in spirit to early Impressionism, i.e., to the work of Monet and Renoir in the sixties and seventies. It was a time when he was using a relatively subdued, naturalistic palette (especially compared to his use of vivid color after 1920) and maintaining a balance in his work between a quality of intimacy and a certain detachment from his subject. The *Bridge in Paris* well illustrates this psychological ambiguity; it is notable, too, for an odd disjunction between foreground and background and between the left and right sides of the painting. Bonnard's modernism, or the quality which distinguishes him from the nineteenth century to which he more than half belongs, is discerned more in such subtle qualities of spatial peculiarity or atmospheric opacity than in any dramatic moves away from the older "representational" conventions.

100

Pablo Picasso
Spanish, 1881-1973
Portrait of Sebastian Juñer Vidal, 1903
Oil on canvas
49¾ x 37 in. (126.4 x 94.0 cm.)
Signed and dated lower right: A Sebastian Juñer, Picasso, junio, 1903
Bequest of David E. Bright, 1967
M.67.25.18

Collections: Sebastian Juñer, Barcelona; Carlos and Xavier Junyer, Perpignan; Frank Gabriel Dereppe, Lugano; David E. Bright, Los Angeles

Exhibitions: Paris, Musées Nationaux, *Exposition Picasso,* Nov. 1966-Feb. 1967; Los Angeles County Museum of Art, *David E. Bright Collection,* Oct. 17-Dec. 17, 1967, repr. in color in cat., p. 25; Berkeley, University Art Museum, University of California, *Excellence: Art from the University Community,* Nov. 6, 1970-Mar. 9, 1971, no. 537 repr. in cat.

Literature: C. Zervos, *Pablo Picasso,* Paris: Editions Cahiers d'Art, 1932, vol. I, repr. no. 174 as "Le Peintre Sebastian Juñer"; A. C. Pellicer, *Picasso avant Picasso,* Geneva: Editions Pierre Caillier, 1950, repr. p. 80; *Picasso 75th Anniversary,* New York: Museum of Modern Art, 1957; *Picasso,* Philadelphia: Philadelphia Museum of Art, 1958, repr. no. 11; *Spanish Masters,* University of California, 1960; *Bonne Fête, Monsieur Picasso,* Los Angeles: University of California, 1961, repr. no. 4; P. Daix and G. Boudaille, *Picasso: the Blue and Rose Periods,* Greenwich, Connecticut: New York Graphic Society Ltd., 1966, repr. no. IX.21

The painter Sebastian Juñer-Vidal was a close friend of Picasso during the Barcelona years. Both belonged to the *fin de siecle* circle of artists and writers in Barcelona whose meeting place was the famous cafe Els Quatre Gats. In this portrait, Juñer-Vidal's dramatically whitened face stares directly from the upper center of the canvas; the psychological power of characterization, however, resides more in the close-valued handling of the body, a stiff and yet powerful mass, and in the sad, oddly dehumanized presence of the woman seated next to the portrait's subject as though appended to him. Picasso's somewhat romantic view of his artist friend—and probably of himself at this time—is implicit in his rather theatrical depiction here. And yet by virtue of the painting's very simplicity and its unforced directness the characterization is unsentimental.

101

Henri Matisse
French, 1869-1954
Heads of Jeannette, 1910-1913
Jeannette I, bronze, fourth cast of ten, h: 13 in.
(33.0 cm.) M.68.3.1
Jeannette II, bronze, fifth cast of ten, h: 10⅜ in.
(26.4 cm.) M.68.3.2
Jeannette III, bronze, fourth cast of ten, h: 23¾ in.
(60.3 cm.) M.68.48.1
Jeannette IV, bronze, fourth cast of ten, h: 24⅛ in.
(61.3 cm.) M. 68.48.2
Jeannette V, bronze, first cast of ten, h: 22⅞ in.
(58.1 cm.) M.68.48.3
All bear caster's stamp: Cire C. Valsuani, Perdue
Gift of the Art Museum Council in memory of Penelope Rigby, 1968

Collections: Mme. Georges Duthuit-Matisse, Paris; Frank Perls, Beverly Hills

Exhibitions: New York, 291 Gallery, Mar. 1912; London, *Second Post-Impressionist Exhibition,* 1912; Paris, Galerie Bernheim-Jeune, 1913; New York, Montross Gallery, 1915; Paris, Maison de la Pensée Française, 1950; Los Angeles, UCLA Art Galleries, *Matisse,* 1966, no. 116, repr. in cat., p. 142; Beverly Hills, Frank Perls Gallery, *Six Sculptures by Henri Matisse,* Jan. 15-Feb. 16, 1968, repr. in cat., pp. 30-31; Des Moines Art Center, Dec. 30, 1968-Mar. 31, 1969; New York, Museum of Modern Art, *Sculpture of Matisse,* Feb. 24-May 8, 1972; traveled to Minneapolis, Walker Art Center, June 20-Aug. 6, 1972, and Berkeley, University of California, University Art Museum, Sept. 18-Oct. 29, 1972; Los Angeles County Museum of Art, *Two Decades of Art Museum Council Gifts,* Nov. 11, 1972-Jan. 7, 1973

Literature: A. H. Barr, Jr., *Matisse, His Art and His Public,* New York: Museum of Modern Art, 1951, pp. 140-142, repr., pp. 368-371; A. Legg, *The Sculpture of Matisse,* New York: Museum of Modern Art, 1972, nos. 42-46

The five *Heads of Jeannette* by Henri Matisse are among the most important sculptural holdings of the Museum. Widely considered to be Matisse's greatest work in portraiture, they are of considerable significance for any study of Matisse's sculpture and of his painting.

Matisse began working in sculpture in order to clarify issues in his painting. He said, "…it was done for the purposes of organization, to put order into my feelings and find a style to suit me. When I found it in sculpture, it helped me in my painting."

In the *Heads*—his first series of sculpture based on one model—a step-by-step progression in the artist's approach to sculptural form can be traced in the alteration from the original life-size naturalistic conception to the radically stylized and abstract fifth version. In 1910 he worked on the first two versions from the model, a young woman named Jeanne Vaderin. "Jeannette" was staying at Clamart, near Matisse's studio in Issy-les-Moulineaux, while convalescing from an illness. Within three years after the initial portraits, the remaining three heads were produced specifically as variations, exaggerating the pear-shaped face, aquiline features, and bouffant hair in the third and fourth versions, and drastically simplifying the structure in the fifth. In conceiving the startlingly "Cubist" fifth head, Matisse worked from the plaster cast of the third version. He eliminated the center roll of hair, built up the brow area, and reduced the width of the head. The left eye socket was filled in with an abstract block giving an ambiguous but unmistakable intensity to the face and an assertive strength to the form. The Matisse scholar, Alfred H. Barr, finds *Jeannette V* bolder than any Cubist sculpture of the period.

All five heads were cast by the master bronze-caster, C. Valsuani, during the artist's lifetime.

102

Frank Kupka
Czechoslovakian, 1871-1957
Irregular Forms: Creation, 1911
Oil on canvas
42½ x 42½ in. (108.0 x 108.0 cm.)
Signed lower right: Kupka
Inscribed lower left: Formes Irregulières: Création
Bequest of David E. Bright, 1967
M.67.25.10

Collections: Mme. Eugénie Kupka, Paris; Richard Feigen
Gallery, Chicago; David E. Bright, Los Angeles

Exhibitions: São Paulo, Brazil, *IV Bienal de Arte Moderna,*
1957; Paris, Musée National d'Art Moderne, *Kupka,*
1958, no. 16, repr. in cat., p. 19; Los Angeles, Ambassador
Hotel, *Living with Famous Paintings,* Feb. 1961; Los
Angeles County Museum of Art, *David E. Bright Collection,*
Oct. 17-Dec. 17, 1967, repr. in color in cat., p. 17;
New York, Spencer A. Samuels and Company, Ltd.,
The Work of Kupka (1871-1957), Mar. 25-Apr. 27, 1968;
San Diego, Fine Arts Gallery, *Color and Form 1909-1914,*
Nov. 20, 1971-Jan. 2, 1972; traveled to the Oakland Museum,
Jan. 26-Mar. 5, 1972, and Seattle Art Museum Pavilion,
Mar. 24-May 7, 1972; Pittsburgh, Carnegie Institute
Museum of Art, *Celebration,* Oct. 25, 1974-Jan. 5, 1975

Frank Kupka, born in Czechoslovakia, first came to Paris
in 1894, settled there in 1900, and continued to work in
France until his death. Kupka is one of the first artists to
have painted totally abstract works. Innovations in abstract
painting parallel to Kupka's were made more or less
simultaneously, ca. 1910-1911, by Delaunay in Paris,
Kandinsky in Munich, and Larionov in Moscow. These
artists shared an interest in making paintings which,
through the qualities inherent in their construction and
color, would awaken feelings similar to those aroused
by elements in visible nature.

Kupka's special interest lay in a study of the properties
of color as a means of expressing the vital forces of the
cosmos. In 1910-1911, he became associated with a group of
young painters, among them Delaunay, who were
influenced by the color theories of the Neoimpressionists
and the daring color of the Fauves. They began to consider the possibility of painting works whose subject matter
would be the interrelational functioning of color.
Delaunay's Orphism successfully combined Fauve color
with Cubist form. Kupka, however, arrived at abstract
color painting by way of Seurat's color theories without
utilizing the structure of Cubism.

Irregular Forms: Creation is one of a series of works,
begun in 1911, known as the Organic Cycle. In this series,
Kupka sought to express the essence of the cosmic drama,
to create a plastic parallel to the natural order. Undoubtedly
influenced by his extensive biological studies and interest
in theosophy, the series is based on Kupka's philosophical
belief that everything, even thought, is a material process.
Kupka's quest for this plastic expression of movement in
time and space is evidenced consummately in this work.
The contemporaneous explorations of a similar theme by
the Italian Futurists employed literal real-world machine
imagery, while Kupka's evocations of the dynamism
of life forces are created entirely by the means of abstract
form and color.

103

Jacques Villon
French, 1875-1963
Yvonne in Profile, 1913
Drypoint on Delâtre paper
Second state of two; edition: 7/23
21⅝ x 16⅞ in. (54.9 x 41.4 cm.)
Signed in pencil lower right: Jacques Villon
Los Angeles County Funds, 1965
65.19

Collection: Peter Deitsch, New York

Literature: J. Auberty and C. Perussaux, *Jacques Villon,
oeuvre gravé,* Paris: Paul Prouté et ses fils, 1950, p. 19, no. 194

In 1913 Villon made three Cubist drypoint portraits.
Two were of his sister, Yvonne Duchamp, the third is titled
Portrait of a Young Woman. The young woman was
depicted in a three-quarter view, truncated below her knees.
Of the prints of his sister, one showed her full face, in an
almost bustlike portrait, while *Yvonne in Profile* is a full-
length figure of Yvonne seated in an armchair. The latter
print was inspired by and is in reverse to Villon's oil
painting *Portrait of Mlle. Yvonne Duchamp* of the same
year which is in the Museum's collection. Among numerous
changes apparent in the drypoint are the artist's alterations
of the proportions of the sitter. In contrast to the attenuated
figure in the painting, the print depicts the seated woman
with a larger head, further emphasizing the portrait quality
of the print. Other substitutions include the more frontal
portrayal found in the print, in contrast to the sweeping,
diagonally foreshortened view found in the painting.

The drypoint is a tightly resolved composition, meticulously constructed of clearly defined polygonal forms which
suggest a total Cubist environment enclosing a prismatically faceted representation of a seated woman. Whereas the
painting incorporates various hues which are often in
dramatic juxtaposition, in the drypoint Villon relied on
dark and light tonalities of ink in contrast to the whiteness
of the unprinted paper. The resulting print suggests the

permeating flicker of firelight while further reaffirming and masterfully integrating the Cubist composition.

The Museum's impression of *Yvonne in Profile* is of the second state, number seven in an edition of twenty-three. (The edition of the first state consisted of only eleven proofs.) As an early impression, this print is extremely rich in the velvety blacks of the long, parallel drypoint lines. They are drawn with a bold assurance that creates a decisive, unifying pattern of faceting that implies layers of depth as well as prismatic sculptural forms. In *Yvonne in Profile,* one of the masterpieces of Cubist printmaking, Jacques Villon attained a greater dramatic impact than either Picasso or Braque had achieved in their own Cubist prints.

104

Raymond Duchamp-Villon
French, 1876-1918
The Large Horse, 1914
Bronze, second cast of nine, 1966
h: 59 in. (149.9 cm.)
Incised: R. Duchamp-Villon/1914
Louis Carré, Editeur/Susse Fondeur Paris
Gift of Anna Bing Arnold, 1968
M.68.44

Collections: Louis Carré, Paris, 1966; M. Knoedler & Co., New York, 1967-1968

Exhibitions: Paris, Galerie Carré, *Duchamp-Villon: Le cheval majeur,* June 23-Dec. 24, 1966; New York, M. Knoedler & Co., *Raymond Duchamp-Villon,* Oct. 10-Nov. 4, 1967, no. 25.9; Berkeley, University of California, University Art Museum, *Excellence: Art from the University Community,* Nov. 6, 1970-Mar. 9, 1971, no. 364 in cat.

Literature: J. Cassou, *Duchamp-Villon: Le cheval majeur,* Paris, Galerie Carré, 1966; G. H. Hamilton and W. C. Agee, *Raymond Duchamp-Villon,* New York: M. Knoedler & Co., 1967, comprehensive study of the development of the image and the history of the casts with notes and bibliography pp. 86-103, repr. fig. 69

In 1913, Duchamp-Villon wrote, "The power of the machine is upon us, and we can no longer conceive of living beings without it." In his most important work, *The Horse,* he combined his optimistic acceptance of the machine with a sculptural realization of Cubist principles.

The Horse was begun in the spring of 1914 before the outbreak of war on August 3, and was finished in the fall of 1914 when the sculptor was on leave from military service. Duchamp-Villon died at the front in 1918 before he could see a large version cast in bronze and another in

steel according to the plans communicated to his brothers, Jacques Villon and Marcel Duchamp. In 1930-1931, his brothers directed the first enlargement of the horse to 39⅜ inches in height. Marcel Duchamp supervised the casting of the present final enlargement in 1966. (Also in the collection of the Los Angeles County Museum of Art is a small, early bronze maquette of the sculpture.)

The Horse synthesizes a half-century of prevailing intellectual trends. It is a visible transformation of the moving horse into the twentieth-century machine, and it is clear that its conception was influenced by the ideas published in the 1909 Futurist Manifesto, in which the horse figured as the embodiment of dynamism and energy. Its open forms interwoven with spatial voids indicate Duchamp-Villon's familiarity with the Cubist paintings of Picasso and Braque. Darwinian theory had stimulated an investigation of animal movement and the sculptor knew Muybridge's and Morey's important studies of the sequential movement of the horse. The philosophy of Henri Bergson, who believed that the true state of existence was change itself, and the "simultaneous" poetry of Guillaume Apollinaire were also important for Duchamp-Villon. A similar interest in the machine as the embodiment of a new age is seen in the con-temporaneous works of the artist's colleagues: Léger, Delaunay, Picabia, and his younger brother, Marcel Duchamp, as well as in creations as diverse as Stravinsky's *Sacre du Printemps* and the poetry of Blaise Cendrars.

105

Lyonel Feininger
German, 1871-1956
Vollersroda, 1918
Black pen and wash
7⅞ x 9⅞ in. (20.0 x 25.1 cm.)
Signed, titled, and dated: Sonntag d.6 Jan. 1918
Gift of the Graphic Arts Council, 1968
M.68.23

Collections: The Feininger family; Robert M. Light, Boston

In the summer of 1913, Feininger made a solitary tour of the hundred villages of Thuringia, near Weimar. The churches there inspired compositions that he used through-out his life in paintings, watercolors, and woodcuts.

The drawing of the church, *Vollersroda,* comes closest to Feininger's painting, *The Cathedral,* 1920 (private collection, Pennsylvania). Here, occupied with the dynamism of light, curves, and spirals, and the simultaneous view, he summed up the explorations of Robert Delaunay, Orphism, Futurism, and Cubism. But Feininger wished to transcend some of the more mechanical elements of these revolutionary movements. *Vollersroda* is more architectonic than *The Cathedral,* and less mechanical in its curved bell motifs which were intended to suggest sound, as well

as time. The intersection of shifting lines and planes—
with their space, light, and shadow—creates forces that
evoke the soaring interior of the cathedral and suggest the
mysterious and infinite.

106

Fernand Léger
French, 1881-1955
Discs, 1918-1919
Oil on canvas
51⅛ x 38¼ in. (129.8 x 97.1 cm.)
Signed and dated lower right: 18.19 F. Léger
Bequest of David E. Bright, 1967
M.67.25.2

Collections: Galerie Louis Carré, Paris; David E. Bright,
Los Angeles

Exhibitions: Paris, Galerie Louis Carré, *70th Anniversary
Exhibition,* 1951, no. 3, repr. in cat., pl. 3; Los Angeles
County Museum of Art, *David E. Bright Collection,* Oct. 17-
Dec. 17, 1967, repr. in color in cat., p. 19; Honolulu
Academy of Arts, *Léger and the Machine,* Sept. 18-Oct. 26,
1969, no. 6, repr. in cat., p. 4

Literature: "Fire," *Time,* Oct. 31, 1949, p. 40; D. Cooper,
Fernand Léger et le nouvel espace, Switzerland: Nouvel
Espace Editions, 1949, Lund Humphries Company, 1949,
repr. p. 80; C. Zervos, *Fernand Léger: Oeuvres de 1905 à
1952,* Paris: Cahiers d'Art, 1952, repr. p. 38; K. Kuh,
Léger, Urbana: University of Illinois Press, 1953, repr.
p. 105; R. M. Coates, "A Léger Retrospective," *The New
Yorker,* Feb. 5, 1955, pp. 155-156; A. Lieberman,
The Artist in His Studio, New York: The Viking Press,
1960, pp. 49-52; R. L. Deleroy, *Léger,* Geneva and Paris:
Skira, 1962, repr. p. 64

In 1910, through Léger's friendships with Delaunay,
Apollinaire, and Max Jacob, he became acquainted with
the theories of Cubism. Seeing Picasso's and Braque's Cubist
works strengthened Léger's interest in exploring geometrically simplified forms. His color handling, however,
remained more closely allied with the pure, luminous hues
of Delaunay's Orphism, and he joined Delaunay in
exhibiting with the Section d'Or in 1911-1912.

Léger's distinctive mark within the context of French
Cubism was his focus on mechanical imagery. In his
optimistic and heroic view of the machine as the symbol
of modern life, he is allied with Raymond Duchamp-Villon
and the Italian Futurists. For Léger, however, it was the
inherent abstract beauty of the machine form which provided the point of departure for his art, rather than
the dynamism of the machine-in-motion celebrated by
the Futurists.

Léger's aesthetic commitment to the objects of modern
industrial civilization as the legitimate subject matter for

painting is well represented by *Discs.* The feel and look
of modern industry, moving machine parts, artificial lighting, and the integration of modern man with the world of
technology are communicated by this highly colored Cubist
composition. But in his finest paintings, such as this one,
Léger achieves much more than a mere version of mechanic-
Cubist style: *Discs* is deeply evocative of biomorphism
as well as its opposite and is as successful coloristically as
any painting of its era.

107

Henri Matisse
French, 1869-1954
Tea, 1919
Oil on canvas
55 x 83 in. (139.7 x 210.8 cm.)
Bequest of David L. Loew in memory of his father,
Marcus Loew, 1974
M.74.52.2

Collections: Galerie Bernheim-Jeune, Paris, 1920;
Paul Ebstein, Paris, 1920-1925; Michael and Sarah Stein,
Paris, 1925-1951; Earl Stendahl Galleries, Los Angeles,
1951-1954; David L. Loew, Beverly Hills, 1954-1973

Exhibitions: Paris, Salon d'Automne, 1919; Paris, Galerie
Bernheim-Jeune, Oct. 15-Nov. 11, 1920, no. 18 in cat.;
Pomona, California, Los Angeles County Fair, *Masters of
Art from 1790-1950,* Sept. 15-Oct. 1, 1950, repr. in cat.;
New York, Museum of Modern Art, *Henri Matisse,*
Nov. 13, 1951-Jan. 13, 1952; Cleveland Museum of Art,
Feb. 5-Mar. 16, 1952; Chicago Art Institute, Apr. 1-
May 4, 1952; San Francisco Museum of Art, May 22-July 6,
1952, no. 33, repr. in cat.; Los Angeles, Municipal Art
Department, *Henri Matisse,* July 24-Aug. 17, 1952,
no. 33, ill. p. 21 (extension of Museum of Modern Art
exhibition); Denver Art Museum, *Origins and Trends
of Contemporary Art,* Jan. 11-Feb. 15, 1953, no. 38;
London, The Arts Council of Great Britain, *Matisse,*
July 9-Sept. 8, 1968, no. 82, repr. in color in cat., p. 39

Literature: C. Einstein, *Die Kunst des 20 Jahrhunderts,*
Berlin: Propylaen Kunstgeschichte, 1926, vol. 16, ill. p. 193;
F. Fels, *Henri-Matisse,* Paris: Chroniques du Jour, 1929,
fig. 14; R. Fry, *Henri-Matisse,* Paris: Chroniques du Jour,
1930, p. 50, and New York: E. Weyhe, 1935, p. 25,
fig. 35; A. H. Barr, Jr., *Matisse: His Art and His Public,*
New York: Museum of Modern Art, 1951, pp. 42, 197,
199, 203, 208, 529, ill. p. 426; G. Diehl, *Henri Matisse,*
Paris: Editions Pierre Tisné, 1954, p. 75; L. M. Golson,
"The Michael Steins of San Francisco: Art Patrons
and Collectors," in *Four Americans in Paris,* New York:
Museum of Modern Art, 1970, p. 44; J. Livingston,
"Matisse's *Tea,*" *Los Angeles County Museum of Art Bulletin,*
1974, vol. XX, no. 1, repr. in color

Henri Matisse's *Tea* of 1919 is stylistically a rather unusual work within the oeuvre of this twentieth-century master, and one of the major canvases of its period. Given its importance, the picture is relatively little known. *Tea* depicts the artist's daughter, Marguerite; Henriette, a model, at the right; and the artist's dog Lili in the garden of the Matisse family home at Issy-les-Moulineaux near Paris. The genre is one familiar in French painting—*plein air* scenes with figures were depicted often by the Impressionists and their Barbizon predecessors—but is atypical for Matisse. His better-known works of the postwar period are the interiors, often with open or shuttered windows, painted at Nice. Both the subject and palette in *Tea* distinguish it from his more characteristic approach. In contrast to the highly pitched, boldly arbitrary coloration initiated in Matisse's Fauve period, the relatively naturalistic, subdued, and extraordinarily subtle use of color here at first appears to refer back to an earlier painting tradition. However, as one examines this picture its unmistakable modernism becomes more and more apparent on a psychological plane. It is most evident perhaps in the Cubist-like distortion of Marguerite's face. The odd discreteness of style from one passage to another—for instance, in the contrast between the faces of the two women and in the difference in paint texture from one area to another over the entire surface—establishes a complexity which nevertheless does not disrupt the overall unity of the picture.

Tea is full of witty and whimsical elements like the scratching dog and the dangling shoe on Marguerite's foot; it is a richly inventive painting on every level. Interestingly, it was the last major Matisse acquired by Michael and Sarah Stein, the artist's devoted and perceptive patrons during his formative years.

108

Henri Matisse
French, 1869-1954
Warrior Costume and Design for "Le Chant du Rossignol,"
1920
Costume: wool felt, velvet, silk
Costume Council Fund, 1968
M.68.51.20 a-c
Design: pencil on paper
16¾ x 8½ in. (42.5 x 21.6 cm.)
Costume Council Fund, 1968
M.68.51.23

Costume

Collection: Diaghilev and de Basil Ballets Foundation, Ltd. (Sale, London, Sotheby, July 17, 1968, no. 78 ii)

Literature: Sale catalog, *Costumes and Curtains from Diaghilev and de Basil Ballets,* London, Sotheby, July 17, 1968, no. 78 ii, repr. in color p. 86, pl XXXVII (g)

Design

Collection: Nigel Seymer, London (Sale, London, Sotheby, July 18, 1968, no. 139)

Literature: *Comoedia Illustré,* May-June 1920, repr.; Sale catalog, *Diaghilev Ballet Material: Décor and Costume Designs, Portraits and Posters,* London, Sotheby, July 18, 1968, no. 139, repr. p. 128

Costume and design

Exhibition: Los Angeles County Museum of Art, *Serge Diaghilev Ballet Costumes,* Feb. 25-Apr. 4, 1969

As the originator of the Ballets Russes, Serge Diaghilev revolutionized scenic design. During the first great period of the Ballets Russes (1909-1929), Diaghilev called upon known painters rather than theatrical designers. Derain, Braque, Gris, Miró, Picasso, Matisse, and Rouault are a few of the artists who designed for Ballets Russes and for whom the theater offered a means of exploring new forms and ideas.

Matisse designed set and costumes for "Le Chant du Rossignol" which was first produced by Diaghilev at the Théâtre National de l'Opéra on February 2, 1920. The one-act ballet, based on a fairy tale by Hans Christian Andersen, with music by Stravinsky and choreography by Massine, was adapted from the 1914 opera "Le Rossignol." Léonide Massine recalls that Matisse made many of his designs for this ballet in the Musée Guimet in Paris.

The ferocious quality of the warrior in Matisse's pencil drawing was not lost in translating from sketch to costume. The short-skirted military tunic is made of white felt with a pleated band of blue china silk bordering the hem. The flared sleeves are elbow length and beneath the tunic are knee-length blue silk pantaloons. Bold geometric shapes and stylized armor elements of brown velvet covered with a grill pattern of gold braid decorate the tunic. Hand-painted black lines border the velvet areas and edges of the tunic. A painted scalloped border around the bottom is suggestive of tabs or lappets on military costumes. The tunic skirt is shaped like the lower section of a suit of armor. Inverted brass *L's* border the top of the tunic at chest height and at the waist, and decorative felt arabesques below the waist at front and sides are similar to decorative embellishments on armor pieces. According to Serge Grigoriev, Matisse himself painted much of the decoration on his costumes. Missing are the white felt paulfrons or shoulder segments indicated in the sketch. Completing the costume is a white felt skull cap with a top knot; painted black lines simulating creases radiate from the crown.

109

Mariano Fortuny
Spanish, 1871-1929
Coat, ca. 1925
Beige silk stenciled in brown, glass beads
Gift of Mrs. Harry D'Arrast, 1973
M.73.35.2

Mariano Fortuny y Madrazo, a notable Venetian designer at the turn of the century, recreated medieval and Renaissance design motifs utilizing a secret process of textile printing which he developed. Fortuny fashions embodied the new look of the twentieth century. European couture led by Worth and Poiret freed the female figure from corsets and heavily constructed garments, wrapping it instead in flowing fabrics and graceful draping. Fortuny as a leader in this movement was inspired by historical costume styles. The elegance of his designs is achieved through classic simplicity of construction, and by the use of flowing lines and sumptuous fabrics.

The colors and motifs of this coat of beige silk stenciled in brown are not typical of Fortuny designs. In the printing process he developed, light and gilded colors were usually printed on opulent dark grounds of velvet or cotton, rather than dark colors on a light ground. And while most Fortuny prints are based on Renaissance floral motifs, the printed design on this coat is abstract rectilinear leaf forms, rosettes, and geometric shapes of Coptic origin rather than curvi-linear floral forms. Its appearance in 1925 was in striking contrast to the floral patterns popularized by the Art Nouveau movement.

The coat utilizes a device characteristic of Fortuny: finished panels of fabric joined together with glass beads. Constructed from eight rectangular panels, each sleeve consists of four smaller panels. Sleeve panels are set into the coat body in a kimono fashion. Every panel is bordered by a linear pattern of alternating vine leaves, and the continuous vine is broken by rosettes containing geometric motifs. The border design is very similar to borders of trailing stem patterns in Coptic textiles. The Coptic rosettes denote the placement for the joining of the beads: five for each sleeve panel and four for each coat panel. The entire coat is lined with pale green china silk.

The sleeves are extreme in length, measuring 39½ inches (100.3 cm.) and only 10 inches (25.4 cm.) in width. The sleeves can be worn either folded or by placing the arms through the openings formed by the beads. The shoulder area of the coat and the sleeves are printed with a linear design of strands of rope. The manner in which the strands radiate suggests the coat panels were assembled before printing, as the motifs radiate from the neckline in the shape of the panels and do not interfere with the seam lines. The area between the borders on the coat panels shows further evidence of Coptic motifs with square medallions containing a variation of the Coptic hidden cross motif and linked in a linear manner by a printed form of the wheat-ear embroidery stitch. Three of these linear patterns are printed on each coat panel. The hem is a border of squares containing four vine leaves in a cruciform design, a typical fifth-century Coptic motif.

While Fortuny relied upon Coptic motifs for the printed decoration of the coat, the cut of the garment has definite stylistic traits from the Renaissance. The loose flowing shape of the coat is similar to a sixteenth-century Italian man's shirt. Both garments have long straight sleeves constructed of panels bordered with a decorative motif. The Renaissance shirt sleeves are bordered along the hem and the side sleeve panels with a design of reticella work in a rosette pattern.

110

Käthe Kollwitz
German, 1867-1945
Self-Portrait, 1934
Charcoal
13¼ x 17 in. (33.7 x 43.2 cm.)
Signed and dated in pencil lower right: Kathe Kollwitz 1934
Los Angeles County Funds, 1969
69.1

Collection: Jan Hoowij, Encino, California

Literature: O. Nagel, *The Drawings of Käthe Kollwitz,* New York, 1972, p. 442, cat. no. 1246, repr.

Käthe Kollwitz occupies an individual place among the German artists of the first half of our century. A pupil of Stauffer-Bern, and first influenced by Max Klinger, she did not follow the latter's mystical-allegorical approach or the "primitivistic," subjective style of the Expressionists. The life of the people, the poor and oppressed, became the central theme of her life's work, inspired in part by the social writers of the late nineteenth and early twentieth century, Gerhart Hauptmann, Ibsen, Zola, Dickens, and, later, Henri Barbusse.

Although primarily a graphic artist, Kollwitz was already working in sculpture in 1901. The monumental *Self-Portrait* of 1934 is strikingly plastic in the forceful reworking and chiaroscuro modeling of the face. The artist reinforced the broad strokes of charcoal with deep accents on the head and around the eyes as though she were engaged in a still developing definition of the form.

Käthe Kollwitz represented herself many times in lithographs and drawings. Her stern, unsparing *Self-Portrait* with its penetrating eyes and relentless character lines, shows her worn out by age and suffering, but controlled by *schmerzvoller Ruhe* ("painful calm"). This heroic and searching declaration is in the long tradition of the revela-tory self-studies of the Northern schools, exemplified by the great self-confessional portraits of Dürer and Rembrandt.

Joan Miró
Spanish, b. 1893
Animated Forms, 1935
Oil on canvas
76½ x 68 in. (194.3 x 172.7 cm.)
Signed lower right: Miró
Bequest of David E. Bright, 1967
M.67.25.3

Collections: Pierre Matisse Gallery, New York;
David E. Bright, Los Angeles

Exhibitions: Beverly Hills, Southern California Savings
and Loan Association, *Spanish Paintings,* Jan. 1965;
Los Angeles County Museum of Art, *David E. Bright
Collection,* Oct. 17-Dec. 17, 1967, repr. in color in cat.,
p. 35; New York, Museum of Modern Art, *Dada, Surrealism,
and Their Heritage,* Mar. 25-June 9, 1968, no. 193, repr.
in cat., p. 134; in collaboration with the Los Angeles
County Museum of Art, July 17-Sept. 8, 1968, and the Art
Institute of Chicago, Oct. 4-Dec. 1, 1968

Literature: J. Dupin, *Joan Miró: Life and Work,* New York:
Harry N. Abrams, 1962, no. 416, repr. as "Animated Forms"

This picture, which contrasts linear graphic marks with
summary forms composed of pure color, recaptures the
spontaneity of Miró's earlier Surrealist automatic pictures.
It has both a breadth and abandon in the arrangement
of forms, and a sumptuousness and purity of color.

The work is fresh and intimate in feeling despite its
large size, largely due to the springy vitality of the forms
and their isolated arrangement in a free-wheeling all-over
composition. The lively black calligraphic markings are
full of movement and vigor, while the strong vertical shapes
and other colored forms contribute an element of stability
and majestic monumentality to the large painting.

Miró has said of his art, "For me a form is never
something abstract, it is always a sign of something." The
drawn forms, while not referring to specific organisms,
seem evocative of meanings and function as pictorial
metaphors for animated biomorphic life. A testimony to
the life forces implied by the forms is seen in their
metamorphoses in color whenever they intersect.

The radical simplicity and abstractness of the colored
forms—Miró uses black as a color, not as a means of
modeling form—reveal the artist's considerable ability to
compose in flat colors and his feeling for the sumptuousness
of those colors: intense yellow and red, and dense,
saturated green and purple.

Pablo Picasso
Spanish, 1881-1973
Young Woman in Striped Dress, 1949
Oil on canvas
45⅝ x 35 in. (115.9 x 88.9 cm.)
Signed lower left: Picasso; dated on back: 15 mars 1949
Bequest of David E. Bright, 1967
M.67.25.12

Collections: Perls Galleries, Inc., New York;
David E. Bright, Los Angeles

Exhibitions: Los Angeles, University of California,
Bonne Fête, Monsieur Picasso, 1961, no. 37; Los Angeles
County Museum of Art, *David E. Bright Collection,*
Oct. 17-Dec. 17, 1967, repr. in cat., p. 27; San Diego, The
Fine Arts Gallery, *Modern Masters of Spanish Painting:
Legacy of Spain, 20th Century,* Jan. 2-Mar. 4, 1969

Literature: C. Zervos, *Pablo Picasso,* Paris: Editions
Cahiers d'Art, 1967, vol. 5, ill. no. 131

Young Woman in Striped Dress, 1949, is one of the
artist's most important portrayals of Françoise Gilot.
During the late forties and fifties, Picasso often worked in
series, rendering the same subject in variations over a
short period of time; this painting is one of many made at
the time of seated women. In this highly stylized and witty
picture, the female form, and perhaps Picasso's view of the
female psyche, are represented through shapes and motifs
recollective of both flower parts and insectlike elements.
The painting is at the same time exuberantly bold and
playfully evocative. By this point in his career Picasso is
able to actually parody his own earlier styles—here, synthetic
Cubist devices are referred to but without the intense
seriousness of the twenties period. The figure is made up
of flat, superimposed, and interlocking planes; however,
color and decorative pattern rather than structural experi-
mentation dominate the spirit of the painting. It combines
an emphatically clear linearity with a warm palette.
Color in this portrait is in fact considerably more high-keyed
and sensuous than in the majority of Picasso's postwar
paintings. The quality of color and design here is
slightly reminiscent of Matisse; we are also reminded of
Picasso's own style of the early 1930s, culminatively
represented in the famous *Girl Before a Mirror*
(Museum of Modern Art).

A comparison of this late work with others of women by
Picasso in the Museum's collection indicates the extraordinary range of the artist's handling of the female image
during his career. The *Woman with a Blue Veil* is a
classicized image from the 1920s; beside it both the stylized
decorativeness and psychologically expressive distortion
of the *Woman in Striped Dress* are emphasized. Yet next to

our small, powerful *Study for Guernica* of 1937, an almost abrasive image conveying human suffering, or the angular distortion of the *Arlesienne* of 1958, this picture becomes comparatively lyrical and abstractly sensuous.

113

Pablo Picasso
Spanish, 1881-1973
Woman with Hairnet, 1949-1956
Color lithograph, fourth and final state; edition: 36/50
26 x 19¼ in. (66.0 x 48.9 cm.)
Signed by the artist in red: Picasso
Gift of Mr. and Mrs. Harry Lenart, 1966
M.66.44

Collection: Mr. and Mrs. Harry Lenart, Los Angeles

Exhibition: Los Angeles County Museum of Art,
Picasso: Sixty Years of Graphic Works, Oct. 25, 1966-
Jan. 8, 1967, no. 244, repr. in cat., p. 110

Literature: F. Mourlot, *Picasso lithographe,* Monte Carlo:
André Sauret, 1956, vol. III, pp. 14-15, 178ter; idem,
Picasso Lithographs, Boston Book and Art, 1970,
pp. 148, 178 (a)

In March 1949, Picasso started work on his most important color lithograph. Using the theme of a woman with green hair, the artist began the print as a wash drawing on lithographic paper which was then transferred to a zinc plate and printed in four colors. The work was further developed to a second state in April of the same year when the four zinc plates were reworked. Then, in May 1949, the black plate was reworked by Picasso who refined the harshness of the drawing found in the earlier second state. The final color state of this print was achieved in September 1956 when Picasso again resumed work on the print, chiefly in the area of the hair. The lithograph was finally issued in an edition of fifty impressions with an additional five artist's proofs.

In her *Life with Picasso,* Françoise Gilot recounts a visit that she and Picasso made in 1946 to Matisse who was then bedridden in Vence. After Picasso criticized the color of a nude Matisse had been painting, Matisse laughed and said that if he ever painted Françoise he would make her hair green. As the couple left, Picasso appeared displeased at the thought of Matisse portraying his young mistress, but he told Françoise that now he knew how to portray her. The green-haired woman depicted in this lithograph was apparently the result.

114

Burial Mantle
Peru (Paracas Necropolis), 300 B.C.-A.D. 300
Embroidery, stem, buttonhole, and knit stitches
on plain weave ground, alpaca
97⅛ x 51⅜ in. (247.6 x 130.5 cm.)
Los Angeles County Funds, 1967
67.4

Collection: John Wise, New York

In the four thousand years preceding the Spanish conquest of the central Andes—an area which includes the Peruvian coast and highlands as well as most of the Bolivian highlands—weavers attained a high degree of excellence in both design and technique. Several strong cultures flourished during these millennia, and each developed its own distinctive style of textile and costume.

The costumes not only give us a clue to the character of ancient Peruvian life, but also provide a glimpse into beliefs about the afterlife. In a culture where material objects were provided for the next life, many of the most elaborate costumes and accoutrements were made exclusively for inclusion in mummy bundles. One mummy bundle of a Paracas Necropolis inhabitant, for example, consisted of this extensive wardrobe: eleven mantles, twenty ponchos, twelve shirts, six turbans, five belts, and more than one hundred yards of plain weave fabric.

The Museum's mantle was originally excavated at Paracas Necropolis, a vast grave site in southwestern Peru that has yielded considerable archeological material. Though the textile has the shape of a mantle, its dimensions indicate that it was made for inclusion in a burial, rather than to be worn. Alpaca fiber was used to weave four complete fabrics which were sewn together to form the base fabric. The central area is of two pieces seamed longitudinally at the center; two narrow pieces form the border. It is interesting to note that fabrics were never cut, but were woven to the exact shape required, which accounts for the fact that each piece has a selvage on all four sides. The design areas are all worked in a stem embroidery stitch. The central field alternates embroidered vertical bands with bands of plain ground fabric. The four corner blocks and the borders are also solidly embroidered.

In each of the design units—borders, corners, and vertical bands—the primary motif appears: a double-headed serpent with feline heads, identifiable by their chin whiskers. Feline attributes are also used for the secondary motif which appears in the borders and transverse bands. These incorporate similar figures within their bellies, a form of duality or fertility. A third distinctively feline motif, identified by chin whiskers and pointed ears, and a crab design are also used as smaller units in the borders and corner blocks. These secondary and minor elements fill spaces between the edges of the borders and the constantly repeated Z-shaped serpent bodies.

The importance of the felines, probably the jaguar, as the most widely used motif in Paracas embroidery began in the earlier Chavín culture. The jaguar is admired for its superb hunting skills, and a number of Peruvian cultures present the ideal of duality between the jaguar and man in their textile designs; there appears to be no clear line between an anthropomorphized jaguar and a man with feline characteristics. In addition to their aggressiveness in the hunt, the felines were symbols of fertility and their roar was thought to effect the rain needed for crops.

115

Feather Tunic
Peru (Inca, central coast?), 1100-1400
Rows of feathers knotted on cords, stitched
to plain weave cotton ground
71 x 33 in. (180.5 x 83.5 cm.)
Gift of Mr. and Mrs. William T. Sesnon, Jr., 1974
M.74.49

Collection: John Wise, New York

Exhibition: Los Angeles County Museum of Art,
*Ornamental Costumes from the John Wise Collection of
Ancient Peruvian Textiles,* Nov. 2-Feb. 6, 1972,
repr. in color on cover

Beginning as a small tribe in the highlands of Peru, the Incas extended their power and influence by military conquest until they were themselves conquered by the Spaniard Pizarro in 1532; at that time their empire was only about one hundred years old and included the coastal areas and highlands from Ecuador to Chile and Argentina. A model of organization, the Inca civilization had a sophisticated system of roads, an effective method of trans-empire communication, a complex bureaucracy, and a highly developed skill in engineering. The Incas were further enriched by the artistic heritage of other cultures such as the Tiahuanaco which passed along an extensive repertoire of decorative motifs as well as proficiency in arts such as weaving.

The Incas apparently added no new motifs in textile design, but instead drew on those learned from conquered tribes. Their design was characterized by highly geometricized and schematized forms and by repetition. The detailed and imaginative forms found in earlier textiles, such as those of Paracas, were largely abandoned by the Inca artisans in favor of more generalized and simplified ones.

In addition to the traditional types of weaving, the Incas also produced garments overlaid with colored feathers. Such feather mosaics had been produced by earlier cultures in the Andean area, but for the Incas, they seem to have held a special appeal. Feathers were conscientiously collected and stored in great quantity for such use. The

tribute the Incas normally exacted from conquered tribes was sometimes paid in feathers, especially by tribes which could offer no precious metals. Feathers were used not only for mantles and ponchos, but for headdresses, fans, collars, and other articles of clothing; the hand shield of the Inca soldier was sometimes decorated with a feather mosaic. Feather garments were for the most part restricted to the royal family and to the nobility. But the popularity of feather clothing was so widespread that while the common people possessed no splendid feather mosaics, they nevertheless decorated with feathers in a less elaborate way.

Brilliantly colored feathers were taken from native birds such as the toucan, macaw, parrot, parakeet, and even the tiny hummingbird. The sturdy cloth to which they were attached was left undecorated as it would be entirely covered by feathers. The stiff quill of the feather was bent back and hooked over a cord, then secured by knots in a second cord which ran just below the first. A row of feathers tied to the cords was then stitched to the ground fabric; each new row slightly overlaid the one before it, hiding the cords and stitching. Occasionally the feathers were cemented down, but the stitch method was far more common and may have encouraged the geometrical regularity of Inca design.

As a basically agricultural god, the sun became pre-eminent among the other deities in the Inca religion. It came to symbolize the Inca Empire, and from it the emperor was said to have descended. The sun was thought to be male (while the moon was his wife) and was often depicted with a human face. In the Museum's feather tunic, the sun and its rays are interpreted geometrically in a schematized way that is characteristic of Inca art. The face has been reduced to a simple combination of rectangles, and the broad flat areas of color produce an aggressive and dazzling design.

116

John Singleton Copley
American, 1738-1815
Portrait of Hugh Montgomerie, 12th Earl of Eglinton, 1780
Oil on canvas
94½ x 59¾ in. (238.7 x 151.8 cm.)
Gift of the Andrew Norman Foundation and
Museum Acquisitions Fund
M.68.74

Collections: Hugh Montgomerie, Coilsfield, Scotland, 1821;
Lady Jane Montgomerie (Hugh Montgomerie's daughter,
Mrs. Edward Archibald Hamilton), Rozelle, Ayr;
by descent to Lt. Commander John Hamilton, R.N.
(Sale, London, Christie's, July 7, 1967, no. 109);
Knoedler & Co., Inc., New York

Exhibitions: London, The Royal Academy of Arts,
Twelfth Exhibition, 1780, no. 172, as "Portrait of a Highland
Officer"; Washington, D.C., National Collection of Fine

Arts, *Survey of American Art* (opening exhibition),
May-June 1968, p. 7; Washington, D.C., National Gallery
of Art, special loan, June-Aug. 1969; Oakland Museum,
Art Treasures in California, Nov. 29-Dec. 31, 1969, repr.

Literature: (by an Artist), *A Candid Review of the
Exhibition (Being the Twelfth) of the Royal Academy,*
2nd edition, London, 1780, p. 26, no. CLXXII; F. W. Bayley,
The Life and Works of John Singleton Copley, Boston,
1915, p. 179; J. D. Prown, *John Singleton Copley,*
Cambridge: published for the National Gallery of Art by
Harvard University Press, 1966, vol. 2, pp. 275, 276,
328, 387, 427, four Copley sketches for the portrait, fig. 390-
390a, copy in the National Portrait Gallery of Scotland,
fig. 389; Sale catalog, *Important English Pictures,* London,
Christie's, July 7, 1967, no. 109, repr. opp. p. 46;
*Los Angeles County Museum of Art Annual Report
1968-1969,* pp. 15-16, repr.; *Gazette des Beaux-Arts,*
Feb. 1970, suppl., p. 75, repr.

In 1775, John Singleton Copley, the greatest native
American portrait painter of the eighteenth century, took
up residence in London. He brought with him a talent
fully matured in America during the preceding decade, and
quickly settled into an active career in his adopted city.
Under the influence of Benjamin West, then historical
painter to King George III, Copley enlarged upon straightforward portrait painting to include group portraits and
scenes from history. His first major effort in this vein,
The Death of the Earl of Chatham, 1779-1781 (The Tate
Gallery, London) partakes of both interests. Thus when
Copley was commissioned to paint the *Portrait of Major
Hugh Montgomerie* in 1780 he was already engrossed
in the Chatham picture. The background elements of the
Montgomerie portrait attest to Copley's awakened interest
in action subjects which he first essayed with considerable
verve in *Watson and the Shark* of 1778 (National Gallery
of Art, Washington, D.C.) and was to culminate in *The Death
of Major Peirson,* 1782-1784 (The Tate Gallery, London).
In composing the Montgomerie portrait, Copley indulged in
the practice of borrowing from the modes then fashionable
in European painting. The so-called grand manner
portrait, in which this work is cast, has a noble stylistic
ancestry reaching back to Peter Paul Rubens, and his
principal follower, Anthony van Dyck, who introduced it to
the English court in the seventeenth century. By Copley's
time, English painting was dominated by the Royal
Academy, founded by George III in 1768, and led by
Sir Joshua Reynolds, its first president and a champion of
neoclassicism. Montgomerie's stance as a modern Apollo
Belvedere is, therefore, Copley's concession to this fashion
and to the Academy's approval. Yet Copley was still
close enough to his American experience to lend the
Montgomerie portrait precision and objectivity. As Jules
Prown has observed, "Copley was at the peak of his

English career in the early 1780s and during the next four
years he produced a number of pictures that in their bravura
brushwork, brilliant heightened palette and masterful
chiaroscuro rival the more sober triumphs of his
American style."

The portrait of Hugh Montgomerie was painted in 1780,
just after Major Montgomerie (1736-1819) had been
elected a member of Parliament for Ayrshire. Though the
portrait shows him as a forty-four-year-old man, he stands
before a battle in which he participated twenty years
earlier. In 1756 Montgomerie entered the 77th Regiment
as lieutenant and embarked shortly after for duty in
America where he participated in several campaigns against
the French and the Indians. The battle shown in the background is either the triumph over the Cherokees in the battle
of Etchocy in 1760 or that of War-Women's Creek in
1761. Montgomerie is shown in full Highland uniform—
kilt of government or Black Watch tartan, red and white
hose, red jacket faced with green and laced with silver,
and feathered bonnet.

117

Gilbert Stuart
American, 1755-1828
Portrait of Richard, 4th Viscount Barrington
Oil on canvas
30 x 25 in. (76.2 x 63.5 cm.)
Museum Purchase, 1968
68.2

Collections: Richard, 4th Viscount Barrington, descending
in his family to George (5th Viscount), William Keppel
(6th Viscount), George William (7th Viscount), Percy
(8th Viscount), Walter Buckley (9th Viscount), and to
Sir C. B. Barrington; F. Kleinberger & Co. Inc., New York

Literature: *Los Angeles County Museum of Art
Annual Report 1968-1969,* p. 17, repr.

The subject of this portrait—surely one of Stuart's most
sensitively felt works—was a direct descendant of John Shute
Barrington (1678-1734) who became Viscount Barrington
of Ardglass and Baron Barrington of Newcastle simultaneously in 1720. The date of birth of Richard, who became
4th Viscount Barrington upon succession in 1801, is not
known. Indeed, few facts are well established concerning
his life beyond the date of his marriage to Susan Budden
of Philadelphia in 1783 and his death in Valenciennes,
France, in 1814. His marriage date coincides with that of
the signing of a treaty of peace between Britain and the
American States ending the Revolutionary War. No marriage
record exists in the archives of the Pennsylvania Historical
Society to support an assumption that the marriage
occurred in Philadelphia, the bride's home. Since many

Philadelphians were Tories it may well be that Susan Budden and Richard Barrington were married abroad. There was no issue to this marriage, and the title passed to a brother. Lady Barrington died in 1830, and the portrait descended in the Barrington family through the male heirs to the title, the last of whom died in 1935.

It has been conjectured that because of the subject's nationality, the portrait may have been painted in Ireland during Stuart's residence there between 1787 and 1792. Richard Barrington's uncle, Admiral Samuel Barrington, R.N., did sit for Stuart in London in 1785, so that the nephew may have known of Stuart through the family. However, the manner in which the Los Angeles portrait is painted does not suggest either London or Dublin. Rather it is executed in the same fluid and easy brushwork that distinguishes Stuart's best portraits in the period immediately following his return to America in 1793. It is particularly like that of Major General Matthew Clarkson of about 1794 (The Metropolitan Museum of Art). In both portraits an analogous composition is adopted, a similar scumbling of the background is to be noted, and, most importantly, the same careful differentiations between textures of hair, flesh, and clothing are observed in each, all executed with the easy assurance that marks Stuart's matured talent.

In attempting to date the portrait, therefore, the stylistic evidence suggests Stuart's Philadelphia period—1794 to 1803. Considering Lord Barrington's Philadelphia connections through his wife's family, it would not be unlikely that he visited the city during Stuart's residence there.

118

Gilbert Stuart
American, 1755-1828
Portrait of George Washington, 1822
Oil on canvas
44⅛ x 34½ in. (112.0 x 87.6 cm.)
Promised gift of the Armand Hammer Foundation

Collections: William D. Lewis, Philadelphia; Estate of William D. Lewis (on loan to Pennsylvania Academy of the Fine Arts, Philadelphia, 1881-1928); Howard Young Galleries, New York; Mr. and Mrs. Alfred G. Wilson, Detroit (Sale, New York, Parke-Bernet Galleries, Dec. 10, 1970, no. 12); Armand Hammer, Los Angeles

Exhibitions: The Detroit Institute of Arts, *The Eleventh Loan Exhibition, American Colonial and Early Federal Art,* Feb. 4-Mar. 2, 1930, no. 81; The Detroit Institute of Arts, *Masterpieces of Painting from Detroit Private Collections,* Apr. 23-May 22, 1949, no. 30 (lent by Mr. and Mrs. Alfred G. Wilson in 1930 and 1949); Little Rock, Arkansas Art Center, Smithsonian Institution Traveling Exhibition Service, *The Armand Hammer Collection,* Nov. 21, 1970-Jan. 12, 1971; San Francisco, California Palace of the

Legion of Honor, *The Armand Hammer Collection,* Feb. 11-Mar. 14, 1971; Oklahoma City, Oklahoma Art Center, *The Armand Hammer Collection,* June 15-July 11, 1971; Los Angeles County Museum of Art, *The Armand Hammer Collection,* Dec. 21, 1971-Feb. 27, 1972, no. 51, repr. in color in cat.; traveled to London, Royal Academy, June 24-July 24, 1972; Dublin, National Gallery of Ireland, Aug. 8-Oct. 1, 1972; Leningrad, State Hermitage Museum, Oct. 23-Dec. 2, 1972; Moscow, State Pushkin Museum of Fine Arts, Dec. 8, 1972-Feb. 11, 1973; Kiev, State Museum of Ukrainian Art, Mar. 6-31, 1973; Minsk, Belorussian State Museum of Fine Arts, Apr. 26-May 26, 1973; Riga, State Museum of Latvian and Russian Art, June 8-July 8, 1973; Odessa, State Picture Gallery, July 25-Aug. 25, 1973

Literature: H. T. Tuckerman, *Book of the Artists,* New York: G. P. Putnam & Son, 1867, p. 120; G. C. Mason, *Life and Works of Gilbert Stuart,* New York: Charles Scribner's Sons, 1879, p. 113; E. B. Johnston, *Original Portraits of Washington,* Boston: J. R. Osgood & Co., 1882, pp. 81, 82; M. Fielding, *Gilbert Stuart's Portraits of Washington,* Philadelphia, 1923, no. 30, p. 148; L. Park, *Gilbert Stuart, An Illustrated Descriptive List of His Works,* New York: William Edwin Rudge, 1926, vol. II, no. 31, p. 862; J. H. Morgan and M. Fielding, *The Life Portraits of Washington and Their Replicas,* Philadelphia: Lancaster Press, Inc., 1931, no. 31, p. 271; G. A. Eisen, *Portraits of Washington,* New York: Robert Hamilton & Associates, 1932, p. 126, repr. p. 255; Sale catalog, *Important American Paintings, Sculpture and Drawings,* New York, Parke-Bernet Galleries, Dec. 10, 1970, no. 12, p. 14, repr. in color; *Antiques,* Nov. 1970, p. 693, repr.; *Apollo,* June 1972, p. 452

Whatever Stuart's reasons for leaving Ireland in 1793, he returned to this country expecting to capitalize on the demand for portraits of George Washington. It was an astute and logical move for one of the greatest portrait painters of the period. Such was the stature of Washington, already the personification of the nation, that Stuart and his competitors, the Peales, found it profitable to devote a great part of their energy and time to recording his image.

Although a list dated April 20, 1795, with orders for thirty-nine portraits indicates that Stuart already had received permission for sittings from Washington, the first session did not take place until autumn of that year. There were three sittings of several days each, from which three different but original portraits were painted. The first sittings in the autumn of 1795 produced the "Vaughan" type (bust portraits with face to the right); the second series of sittings, begun about April 21, 1796, resulted in the "Brook" type (bust portraits with face to left); the third series in September 1796 produced the famous unfinished bust portrait (face to left and greatly idealized), now in the Boston Museum, which is referred to as the "Athenaeum" type. From these three prototypes Stuart painted more than 100 variants ranging from bust to full-length portraits.

When Senator William Bingham asked for a full-length portrait of Washington in 1796, the "Athenaeum" portrait was used as the model for the head in the composition which became known as the "Lansdowne" type. The Hammer portrait, painted for William D. Lewis in 1822, is based on the "Lansdowne" full-length, specifically on the later version now in the New York Public Library (Lenox Collection) painted at the request of Peter Jay Munro. The background with a landscape to the left and the pillar and curtain to the right is closely related to the Constable-Hamilton half-length of 1797, also in the New York Public Library. Other details used in "classification" studies are the hairband, thin here rather than wide as in some other portraits, and the jabot, or neck ruffle, here of closed lace.

119

Thomas Cole
American, 1801-1848
L'Allegro, 1845
Oil on canvas
32 x 48 in. (81.3 x 121.9 cm.)
Art Museum Council and the Michael J. Connell Foundation, 1974
M.74.53

Collections: Charles M. Parker, descended to James V. Parker (Sale, American Art Association, New York, Jan. 14, 1918, no. 101); William H. Payne (Sale, American Art Association, Jan. 6, 1919, no. 77); (Sale, Anderson Galleries, New York, Mar. 5, 1925, no. 112) Mrs. Cecelia Ober, New York, 1925-1931; Dr. and Mrs. Samuel Kleinberg, New York, 1931-1957; Private collection, Washington, D.C., 1957-1965; Private collection, New York, 1965-1969; Hirschl & Adler Galleries, New York; Douglas Collins, 1969-1974; Vose Galleries, Boston

Exhibitions: New York, National Academy of Design, *Annual Exhibition,* 1846, no. 174 (as "Italian Sunset"); New York, American Art Union, *Exhibition of the Paintings of the Late Thomas Cole at the Gallery of the American Art Union* (March?) 1848, no. 50; New York, Hirschl & Adler Galleries, *The American Scene,* Oct. 29-Nov. 22, 1969, no. 13, repr. in color in cat.

Literature: H. T. Tuckerman, *Book of the Artists,* New York: G. P. Putnam & Son, 1867, p. 231; *Thomas Cole, 1801-1848, One Hundred Years Later, A Loan Exhibition,* Hartford: Wadsworth Atheneum, 1948, p. 11; L. L. Noble, *Life and Works of Thomas Cole,* Cambridge: Harvard University Press, 1964, pp. 266, 271; H. S. Merritt, *Thomas Cole,* Rochester: University of Rochester, 1969, p. 18; *Antiques,* Feb. 1973, p. 229, repr. in color; *American Art Review,* Sept.-Oct. 1973, p. (4), repr. in color

As a young artist working in New York by 1825, Cole contented himself almost entirely with observing the changing moods of nature along the Hudson River, and was little more than a landscape painter given to romantic fantasies. After 1828, as his works matured, he began to favor "serial" compositions in which a single theme is expressed in two or more pictures that form a set. These subjects often have as their central idea the complementary opposites which Cole saw everywhere. The inception of these narrative themes that play such a paramount role in Cole's art can be traced to the artist's exposure to European culture during an extended visit to England, France, and Italy between June 1829 and November 1832.

He was probably familiar with the writings of the French skeptic C. F. Volney (1757-1820) whose *Ruines, ou méditations sur les révolutions des empires,* published in 1791, seems to have been a seminal influence on Cole's philosophy. Volney's thesis that civilizations evolve from their foundation through maturity to their final overthrow was an idea that corroborated Cole's own innate romanticism. Indeed, Volney seems to have provided Cole with an exact scenario for his first serial subject, *Course of Empire* of 1836, an enormously ambitious work in five parts begun immediately following the artist's return to New York from Europe.

However, the majority of Cole's allegorical serial paintings which he called "a higher style of landscape" are in pairs, with the opposites of nature frequently cast in the roles of past and present time. Indeed, Cole so named a pair of large pictures *The Past* and *The Present,* painted in 1838 (Amherst College). A year later he completed another paired set, *The Departure* and *The Return* (Corcoran Gallery of Art, Washington, D.C.), in which the passage of time is also considered in relation to life and death. Symbolically, Cole usually associated life with the morning; conversely his scenes of decay, death, or desolation are illuminated by the setting sun.

L'Allegro corresponds exactly to this kind of plan. Together with its now-lost companion, *Il Penseroso,* it represents the final flowering of Cole's work in the idiom of the allegorical serial composition. Cole adopted the titles and themes of these paintings from John Milton's poems of 1632. *L'Allegro,* meaning "the merry one," is a pastoral idyl characterized by gaiety of spirit and was intended to contrast with its companion, giving the viewer a poetic reflection upon the joys and sorrows of the human experience.

In a letter dated January 8, 1844, to Charles Parker, for whom the set was painted, Cole stated, "I now write to say, unless you suggest something from nature, of which I have sketches, or from poetry or history, I intend

to commence two pictures, to be called L'Allegro and
Il Penseroso. In the first, I should represent a sunny luxuriant
landscape, with figures engaged in gay pastimes or pleasant
occupation. In the second, I would represent some ivy
clad ruin in the solemn twilight, with a solitary figure
musing amid the decaying grandeur around. I hope the
subject will suit your taste, for it is one on which I can
work con amore...."

120

Ball Dress
United States, 1865
Silk taffeta
Gift of Mr. and Mrs. Parker Huntington, 1969
M.69.33.1 a-d

Exhibition: Los Angeles County Museum of Art,
If the Crinoline Comes Back, Oct. 16, 1973-Jan. 6, 1974

Constructed for Abraham Lincoln's Second Inaugural
Ball on March 4, 1865, this gown is part of an ensemble
including a day bodice, evening bodice, trained skirt, and
overskirt. The four-piece ensemble allowed changes of
costume for the many events of inaugural ceremonies with
a minimum of garments. The brilliant tones of the taffeta
are enriched by the corresponding green silk organza trim.
The applied decoration provides a subtle contrast with a
slight hue variation between the blue green organza and the
yellow green taffeta. The delicate evening bodice has a
wide V-neckline front and back. Narrow bias folds of darker
organza extend over the shoulders culminating in a deep
point at the back. Rever shapes are covered with five rows of
bias folds; a soft pleated section of white organza fills the
back section between the revers. A back peplum is of two
French folds and is accented with fabric bows and tabs.
A narrow front peplum curves to the side seam; its
decoration consists of two rows of taffeta bias and three
rows of organza bias.

The bodice construction with a typical three-piece back
is characteristic of this period. Boning and bust padding
are used to mold the figure to the popular silhouette. The
shoulder seams slant to the back with the sleeve seams
extending onto the arms to achieve the desired look of
sloping shoulders.

The day bodice is trimmed in the same manner as the
evening bodice; its deep V-neckline, emphasizing the
shoulders and diminishing the waist, is accented by four
rows of organza bias and one row of taffeta bias. The front
decoration also extends over the shoulders to the center
back. A smaller V-shape originating at the shoulders is set

inside the other and trimmed in an identical manner.
A small lace collar is the only trim not made of bias bands.

The three-quarter-length two-piece coat sleeves of the
day bodice are set into the armscyes with a small decorative
cording. Concentrated at the bottom, bias bands accent
the hem of the sleeve. The addition of a box-pleated flounce
at the back gives the straight sleeve the flared silhouette
fashionable at this time.

A transitional shape between the crinoline and the bustle,
the dome-shaped skirt had flattened in front and increased
in back. This voluminous skirt is constructed of eleven gores
of fabric with slight shaping at the top that allows the skirt
to fall flat in front and flare smoothly to the rear. Center
back cartridge pleating controls the extra fabric needed to
achieve the full train of the back skirt. The fabric has
enough body not to require lining and only slight stiffening
is needed around the hem to prevent it from falling in
under the petticoat. A pocket in the right front side of the
skirt is hidden under the overskirt. Horizontal bias bands
border the hem using bands of taffeta and organza.

Completing the ensemble is an overskirt. The petal effect
of the leaf shapes was first designed by Charles Frederick
Worth of Paris for the empress Eugénie and copied in
America. The back of the overskirt is pleated to give it
enough fullness to cover the ample skirt. Taffeta and organza
bands border each of the four overlapping leaf shapes.

The demure style of the gown emphasizes the fashionable
figure traits of broad, sloping shoulders and a diminished
waist. The simplicity of trimming emphasizes the grace of
the sumptuous trained skirt. The conservative styling of
this gown is indicative of the concern and turmoil of this
period. The flounces and beribboned gowns then popular
in European fashion were unsuitable for inaugural functions
of a nation engaged in civil war.

121

Jasper Francis Cropsey
American, 1823-1900
*Sidney Plains—With the Union of the Susquehanna
and Unadilla Rivers,* 1874
Oil on canvas
42 x 72 in. (106.6 x 182.9 cm.)
Jessie R. McMahan Memorial and Museum
Acquisitions Fund, 1970
M.70.2

Collections: John N. Johnston (original owner); Newhouse
Galleries, New York, 1970

Exhibitions: New York, National Academy of Design,
Annual Exhibition, 1875, no. 375; Philadelphia Museum of
Art (no exhibition title), Mar. 9-June 9, 1970

Literature: C. Clement and L. Hutton, *Artists of the
Nineteenth Century and Their Works,* St. Louis:
North Point, Inc., 1969, p. 173

In the early 1850s Jasper F. Cropsey produced four sets of paintings representing the four seasons, and it may be in those autumn scenes that the germ of his later specialty can be found. He was encouraged in this direction by the success of his most famous autumn scene, *Autumn—on the Hudson River* (National Gallery of Art, Washington, D.C.), painted in 1860 in London. It was praised by reviewers for its beautiful coloring, although some critics who had never seen America in the fall doubted the authenticity of the brilliant colors.

During the ten years after his return to America in 1863, Cropsey painted other scenes similar to it in scope and coloring, for example: *Starrucca Viaduct* (Toledo Museum of Art), *Valley of Wyoming* (The Metropolitan Museum of Art), *Mt. Washington, New Hampshire* (Cleveland Museum of Art), *Indian Summer* (University of Cincinnati Fine Arts Collection), and the Los Angeles *Sidney Plains*. All are large works in which a wide panorama opens before the viewer, inviting him into vast space bounded only by low hills in the distant background. In *Sidney Plains* the viewer is drawn into the totality of the landscape, partly attracted to the far distance by the railroad train. This directness is typical of Cropsey's work, in contrast to that of painters who employed devices such as a path winding through woods to lead the viewer circuitously into the open distance. The large size was not only in vogue in America of the 1860s, but gave Cropsey ample space to display his mastery of detail.

A detailed drawing with color notes for this painting is in the collection of the Sheldon Art Gallery of the University of Nebraska. A comparison of the drawing with the finished painting shows that Cropsey transferred the scene almost exactly from the sketch onto his canvas. Because of its inscriptions and closeness in composition to our painting, we were able to correctly name the Museum's work which had been erroneously labeled *Wyoming Valley* by New York dealers. Sidney Plains in New York State and the Wyoming Valley in Pennsylvania are separated by only about seventy miles; both lie on the Susquehanna River and their geography and flora are so similar it would have been impossible to identify the painting correctly without the drawing.

Of even more aid in the study of the painting is the insight into Cropsey's working procedure provided by the color notes inscribed in the upper right hand corner of the drawing: "1. a few patches of Emerald green, grain fields, 2. light and thin foliage—soft grey in (?); and stems of trees—with splotches of brilliant red…7 silvery gray…." The notes jotted down in the landscape were closely followed. In this work the sky is cut prismatically by light rays from a brilliant midday sun. It is this clarity of light and emphasis on a specific time of day that link this work to the luminist tradition in mid-nineteenth-century America.

Cropsey made the drawing in October 1873, and had finished the large painting by 1874. It was shown in 1875 at the National Academy of Design exhibition by its owner, John Johnston, but then all trace of the work was lost until it was offered for sale by Newhouse Galleries, New York, in 1970.

122

John Singer Sargent
American, 1856-1925
Doctor Pozzi at Home, 1881
Oil on canvas
80½ x 43⅞ in. (204.5 x 111.5 cm.)
Promised gift of the Armand Hammer Foundation

Collections: Estate of the Hon. Jean Pozzi (Sale, Paris, Palais Galliera, Dec. 4, 1970, no. 84); Armand Hammer, Los Angeles

Exhibitions: San Francisco, California Palace of the Legion of Honor, *The Armand Hammer Collection,* Feb. 11-Mar. 14, 1971; Oklahoma City, Oklahoma Art Center, *The Armand Hammer Collection,* June 15-July 11, 1971; Fine Arts Gallery of San Diego, *The Armand Hammer Collection,* July 23-Sept. 5, 1971; Los Angeles County Museum of Art, *The Armand Hammer Collection,* Dec. 21-1971-Feb. 27, 1972, no. 53, repr. in color in cat.; traveled to London, Royal Academy, June 24-July 24, 1972; Dublin, National Gallery of Ireland, Aug. 8-Oct. 1, 1972; Leningrad, State Hermitage Museum, Oct. 23-Dec. 2, 1972; Moscow, State Pushkin Museum of Fine Arts, Dec. 8, 1972-Feb. 11, 1973; Kiev, State Museum of Ukrainian Art, Mar. 6-31, 1973; Minsk, Belorussian State Museum of Fine Arts, Apr. 26-May 26, 1973; Riga, State Museum of Latvian and Russian Art, June 8-July 8, 1973; Odessa, State Picture Gallery, July 25-Aug. 25, 1973

Literature: *L'Art et les artistes,* Jan. 1907, repr., p. 370; *La renaissance de l'art française,* June 1919, repr., p. 280; W. H. Downes, *John S. Sargent, His Life and Work,* Boston: Little, Brown & Co., 1925, pp. 10-11, 113; Hon. E. Charteris, *John Sargent,* New York: Charles Scribner's Sons, 1927, p. 258; C. M. Mount, *John Singer Sargent,* London: The Cresset Press, 1957, pp. 61, 65, 67, 69, 116, 153, 337; R. Ormond, *John Singer Sargent, Paintings, Drawings, Watercolors,* New York: Harper & Row, 1970, p. 34; Sale catalog, *Tableaux modernes, sculptures,* Paris, Palais Galliera, Dec. 4, 1970, no. 84, repr., also in color on cat. cover; *Connaissance des arts,* Feb. 1971, p. 93, repr.; *Connoisseur,* Feb. 1971, p. 146, repr.; *Apollo,* June 1972, p. 455, repr.; *Detroit Institute of Arts Bulletin,* Fourth quarter, 1972, p. 101, repr.

While there was still a decidedly youthful quality in Sargent's work in 1881, he was rapidly reaching full stride as an artist. Already honored in the Salon of 1879 for the dramatic portrait of his teacher, Carolus-Duran, in 1881 he received a medal second class, making him "...*hors concours* and a great swell," as he jokingly put it. The portrait of *Doctor Pozzi at Home* was eagerly undertaken by an artist brimming with enthusiasm and confidence. Dr. S. L. Pozzi (1846-1918), a distinguished Paris physician and innovative gynecologist, was a friend of Carolus-Duran; and the friendship may have led to the painting of this noncommissioned portrait. In turn, the doctor may have been instrumental in acquainting Sargent with Pozzi's reputed mistress, the infamous Mme. Gautreau. The result was the notorious *Portrait of Madame X,* cause of the scandal that probably forced the artist's subsequent move to London.

Innovative from the beginning, Sargent was never content with a formal, straightforward likeness. Even in the early portrait of Carolus, the teacher assumes a special vitality in a dynamic pose conveying force and movement. Some of Sargent's greatest portraits are the most informal ones, catching the subject engaged in life; the portrait of Dr. Pozzi is a powerful statement of this kind. Moving beyond the snapshot effect which could so easily result from this approach, the artist brings to the painting much more than the experience of Carolus' studio. The solid grasp of form and light, particularly in the head, reflects the method of his teacher, but Sargent's own personal gift, expanded and refined by a close study of the old masters, is affirmed. The drama of the painting is an extension of the artist's response to the work of Velàsquez and Hals which he had studied so closely in the previous months. In gesture and movement the figure is purely baroque, and, despite the overt drama of the technically superb glazes, there is a subtlety of light and tone which could well have had its source in Velàsquez.

123

William Michael Harnett
American, 1848-1892
Still Life, 1885
Oil on panel
13¾ x 10¼ in. (34.9 x 26.2 cm.)
Promised gift of the Armand Hammer Foundation

Collections: George Richmond, London, 1885 (Studio Sale, Christie, Manson & Woods, May 1, 1897, no. 4); Lord Justice William Rann Kennedy (Sale, London, Christie, Manson & Woods, Feb. 19, 1971, no. 177); Armand Hammer, Los Angeles

Exhibitions: London, Royal Academy of Arts, May 1885, no. 860 (purchased by George Richmond); St. Helens, Victoria Park, *First Summer Exhibition,* 1892, no. 105; Oklahoma City, Oklahoma Art Center, *The Armand*

Hammer Collection, June 15-July 11, 1971; San Diego, Fine Arts Gallery of San Diego, *The Armand Hammer Collection,* July 23-Sept. 5, 1971; Los Angeles County Museum of Art, *The Armand Hammer Collection,* Dec. 21, 1971- Feb. 27, 1972, no. 52, repr. in color in cat.; traveled to London, Royal Academy, June 24-July 24, 1972; Dublin, National Gallery of Ireland, Aug. 8-Oct. 1, 1972; Leningrad, State Hermitage Museum, Oct. 23-Dec. 2, 1972; Moscow, State Pushkin Museum of Fine Arts, Dec. 8, 1972-Feb. 11, 1973; Kiev, State Museum of Ukrainian Art, Mar. 6-31, 1973; Minsk, Belorussian State Museum of Fine Arts, Apr. 26-May 26, 1973; Riga, State Museum of Latvian and Russian Art, June 8-July 8, 1973; Odessa, State Picture Gallery, July 25-Aug. 25, 1973

Literature: A. Graves, *The Royal Academy of Arts, a Complete Dictionary of Contributors and Their Work from Its Foundation in 1769 to 1904,* London: Henry Graves & Co., Ltd. and George Bell & Sons, 1905, no. 860, p. 395; *Magazine of Art,* Feb. 1951, p. 66; A. Frankenstein, *After the Hunt, William Harnett and Other American Still Life Painters,* Berkeley and Los Angeles: University of California Press, 1953, no. 96, pp. 55, 70-71, 170-171, and rev. ed. 1969; Sale catalog, *Pictures, Drawings, Bronzes and Prints of American, Australian, Canadian, New Zealand and South African Interest,* London, Christie, Manson & Woods, Feb. 19, 1971, no. 177, p. 49, repr. opp. in color; *Art News,* Jan. 1971, p. 6, repr.; *Apollo,* Feb. 1971, p. 9, repr.; *Connoisseur,* June 1971, p. 158, repr.; *Art News,* Feb. 1972, p. 46, repr.; *Apollo,* June 1972, p. 453, repr. and p. 454; *Country Life,* Apr. 19, 1973, p. 1088, repr.

Though Harnett's *trompe-l'oeil* painting has a counterpart in the history of European art, it stands as a culmination of a long tradition of American Realism. Five years abroad had an effect on Harnett's work but did not erase the unique, personal elements of his style nor the stamp of forthright vision which characterizes so much of American painting.

Painted in Paris in 1885, this *Still Life* was sent to the Royal Academy in London where it was noted in the *Times* as "...one of the most miraculous representations...that we have ever seen." The writer undoubtedly was referring to the degree of realism of the painting. For, while the arrangement of solid objects in Harnett's *Still Life* does not permit the kind of visual deception typical of the two-dimensional rack paintings in which flat objects such as cards and envelopes are mounted on a board, it nevertheless achieves an almost tangible extension into space. But Harnett achieves more than an illusion of three-dimensionality. In this work he displays his particular genius in the highly sophisticated balance of color, form, and texture. Even the subtle shifts in hue among the variously faded sheets of music are exploited to the fullest, and the qualities of paper, metal, leather, velvet, and wood are explored and juxtaposed to play the full visual scale. While studying in Munich, Harnett had assembled a collection of curios to use as models in his still lifes and one of these may have been the vellum bound copy of Dante's *Divina Commedia* which appears here and in many of his other paintings after 1882. Also, the barely legible paneled cabinet seen in the background was a Munich invention which first appeared the same year. The flute he owned in America (it can be seen in *Music and Literature,* Albright-Knox Art Gallery, painted two years before he went to Europe). The Arnold ink bottle with quill pen and the piece of worn velvet are also pre-European models.

Another almost identical painting at Yale University has been mistaken for this one which was bought by George Richmond from the Royal Academy in 1885. The only obvious difference between the two, probably introduced to avoid exactly the kind of problem which has arisen, is the reversal of the printed word fragments on the roll of music protruding at the left and again on the top sheet of music at the front edge of the cabinet. Apparently Harnett himself was a victim of this confusion, for, on the back of a photograph—owned by Alfred Frankenstein—of the Yale painting, an inscription in the artist's own hand identifies it as the George Richmond still life.

124

John Singer Sargent
American, 1856-1925
Portrait of Mrs. Edward L. Davis and Her Son, Livingston Davis, 1890
Oil on canvas
86 x 48 in. (218.4 x 121.9 cm.)
Signed lower right: John S. Sargent
Frances and Armand Hammer Purchase Fund, 1969
M.69.18

Collections: Edward Livingston Davis, Worcester, Mass.; Livingston Davis, Boston; Mrs. A. Winsor Weld, Boston (Sale, New York, Parke-Bernet Galleries, Mar. 19-20, 1969, no. 74); James Graham & Sons, New York

Exhibitions: New York, National Academy of Design, 1890; New York, Society of American Artists, 1891; Boston Art Museum, 1891; Chicago, *World's Columbian Exhibition,* 1893, no. 875; Boston, Copley Hall, *Loan Collection of Portraits of Women,* 1895, no. 257; Philadelphia, Pennsylvania Academy of the Fine Arts, 1896; Boston, Copley Hall, *Paintings and Sketches by John S. Sargent, R.A.,* Feb. 20-Mar. 13, 1899, no. 5; Worcester, Mass., Worcester Art Museum, 1909; Boston, Museum of Fine Arts: 1913, no. 757; 1916, no. 573; 1918,

no. 480; 1920, no. 340; 1921, no. 420; New York, Grand Central Art Galleries, *Retrospective Exhibition of Important Works of John Singer Sargent,* Feb. 23-Apr. 6, 1924, no. 20, repr. in cat., p. 45; New York, The Metropolitan Museum of Art, *Memorial Exhibition of the Works of John Singer Sargent,* Jan. 4-Feb. 14, 1926, no. 26, repr. in cat.; Boston, Museum of Fine Arts: 1928, no. 168; 1929, no. 993; 1930, no. 530; 1956, no. 20; Boston, Museum of Fine Arts, Centennial Exhibition, *Sargent's Boston,* Jan. 3-Feb. 7, 1956; Memphis, Tennessee, Brooks Memorial Art Gallery, *The Armand Hammer Collection,* Oct. 2-Dec. 30, 1969, no. 57, repr. in cat.; Washington, D.C., Smithsonian Institution, *The Armand Hammer Collection,* Mar. 20-May 17, 1970, no. 63, repr. in color in cat.; San Francisco, California Palace of the Legion of Honor, *The Armand Hammer Collection,* Feb. 11-Mar. 14, 1971; Los Angeles County Museum of Art, *The Armand Hammer Collection,* Dec. 21, 1971-Feb. 27, 1972, no. 54, repr. in color in cat.; traveled to London, Royal Academy, June 24-July 24, 1972; Dublin, National Gallery of Ireland, Aug. 8-Oct. 1, 1972; Leningrad, State Hermitage Museum, Oct. 23-Dec. 2, 1972; Moscow, State Pushkin Museum of Fine Arts, Dec. 8, 1972-Feb. 11, 1973; Kiev, State Museum of Ukrainian Art, Mar. 6-31, 1973; Minsk, Belorussian State Museum of Fine Arts, Apr. 26-May 26, 1973; Riga, State Museum of Latvian and Russian Art, June 8-July 8, 1973; Odessa, State Picture Gallery, July 25-Aug. 25, 1973

Literature: L. Mechlin, "The Sargent Exhibition," *The American Magazine of Art,* vol. XV, no. 4, Apr. 1924, pp. 169-190, repr. p. 184; R. V. S. Berry, "John Singer Sargent: Some of His American Work," *Art and Archaeology throughout the Ages,* vol. XVIII, no. 3, Sept. 1924, pp. 83-112, repr. p. 100; W. H. Downes, *John S. Sargent, His Life and Work,* Boston: Little, Brown & Co., 1925, pp. 33, 157-158, repr. p. 128; E. Charteris, *John Sargent,* New York: Charles Scribner's Sons, 1927, pp. 109, 137, 263; C. M. Mount, *John Singer Sargent,* New York: W. W. Norton, 1955, pp. 183, 433, no. 9024; D. McKibbin, *Sargent's Boston,* Boston: Museum of Fine Arts, 1956, pp. 43, 68, 91, repr. p. 41; Sale catalog, *18th-20th Century American Paintings, etc.—Various Owners,* New York, Parke-Bernet Galleries, Mar. 19-20, 1969, no. 74, repr.; R. Ormond, *John Singer Sargent, Paintings, Drawings, Watercolors,* New York: Harper & Row, 1970, pp. 43, 246, repr.; *Los Angeles County Museum of Art Annual Report 1968-1969,* pp. 17-18, repr.

By 1889 when Sargent came to this country to discuss the mural project for the Boston Public Library, he was already the most renowned portrait painter of his day. When he was not actually involved with plans for the murals, portrait commissions in New York and Boston kept him completely absorbed. One of these commissions, for the *Portrait of Mrs. Edward L. Davis and Her Son, Livingston*

Davis, came from Edward L. Davis, a civic and social leader of Worcester, Massachusetts, who had served as mayor of the city. He married his second wife, Maria Louisa Robbins, of Boston, in 1869; their only son, Livingston, was born in 1882. According to W. H. Downes, Sargent painted the double portrait in the Davis' carriage house in Worcester because it afforded him an excellent studio with proper light. In several of his group portraits Sargent relates his sitters in touching, yet unsentimental poses. Mrs. Davis' relationship to her son is a simple sympathetic one like that seen in both his *Portrait of Mrs. Fiske Warren and Daughter* (Coll. Fiske Warren, Esq.) where the child leans her head on her mother's shoulder, and in the *Portrait of Mr. and Mrs. Field* (Pennsylvania Academy of the Fine Arts) in which the elderly couple are joined arm in arm. The seemingly casual relationship between the two figures in the Davis portrait is actually a relationship of considerable formal and psychological complexity. The precarious movement of the boy is played against the monumentally stable form of his mother who looms forward as she forcefully confronts the viewer. While the broad, loose brushwork continues to reflect Sargent's debt to the Dutch and Spanish masters and even to an extent to the Impressionists, the firm modeling and dramatic lighting of the woman's head seem to have something of the quality of the realist Copley, whose work Sargent discovered in Boston.

125

Thomas W. Eakins
American, 1844-1916
Portrait of Sebastiano Cardinal Martinelli, 1902
Oil on canvas, mounted on panel
78¼ x 59⅞ in. (198.9 x 152.3 cm.)
Signed lower right: Eakins 1902
Inscribed on back: EFFIGIES SEBASTIANI SRE CARDINALIS MARTINELLI QUI ANNOS VI IN STAT FOED AB MDCCCXCVI AD MCMII DELEGATI APOSTOLICI OFFICIO FUNCTUS
and below: THOS. EAKINS PHILADELPHIEN A.D. MCMII PINXIT
Promised gift of the Armand Hammer Foundation

Collections: Catholic University of America, Washington, D.C. (presented by the artist in 1903) (Sale, New York, Parke-Bernet Galleries, May 21, 1970, no. 57); Armand Hammer, Los Angeles

Exhibitions: New York, 1902/3; Philadelphia, Institute, *International Exhibition,* 1903; Chicago, 1903; Pittsburgh, Museum of Art, Carnegie Institute, *International Exhibition,*
Nov. 5, 1903-Jan. 1, 1904; Philadelphia, Pennsylvania Academy of the Fine Arts, *Thomas Eakins Memorial Exhibition,* Dec. 23, 1917-Jan. 23, 1918, no. 20; Baltimore Museum of Art, *Thomas Eakins, A Retrospective Exhibition of His Paintings,* Dec. 1, 1936-Jan. 1, 1937, no. 34; Philadelphia Museum of Art, *Thomas Eakins Centennial Exhibition,* 1944, no. 99; Pittsburgh, Museum of Art, Carnegie Institute, *Thomas Eakins Centennial Exhibition,* Apr. 26-June 1, 1945, no. 15, repr.; Washington, D.C., National Gallery of Art, 1969-1970; Overbrook, Pennsylvania, St. Charles Seminary, *Eakins Portraits,* 1970; Smithsonian Institution Traveling Exhibition Service, *The Armand Hammer Collection,* no. 101, repr. in color on cover of cat. supplement and in black and white on inside page; Kansas City, Missouri, William Rockhill Nelson Gallery of Art, June 30-Aug. 2, 1970, and New Orleans, Isaac Delgado Museum of Art, Aug. 15-Sept. 20, 1970; New York, Whitney Museum of American Art, *Thomas Eakins Retrospective,* Sept. 21-Nov. 29, 1970; Little Rock, Arkansas Art Center, *The Armand Hammer Collection,* Dec. 11, 1970-Jan. 12, 1971; San Francisco, California Palace of the Legion of Honor, *The Armand Hammer Collection,* Feb. 11-Mar. 14, 1971; Oklahoma City, Oklahoma Art Center, *The Armand Hammer Collection,* June 15-July 11, 1971; San Diego, Fine Arts Gallery of San Diego, *The Armand Hammer Collection,* July 23-Sept. 5, 1971; Los Angeles County Museum of Art, *The Armand Hammer Collection,* no. 55, repr. in color in cat.; traveled to London, Royal Academy, June 24-July 24, 1972; Dublin, National Gallery of Ireland, Aug. 8-Oct. 1, 1972; Leningrad, State Hermitage Museum, Oct. 23-Dec. 2, 1972; Moscow, State Pushkin Museum of Fine Arts, Dec. 8, 1972-Feb. 11, 1973; Kiev, State Museum of Ukrainian Art, Mar. 6-31, 1973; Minsk, Belorussian State Museum of Fine Arts, Apr. 26-May 26, 1973; Riga, State Museum of Latvian and Russian Art, June 8-July 8, 1973; Odessa, State Picture Gallery, July 25-Aug. 25, 1973

Literature: L. Goodrich, *Thomas Eakins—His Life and Work,* New York: Macmillan Co., 1933, no. 361, pp. 105-106, 194; F. Porter, *Thomas Eakins,* New York: George Braziller, Inc., 1959, repr. fig. 64; S. Schendler, *Thomas Eakins,* Boston: Little, Brown & Co., 1967, pp. 201, 208, 215, 296, pl. 102; Sale catalog, *18th, 19th and 20th Century American Paintings,* New York, Parke-Bernet Galleries, May 21, 1970, no. 57, p. 58, repr. opp. in color; *Art News,* May 1970, p. 13, repr.; *Arts,* May 1970, p. 11, repr.; *Goya,* Sept. 1970, p. 125, repr.; *Apollo,* June 1972, p. 454, repr.

As Lloyd Goodrich has pointed out, it seems paradoxical that Thomas Eakins, a Quaker and an uncompromising realist, should have begun in his late years a series of portraits of Catholic prelates. Seen as portraits of friends painted at the artist's own request, however, they begin to take their place very logically within his total oeuvre. Rejected as an artist and rather withdrawn from society, Eakins must have felt a close kinship with these learned men whose mission set them apart from the world.

Sebastiano Martinelli (1848-1918), created Cardinal Archbishop of Ephesus in 1901, was the second Apostolic Delegate to the United States (1896-1902). Eakins painted Martinelli's portrait at the cardinal's residence in Washington, D.C., in 1902 shortly before his return to Rome. He wears the black robes of the Order of Hermits of St. Augustine and the cardinal's red skull cap, or zuchetto; in his left hand he holds the cardinal's red biretta. In this portrait Eakins has achieved a perfect balance between the human quality of the individual and the austerity of the holy office. As is often the case in Eakins' full-length portraits, this figure is placed at some distance from the viewer within a very real space, and the ambience eloquently conveys a feeling of solitary contemplation. This effect is further enhanced by the use of the profile view which presents the figure as a hieratic image to be beheld without direct involvement of the spectator. From the casually rubbed earth color suggesting wood paneling and a parquet floor to the subtle design of the rug, more or less monochromatic surroundings act as a foil, intensifying the impact of the cardinal's presence.

126

Mary Cassatt
American, 1844-1926
Reine Lefebvre and Margot, ca. 1902
Pastel on brown paper, mounted on canvas
32¾ x 26½ in. (83.2 x 67.5 cm.)
Signed lower left: Mary Cassatt
Promised gift of the Armand Hammer Foundation

Collections: Felix Doistau, Paris (Sale, Galerie Georges Petit, June 18-19, 1928, no. 6); Durand-Ruel, Paris and New York, 1929; Mrs. A. L. Adams, Jr. (Sale, New York, Parke-Bernet Galleries, Oct. 15, 1969, no. 16); Armand Hammer, Los Angeles

Exhibitions: New York, Durand-Ruel Galleries, *Mary Cassatt,* Apr. 8-20, 1929, no. 1; Washington, D.C., Smithsonian Institution, *The Armand Hammer Collection,* Mar. 20-May 17, 1970, no. 56, repr. in color in cat.; Smithsonian Institution Traveling Exhibition Service, *The Armand Hammer Collection,* Kansas City, Missouri, William Rockhill Nelson Gallery of Art, June 30-Aug. 2, 1970, and New Orleans, Isaac Delgado Museum of Art, Aug. 15-Sept. 20, 1970; Washington, D.C., National Gallery of Art, *Mary Cassatt,* Sept. 27-Nov. 8, 1970, no. 70; Little Rock, Arkansas Art Center, *The Armand Hammer Collection,* Nov. 21, 1970-Jan. 12, 1971; San Francisco, California Palace of the Legion of Honor, *The Armand*

Hammer Collection, Feb. 11-Mar. 14, 1971; Oklahoma City, Oklahoma Art Center, *The Armand Hammer Collection,* June 15-July 11, 1971; San Diego, Fine Arts Gallery of San Diego, *The Armand Hammer Collection,* July 23-Sept. 5, 1971; Los Angeles County Museum of Art, *The Armand Hammer Collection,* Dec. 21, 1971-Feb. 27, 1972, no. 56, repr. in color in cat.; traveled to London, Royal Academy, June 24-July 24, 1972; Dublin, National Gallery of Ireland, Aug. 8-Oct. 1, 1972; Leningrad, State Hermitage Museum, Oct. 23-Dec. 2, 1972; Moscow, State Pushkin Museum of Fine Arts, Dec. 8, 1972-Feb. 11, 1973; Kiev, State Museum of Ukrainian Art, Mar. 6-31, 1973; Minsk, Belorussian State Museum of Fine Arts, Apr. 26-May 26, 1973; Riga, State Museum of Latvian and Russian Art, June 8-July 8, 1973; Odessa, State Picture Gallery, July 25-Aug. 25, 1973

Literature: *Revue de l'Art,* Nov. 1928; *Bulletin de l'Art Ancien et Moderne,* Nov. 1928, p. 357, repr.; A. D. Breeskin, *Mary Cassatt, A Catalogue Raisonné of the Oils, Pastels, Watercolors and Drawings,* Washington, D.C.: Smithsonian Institution Press, 1970, no. 430, p. 170, repr.; Sale catalog, *Important Impressionist and Modern Paintings and Sculpture,* New York, Parke-Bernet Galleries, Oct. 15, 1969, no. 16, repr. in color; *Apollo,* June 1972, p. 134, repr.

Reine Lefebvre, a neighbor living in the village near Mary Cassatt's Chateau de Beaufresne, posed for the artist from 1901 to 1903, sometimes with the child Margot. Though only sixteen and seventeen years old during this association, she is imbued in this painting with a quiet dignity and conveys a very convincing maternal relationship with the child. Typical of Cassatt's pastels of this period, the present work almost disguises the powerful drafts-manship which won her the admiration of Degas. The free and forceful strokes seem to activate the surface in an almost random way, but ultimately the strength of line emerges in the firm design.

127

Gaston Lachaise
French-American, 1882-1935
Floating Figure, 1927
Bronze, edition 2/7, cast 1969 by Lachaise Foundation, Modern Art Foundry, Long Island
51¾ x 96 in. (131.4 x 243.8 cm.)
Promised gift of Mr. and Mrs. Ray Stark

Collections: Robert Schoelkopf Gallery, New York; Mr. and Mrs. Ray Stark, Beverly Hills, 1970

Exhibitions: New York, Museum of Modern Art, *Gaston Lachaise, Retrospective Exhibition,* Jan. 30-Mar. 7, 1935, no. 31, repr. in cat.; Los Angeles County Museum of

Art, *Gaston Lachaise Sculpture and Drawings,* Dec. 3, 1963-Jan. 19, 1964, and New York, Whitney Museum of American Art, Feb. 18-Apr. 5, 1964, no. 63, repr. in cat.; Los Angeles, Otis Art Institute, *Hollywood Collects,* 1970, repr. in cat. pp. 9-10; Los Angeles, Frederick S. Wight Art Gallery, UCLA , *Gaston Lachaise,* Jan. 12-Feb. 23, 1975

Literature: H. Kramer, *The Sculpture of Gaston Lachaise,* New York: Eakins Press, 1967, repr. pls. 38-40; G. Nordland, *Gaston Lachaise, the Man and His Work,* New York: Braziller, 1974, pp. 130-133

Lachaise, born in Paris, had completed his academic sculptural training by the age of sixteen. Lachaise's drive toward an innovative sculptural idiom and his marriage to Isabel Nagle led him to leave his birthplace, renounce the academic success of which he was assured, and move to America in 1906, where he lived and worked until his death. Thus, his artistic approach was born at the junction of his Beaux-Arts training and the tradition of the heroic figure revitalized by Rodin. But it was in America that his unique sculptural style took shape and matured.

Lachaise's oeuvre—which includes portrait sculptures of friends and associates, renderings of animals and birds, and anatomical fragments as well as monumental women— can be divided into two types: the smaller-than-human scale intimate pieces, and those public and monumental works for which he is best known. *Floating Figure* is a signal example of the latter; the heroic vision of woman which it exemplifies is in fact present in most of his statuettes as well as in his major sculptures of the female from 1910 to 1932.

In the *Floating Figure* and in his other monumental sculptures of women, Lachaise proceeded in a boldly radical spirit to amplify and exaggerate the natural components of the human form. By this kind of proportional emphasis without proportional distortion Lachaise imparted a sense of powerful volumetric rhythm to the body. The artist expressed his own guiding principle in the words, "Simplify and amplify: amplification and simplification." In the case of the *Floating Figure,* Lachaise combines the characteristic robustness and volume in his woman with a literal aspect of buoyancy; she is actually lifted into the air.

The women of Lachaise's sculpture are irresistibly equated with concepts of goddess, mother, lover, and the life principle itself. In his 1935 essay on Lachaise, Lincoln Kirstein wrote: "Lachaise, above all other sculptors since the Renaissance, is the interpreter of maturity. He is concerned with forms which have completed their growth, which have achieved their prime; forms, as he would say, in the glory of their fulfillment."

The plaster of the ninety-six-inch *Floating Figure,* created in 1927, was first shown in 1928 at the Brummer Gallery. The first bronze, unnumbered, was cast for the Museum of Modern Art retrospective in 1935 and was there-

after donated to the permanent collection. Of the edition of seven, four have been cast. The city of Philadelphia owns no. 1, Princeton University no. 3, and the University of Nebraska no. 4.

128

Josef Albers
American, b. 1888
Homage to the Square: Beyond Focus, 1969
Oil on masonite
48 x 48 in. (121.9 x 121.9 cm.)
Promised gift of Mr. and Mrs. Taft Schreiber

Collection: Mr. and Mrs. Taft Schreiber

Exhibition: New York, The Metropolitan Museum of Art, *Josef Albers at the Metropolitan Museum of Art,* 1971, no. 92, repr. in color frontis.

Josef Albers' *Homage to the Square: Beyond Focus,* 1969, is a culmination of his disciplined thinking. The "Homage" series, begun in 1949, focuses on one idea: the instrumentation of the infinite possibilities of color relationships. This series is the largest produced by Albers since the early 1950s. The repetition of a single format provides a controlled structure for his systematic exploration of color. In the artist's words, "They (colors) are juxtaposed for various and changing visual effects. They are to challenge or to echo each other, to support or oppose one another. The contacts, respectively boundaries, between them may vary from soft to hard touches, may mean pull and push besides clashes, but also embracing, intersecting, penetrating."

The square has been especially important in modern painting since 1913. For such artists as Malevich and Mondrian, the square and rectangle were used formally more as ends in themselves than they are for Albers; for him the square is more like a receptacle for color and light. In his "Homages" the relativity and instability of color are demonstrated in a manner both sensitive and cogent.

129

Jackson Pollock
American, 1912-1956
Black and White Number 20, 1951
Duco on canvas
57⅛ x 64 in. (45 x 62.4 cm.)
Bequest of David E. Bright, 1967
M.67.25.16

Collections: Marlborough-Gerson Gallery, Inc., New York; David E. Bright, Los Angeles

Exhibitions: Düsseldorf, Kunsthalle, *Jackson Pollock,* Sept.-Oct. 1961; Zurich Kunsthaus, Oct.-Nov. 1961, repr. in cat., no. 88; traveled to Stockholm, Moderna Museet, Feb.-Apr. 1963; Los Angeles County Museum of Art,

New York School, July 16-Aug. 1, 1965, repr. in cat., no. 81; Los Angeles County Museum of Art, *David E. Bright Collection,* Oct. 17-Dec. 17, 1967, repr. in cat., p. 53

Literature: M. Tuchman, *New York School,* Greenwich, Conn.: New York Graphic Society, 1971, repr. no. 87

In 1951, Jackson Pollock wrote concerning his recent black and white paintings, of which *Number 20, 1951,* is an example: "I've had a period of drawing on canvas in black—with some of my early images coming through—think the non-objectivists will find them disturbing—and the kids who think it is simple to dash a Pollock out." In this statement, the artist announced two important aspects of his black and white series of 1951-1952: the use of a more conscious organization in creating the image, and the suggestion of figuration. These distinctive features of Pollock's black and white paintings must be considered in relationship to his earlier painting styles.

The pre-abstract pictures, 1942-1946, bore close affinities to the line of Surrealism represented by André Masson. In the classic drip paintings, 1947-1950, Pollock pioneered a kind of painting which in spontaneity, abstraction, and scale went far beyond anything Surrealist automatism or indeed any previous improvisational art had proposed. The succeeding black and white paintings synthesized aspects of both the early and middle works. In the works from the later series, there is a sense of resonant graveness, a shift away from the characteristically elegant tracery and grace of the earlier colorful mode. In the black and white series (many artists of note seriously experimented with stark value contrast around 1950), Pollock continued to apply paint dynamically in linear webs, but the forms seem somewhat more slowly and deliberately achieved. Further, as seen in *Black and White Number 20,* faces and figures seem to emerge from the black skeins of paint. As a result, an ambivalence and tension between figuration and abstraction exist in these works which demarcate a new phase in Pollock's art.

130

Gertrude and Otto Natzler
American, 1908-1971 and b. 1908
A Selection of Natzler Ceramics
Collection of Mrs. Leonard M. Sperry
Gift of the Rose A. Sperry Revocable Trust, 1972

Bowl, 1952
Gray white mat glaze, black red-rimmed spots
h: 2 in. (5.0 cm.); d: 5¾ in. (14.5 cm.)
M.72.105.49

The glaze of this bowl is a unique example stemming from experiments of the early 1950s. The black spots are produced from small bits of metallic copper added to the glaze; the red rims are caused by reduction of second firing.

Footed Bowl, 1953
"Sang" and blue reduction glaze
h: 1½ in. (4 cm.); d: 5⅝ in. (14.5 cm.)
M.72.105.26

Faint melt fissures are visible on the inside of one of the most sensitively thrown small pieces in the Sperry Collection. Reduction firing has produced a red blush and slight metallic luster. Colors are produced by a small amount of copper in a semi-alkaline base.

Bottle, 1954
"Tiger Eye" reduction glaze
h: 5⅞ in. (15.0 cm.); d: 5⅞ in. (15.0 cm.)
M.72.105.30

This medium dark "tiger eye" glaze shows pronounced melt fissures and elephant skin texture. The color is derived from titanium and antimony in a lead glaze fired twice for oxidation and reduction.

Vase with Flaring Top, 1960
Flame red mat glaze
h: 8¼ in. (21.0 cm.); d: 3⅛ in. (8.0 cm.)
M.72.105.39

The orange brown black of this glaze shows tiny "explosions" on its surface. The glaze color is produced from uranium in a heavy lead glaze, oxidation fired.

Vase, 1963
"Nocturne" reduction glaze
h: 8⅞ in. (22.5 cm.); d: 7⅛ in. (18.0 cm.)
M.72.105.50

This vase is unique in the Natzlers' production in its wide variations from deep olive to magenta red. The glaze displays crystal formations and melt fissures and is derived from copper and titanium in a semi-alkaline base fired twice for oxidation and reduction.

"...Earth, water and fire should not just be so many ingredients that go into the making of ceramics, but they should be retained on the finished piece to tell their story through the ages. Only the pot that is true to the essence of the medium, both as to form and execution, will retain the timelessness inherent in the best ceramic art."

Otto Natzler in the above quotation from his article in *Craft Horizon* (vol. 24, July 1964, p. 24) states the creed which placed the Natzlers in the forefront of American ceramics of the mid-twentieth century.

Over a period of years Mrs. Leonard M. Sperry formed a retrospective collection of the Natzlers' work in America. The collection of some fifty-four pieces, selected with the guidance of the Natzlers, illustrates scope and variety with significant examples of particular periods of their collaboration from 1940 to 1968.

131

Franz Kline
American, 1910-1962
The Ballantine, 1948-1960
Oil on canvas
72 x 72 in. (182.9 x 182.9 cm.)
Bequest of David E. Bright, 1967
M.67.25.20

Collections: Everett Ellin Gallery, Los Angeles;
David E. Bright, Los Angeles

Exhibition: Los Angeles County Museum of Art,
David E. Bright Collection, Oct. 17-Dec. 17, 1967,
repr. in cat., p. 51

Literature: *Connoisseur,* Feb. 1968, vol. 167, repr. p. 132

Kline's first black and white paintings which were to
become his great artistic statement were done in 1950.
Between that time and his death, Kline also worked in color,
though never with the consistent success attained with
black and white. Until 1949 he had painted figurative
pictures. In that year, his "conversion" to abstract gesture
painting occurred when he enlarged one of his drawings
in a Bell-opticon machine. The structure he perceived in its
enlargement caused him to abandon the figurative
mode permanently.

Contact with Pollock and De Kooning was as important
for Kline as for all artists finding their way to "action
painting" in the late 1940s. Like De Kooning, with whom
he is frequently compared, Kline conveyed the dynamism of
contemporary urban life in his paintings; but Kline's
simpler and clearer configurations express a particularly
confident and direct attitude in contrast to De Kooning's
great psychological complexity. Kline's rapidly evolved
style—abstract configurations of colliding black and white
swaths—so strongly characterized an aspect of the sensibility
of the 1950s that it became difficult to look at a black and
white painting without referring to his work.

Each of Kline's dynamic paintings seems the spontaneous
unretouched record of an impulse. In fact, of course, these
canvases are the result of intensive study, of adjustment and
readjustment with edges shifted and areas painstakingly
reworked to arrive at a dynamic formal relationship, the
powerful interplay of dark and light.

Without suggesting specific references, Kline's paintings
often convey the strength and majesty of the raw steel
structures of a modern city, for instance, or the force of a
moving train. But with this quality of mundane dynamism
the artist evinces on another level the precise delicacy
and almost spiritual simplicity associated with Japanese
and Chinese calligraphy.

132

Mark Rothko
American, 1903-1970
White Center, 1957
Oil on canvas
84 x 72 in. (213.4 x 182.9 cm.)
Bequest of David E. Bright, 1967
M.67.25.21

Collections: Lawrence Rubin, New York; David E. Bright,
Los Angeles

Exhibitions: Los Angeles County Museum of Art,
New York School, July 16-Aug. 1, 1964, no. 107, repr. in
cat.; Los Angeles County Museum of Art, *David E. Bright
Collection,* Oct. 17-Dec. 17, 1967, repr. in color in cat.,
p. 47; Newport Beach, California, Newport Harbor Art
Museum, *Mark Rothko,* Jan. 29-Mar. 10, 1974,
repr. in cat. no. 2 in color, p. 11

Literature: M. Tuchman, *New York School,* Greenwich,
Conn.; New York Graphic Society, 1971, repr. p. 115

Mark Rothko, Barnett Newman, and Clifford Still are
generally acknowledged to be the leading figures of the
color field sub-style of Abstract Expressionism. *White Center,*
1957, is a prime work of Rothko's post-1950 mature
abstract style in which soft-edged rectangles of glowing
atmospheric color are symmetrically arranged.

During the 1930s, Rothko painted isolated figures in
urban settings. Around 1942, he adopted the Surrealist
technique of automatism to combine human, animal, and
plant forms into biomorphic inventions which resembled
Gottlieb's pictographs and Gorky's expressionist Surrealism.
Rothko eliminated ideographic symbols and automatist
calligraphy from his painting in 1947 and began to work
with washes of color. In 1950, he moved into the phase
for which he is now celebrated. In these works, he reduced
the number of formal elements in each picture to two or
three, coalesced into large rectangles of approximately
similar width, and he simplified by locating shapes symmetrically one above the other. The rectangular planes are
distinct from one another, but also constitute a field. Rothko
intended his paintings to be perceived at once holistically:
the sense of a monolithic picture surface is reinforced by
bleeding the shapes into the ground, fusing all color into a
single plane while retaining internal relationalism.
While the post-1950 paintings are simpler in format
than Rothko's previous mythological works, they do not
sacrifice complexity of content. Rothko announced in 1949
that he rejected "memory, history or geometry": in subsequent work he continued to express the urge toward a
sense of momentous content even in his drastically
"non-representational" works. Rothko constantly sought
access to primal energies and intuitions. They find expression
in his abstract works through resonant light-filled color.

133

David Smith
American, 1906-1965
Cubi XXIII, 1964
Stainless steel
76¼ x 172⅞ in. (193.7 x 439.1 cm.)
Contemporary Art Council Funds, 1967
M.67.26

Collection: Estate of David Smith, Marlborough-Gerson Gallery, New York

Exhibitions: Los Angeles County Museum of Art, *David Smith—A Memorial Exhibition,* Nov. 3, 1965-Jan. 30, 1966, no. 8, repr. in cat., pp. 16-17; New York, Museum of Modern Art, International Circulating Exhibition, *David Smith 1906-1965;* traveled to Otterlo, Rijksmuseum Kroller-Muller, May 15-July 17, 1966; London, Tate Gallery, Aug. 18-Sept. 25, 1966; Basel, Kunsthalle, Oct. 25-Nov. 23, 1966; Nurnberg, Kunsthalle, Jan. 17-Feb. 20, 1967; Duisberg, Wilhelm Lehmbruck Museum, Apr. 15-May 28, 1967; Los Angeles County Museum of Art, *American Sculpture of the Sixties,* Apr. 28-June 25, 1967, no. 128, repr. in color in cat., p. 186; Philadelphia Museum of Art, Sept. 15-Oct. 29, 1967; New York, Solomon R. Guggenheim Museum, *David Smith Retrospective Exhibition,* Mar. 29-May 11, 1969, no. 96, repr. in color in cat., p. 160; Dallas Museum of Fine Arts, June-Sept. 1969; Washington, D.C., Corcoran Gallery, Oct.-Nov. 1969

Literature: *David Smith—A Retrospective Exhibition,* Cambridge, Mass.: Fogg Art Museum, 1966, no. 534 (not in exhibition), repr. no. 59

Cubi XXIII belongs to the triumphant "Cubi" series made by David Smith in the early 1960s. Smith, America's foremost sculptor of the twentieth century, received his artistic education in the 1920s. The examples of Picasso's and Gonzales' iron sculptures which he saw in the early 1930s were critically important for Smith. He began working in sculpture in 1932 and made his first arc-welded pieces in 1939. He said, "I learned that art could be made with steel, the material...that had previously meant only labor and earning power." Exposure to Surrealism in the 1940s helped free his sculpture from the constraints of specificity, but the structuring of Smith's sculpture, the principles of composition that he used, fundamentally relate to Cubism and Constructivism.

The "Cubi" series comprises works juxtaposing, in various rhythmic schemata, inventively conceived elements of solid geometry. They are truly monumental sculptures, in scale as in quality, their name a fitting tribute to Cubism, the seminal aesthetic revolution of modern art. The "Cubi"

sculptures are distinguished by their burnished, glinting, stainless steel surfaces. Smith intended the series for outdoor settings. He said, "They are conceived for bright light, preferably the sun, to develop the illusion of surface and depth...they are colored by the sky and surroundings."

Cubi XXIII is an important and famous representative of the series. In it, Smith utilized an uncharacteristic, horizontally extended composition. This orientation reflects a probable interaction at that time with the sculpture of the younger British artist, Anthony Caro. *Cubi XXIII* is a milestone in the development of modern sculpture's break with the notion of attachment to a base: the stride of the piece, a metaphor for walking, is not grounded by any form of support.

134

Alexander Calder
American, b. 1898
Hello Girls, 1964
Three mobiles, painted metal
h: 8 ft. 9 in. (2.67 m.); 15 ft. (4.57 m.); 22 ft. 11 in. (6.98 m.)
Commissioned by the Art Museum Council
M.65.10

Exhibition: Los Angeles County Museum of Art, *American Sculpture of the Sixties,* Apr. 28-June 25, 1967, no. 16, repr. in cat.

Literature: H. H. Arnason, *Calder,* Princeton, N.J.: Van Nostrand, 1966, repr. pp. 66-67

Alexander Calder's *Hello Girls,* a three-piece mobile, was commissioned by the Art Museum Council in 1964 for the new Los Angeles County Museum of Art buildings. The sculpture was installed in one of the Museum's outdoor reflecting pools, kept in continual motion by the play of wind and jets of water striking the blades.

Hello Girls consists of a group of standing mobiles mounted on high pylons. Long crossbars support painted circular metal forms. Two arms extend high in the air in a light-hearted gesture of greeting: thus the name, *Hello Girls* which also salutes the commissioning council members.

Calder's mobiles evolved out of abstract wire constructions inspired chiefly by Miró during the latter part of 1930 and 1931. His use of Mondrianesque primary colors developed at an early stage as well, and has continued throughout his career in both sculpture and painting. He has almost always avoided rectilinear forms in favor of the biomorphic and curvilinear. The element of actual motion in his sculpture seems to have stemmed from his late

1920s "circus" and other mechanized wire figures. By 1932, he had begun to explore the possibilities of suspended sculptures activated only by currents of air; this was the inception of the mobile. The mobiles proliferated during the late 1940s and 1950s, in variants from those which stand on bases, like *Hello Girls,* to those attached to walls or ceilings. In the postwar period, Calder has tended to enlarge both the mobiles and the free-standing stabiles to monumental scale.

Because *Hello Girls* was conceived to be propelled by water, it is considered to be one of his "mechanized" mobiles; it is also actually a fountain. Although the design of fountains would seem to be a natural outcome of the mobile concept, Calder has had few commissions for them: the Museum Calder may indeed be the most important. The artist has given his approval to the present installation of the sculpture in the Museum's new sculpture garden as a wind propelled mobile. Because *Hello Girls* can be activated either by water or by wind, it is a unique synthesis of two mobile types—the "mechanized" and the "natural."

135

Claes Oldenburg
American, b. 1929
Giant Pool Balls, 1967
Sixteen plexiglass balls, 24 in. each (61.0 cm.)
Wood rack, 120 x 120 x 108 in. (304.8 x 304.8 x 274.3 cm.)
Anonymous gift through the Contemporary
Art Council, 1969
M.69.88

Exhibitions: New York, The Metropolitan Museum of Art, *New York Painting and Sculpture: 1940-1970,* 1969, no. 294, repr. in color in cat., p. 97; Pasadena Museum of Art, *Claes Oldenburg,* Dec. 7, 1971-Feb. 2, 1972, no. 24, repr. in cat., p. 102; traveled to Berkeley, University Art Museum, Feb. 28-Apr. 9, 1972; Kansas City, Missouri, William Rockhill Nelson Gallery, Atkins Museum of Fine Arts, May 11-June 18, 1972; Fort Worth Art Center Museum, July 10-Aug. 20, 1972; Des Moines Art Center, Sept. 18-Oct. 29, 1972; Philadelphia Museum of Art, Nov. 15-Dec. 27, 1972; and Art Institute of Chicago, Jan. 17-Feb. 25, 1973

Literature: H. Geldzahler, *New York Painting and Sculpture: 1940-1970,* New York: The Metropolitan Museum of Art and E. P. Dutton and Company, 1969, no. 294, repr. in color, p. 97; B. Rose, *Claes Oldenburg,* New York: the Museum of Modern Art, 1969, repr. p. 131

One of the dominant preoccupations of twentieth-century art has been with the common object. Artists as diverse as Picabia, Schwitters, Picasso, Rauschenberg, and Duchamp have introduced "real" objects into their compositions. In the 1960s, Pop Art focused on and apotheosized the mass culture object in varied conceptions and media. Of the several American artists whose startling transformations of commercial imagery became a significant art movement, sculptor Claes Oldenburg is perhaps the definitive figure.

Oldenburg has said, "Nothing is irrelevant, everything can be used." He is for "Kool-art, 7-up art, Pepsi-art, 39 cents art, R_X art, Fire sale art, Last chance art, $9.99 art, Ready-to-eat art, Best-for-less art, Tomato art, Turkey art, Cookie art...." His art is often based on his perceptions of paradox implicit in virtually every man-made artifact. What absorbs Oldenburg is the alterability, real or imagined, of such basic psycho-physical properties as hardness or softness. The ice cream cone and ice bag, for instance, are two forms he has rendered in various ways, even combining the two in sketches. (Oldenburg is an irrepressible and prodigiously gifted draftsman.)

Oldenburg began making huge-scale hard objects in 1962, but much of his work since that time has been sculpture in soft materials, or prints and drawings conceived as proposals for monuments. The *Giant Pool Balls* is one of the largest hard sculptures ever made by the artist and one of the most literally represented. The piece is rather unusual in that it was not conceived as a model or prototype for a monument, nor was it ever executed in soft form, as were many other of his conceptions.

Its genesis was in fact quite specific: "The Pool Balls," Oldenburg wrote, "are now a rather pure piece, like a palette of round colors, but it began as an altogether different piece. *Playboy* magazine commissioned me (and several other artists) to do an apotheosis of the 'Playmate.' To inspire us, they sent tear sheets of 'Playmates' going back to the start of the magazine. As I pored over the hard and shiny breasts in the photographs, I was reminded of pool balls. I followed my impulse to cut them out, using a circle-maker, and arranged the results in a rack. This was the first form of the Pool Balls—the balls were to be different flesh colors and each would have a nipple."

In the *Giant Pool Balls* the disposition of these colorful, uniformly sized "play" objects neatly contained within a triangular frame creates an eminently satisfying abstract sculpture. They are not, of course, perceived abstractly; the association to their prototype in our experience is even more inescapable than the aesthetic seduction. Like certain of Oldenburg's more numerous soft sculptures in comparable scale, the work creates a kind of indelible imprint in visual memory. In this sense it relates to the minimalist tradition with which it shares historical proximity.

136

Robert Rauschenberg
American, b. 1925
Booster, 1967
Color lithograph and silkscreen
Printed on Curtis Rag by Gemini Ltd., Los Angeles, from
two stones in black, two aluminum plates in white, and
silkscreen in red enamel
Edition: 38/38
72 x 36 in. (182.9 x 91.4 cm.)
Gift of the Times Mirror Company, 1973
M.73.64.2

Literature: E. A. Foster, *Robert Rauschenberg:
Prints 1948/1970,* Minneapolis: The Minneapolis
Institute of Arts, 1970

Robert Rauschenberg's *Booster and Seven Studies* of
1967 is this artist's first series of prints to be published as a
group. (The earlier *Dante* lithographs of 1964, although
based on a single theme, were not issued together.) Of the
Booster and Seven Studies the Museum now has in its
collection *Test Stone 2, Test Stone 3,* and *Booster* itself, one
of the most outstanding prints that Rauschenberg has
produced to date.

Created at Gemini G.E.L. in Los Angeles, the *Booster
and Seven Studies* lithographs in some instances are clearly
interrelated pictorially; images appearing in individual
studies, with various degrees of transformation, reappear in
the borders surrounding the dominant X-ray image of the
artist in *Booster.* In *Test Stone 3,* acquired in 1972 for
the Museum's collection, the artist depicted a view of a
human skull in the upper right corner of the print. Later, this
imagery was echoed in the suggested silhouette of a human
skull in the lower left border of *Booster.* Further enhancing
the imagery of this six-foot lithograph is the superimposed
graph of a time chart of 1967 silkscreened in red over the
X-ray portrait of the artist, who was photographed wearing
only his hobnailed boots. For the main image a photographic contact print was made of the separate X-rays. From
these a halftone negative was produced and put on
photolithography plates. Impressions from these plates
were taken on transfer paper and then transferred to two
separate stones. At this point, additional work in tusche
and crayon was done by Rauschenberg directly on the stone.

As early as 1963 at the International Print Exhibition
of Ljubljana, Yugoslavia, Rauschenberg was recognized as
one of the world's leading printmakers. In 1967, when
he created *Booster,* it was the largest lithograph ever printed
on a hand-operated press. Its impressive scale, technical
innovativeness, and superb craftsmanship have made *Booster*
one of the key prints of the past decade, as well as one of
the standards by which all subsequent modern printmaking
efforts will be evaluated.

137

Frank Stella
American, b. 1936
Protractor Variation, 1969
Fluorescent-alkyd on canvas
10 x 20 ft. (3.05 x 6.1 m.)
Museum Purchase, 1969
M.69.68

Collection: Irving Blum Gallery, Los Angeles

A student at Princeton between 1954 and 1958,
Frank Stella internalized the lessons of 1950s New York
painting and has developed, in the works produced from
the late 1950s to the present, a series of radically new stylistic
idioms. The artist's own words from 1959-1960 express
his early ideas: "The solution I arrived at…forces illusionistic space out of painting at a constant rate by using a
regulated pattern." His paintings have developed based on
this central idea, and the patterned flat canvases, including
"shaped" works, have insinuated a new iconic regularity and
structure into modern painting.

Protractor Variation, 1969, is one of a series of large
curvilinear compositions begun by Stella in 1967. These
paintings, known as the "Protractor Series," are based on
the curvilinear, sectional shapes inherent to the geometric
instrument. In them, the artist made an immensely ambitious
foray into the project of complex coloration. Stella
realized this series in three different design types known
as interlaces, rainbows, and fans. The Museum's picture
belongs to the "interlace" category. The "Protractor Series"
is Stella's first truly architectural work—in terms both of
sheer overall scale and the scale relationships established by
the relatively large size of the interlacing units. These
paintings have also been viewed as a sudden shift into the
realm of "high decoration." The basic semicircular forms
are articulated in terms of complex interwoven bands.
Significantly, however intricate the interweavings become,
the illusion of receding space is avoided. This is due partly
to the flat and even application of paint and partly to the fact
that no band of one protractor group is ever placed consistently "behind" all those of another. Further spatial
interest and contradictions are created by the contrasts of
bright day-glo colors with relatively nonreflective mat hues.

138

Larry Bell
American, b. 1939
Untitled, 1971
Coated glass, two panels
Each panel: 108 x 60 x 3/8 in. (274.3 x 152.9 x 1.0 cm.)
Gift of the Kleiner Foundation, 1973
M.73.38.1

Working in a remarkably precocious way—he is now only thirty-four years old—through a progression of rigorously calculated formal decisions, Bell has created a distinctive body of work culminating in the 1971-1973 series of sculptures to which the Museum's work belongs. Beginning as a painter, the artist began incorporating mirrors into geometrically shaped wall works (examples of paintings with and without mirrors belong to the Los Angeles County Museum of Art), leading in 1964 to free-standing cubes made of aluminized glass. The first cubes were faced with geometric shapes—ellipses or linear patterns (an early cube of this type is in our permanent collection). These were followed by variously sized small cubes whose only surface incident was that created by a process of vacuum-coating developed by the artist in his factorylike Venice studio. These cubes, whose quality was at the same time translucent and reflective, richly colored and elusively chameleonlike in tonality, represent by themselves an entire chapter in the art of the sixties. They occupy a place on one hand with the minimalist sculptural movement, and on the other they epitomize the indigenously Southern Californian concern with sensuous, finely crafted, light-activated art.

At a certain point in 1970, Bell decided he no longer wanted to restrict himself to the small-scale, enclosed format of the cube, and he suddenly extended his glass pieces to a larger-than-human scale. He had passed a self-confessed crisis period in his work and successfully invented an environmental art without sacrificing the formal classicism so essential to his aesthetic. The Museum's sculpture is an example of the original, two-sided version of the works in this scale. Bell has said, "In the best (cubes), color was emanating from the corners. I didn't need the cube structure any more: I just needed a corner."

In some pieces of this series the glass panels number eight or more, arranged in zigzagging or mazelike configurations to enable the spectator to be virtually surrounded by half-reflective, shifting glass surfaces. The relative containment and simplicity of the prototypical two-sided work, however, gives it the character of a sort of monolithic emblem of Bell's oeuvre and it is thus a key example of recent Los Angeles art.

139

Richard Diebenkorn
American, b. 1922
Ocean Park Series #49, 1972
Oil on canvas
93 x 81 in. (236.2 x 205.7 cm.)
Signed and dated bottom right: RD 72
Museum Purchase, 1973
M.73.96

Collection: Marlborough Galleries, New York

Exhibitions: San Francisco Museum of Art, *Richard Diebenkorn: Paintings from the Ocean Park Series,* Oct. 14, 1972-Jan. 14, 1973, no. 14, repr. in color in cat.; London, Marlborough Fine Art, *Diebenkorn,* Dec. 4, 1973-Jan. 12, 1974, and Zurich, Marlborough Gallery, Feb. 21-Mar. 23, 1974

Richard Diebenkorn rose to importance during the late 1940s and early 1950s while closely associated with the group of younger San Francisco Abstract Expressionists, among whom were David Park, Elmer Bischoff, Hassel Smith, Frank Lobdell, and Edward Corbett. Though Diebenkorn painted exclusively in an abstract manner in those years, he has said that temperamentally he had "always been a landscape painter."

Diebenkorn's admitted affinity for representing what he sees found expression in the post-1955 decade in his well-known figurative cycle, and contributed to establishing the so-called Bay Area Figurative Style. The subject matter of these paintings is generally intimate and natural in spirit. Whether depicting a figure in a room, a fragment of an interior environment, or a landscape view, the works have a Cézannesque sense of control and structure combined with relatively broad brushwork.

Diebenkorn continued working figuratively until he moved to Los Angeles in 1967 and embarked upon the abstract *Ocean Park Series,* represented here by *#49* from 1972. The title of this series, as in his earlier cycles—*Albuquerque, Urbana,* and *Berkeley*—refers to the locale where the works were painted: the Ocean Park section of Santa Monica. The precise quality of light in any given working location has always been extremely important to Diebenkorn, and he finds its character here uniquely interesting, distinguishable even from nearby coastal locations.

The Ocean Park paintings may be said to represent a culminative point in Diebenkorn's career. They represent not only a return to abstract painting but an unprecedented overall strength of composition and masterful subtlety of color. These works deal with the central problems of painting itself: those of spatiality and of the relationships between color; lateral, flat, and illusionistic space; and depth. Diebenkorn has sought in this series to capture what he calls "the complete visual impression." He has allowed himself "to follow the painting in terms of just what I want for the painting, as opposed to the qualifying I found I had to do in figurative painting."

Ellsworth Kelly
American, b. 1923
Blue Curve III, 1972
Oil on canvas
67¾ x 166½ in. (172.1 x 422.9 cm.)
Museum Purchase, 1973
M.73.76

Exhibition: New York, Leo Castelli Gallery,
Oct. 29, 1973-Feb. 6, 1974

The "tradition" of purified geometric abstraction in the
twentieth century is multipart. In Europe the Russian
Constructivist, Dutch De Stijl, and German Bauhaus schools
are related but quite distinct; in America a handful of
artists, each continuing in a particular way the spirit of
these originating movements, has vastly extended their
possibilities. Among the foremost of those artists are
Tony Smith, Josef Albers, and Ellsworth Kelly.

Kelly is of the generation immediately succeeding the
Abstract Expressionists and thus working under close
critical scrutiny in the wake of that rare efflorescence of
artistic genius. He has managed to remain somewhat
separate from any group or stylistic issue. His work has been
divided among several media—painting, sculpture,
drawing, and prints; and he has followed a rigorous,
privately determined course in refining his approach to
simple color relationships and reductive form. Kelly
tends to be a systematic, intellectually methodical artist who
nevertheless has managed to retain a strongly lyrical
quality in nearly all his work. The paintings have tended
to alternate in series between straight-edged and curvilinear forms. *Blue Curve* is a prime example of Kelly's 1971-
1972 series in which he achieves a heroically expansive,
sweeping conception of the arc form. It refers beyond itself.
The basis of this use of curvature is the circle; the various
permutations of the segment of a circle within straight-
edged formats suggest a kind of universal idea of circularity
itself. It seems to refer to the earth's horizon; the psychology
of seeing the curve of the earth in the ocean's edge only
when one knows intellectually that the earth is round is
analogous to the kind of perceptual tension created in this
phase of Kelly's work between straight and arced lines.
The restriction of the paintings in this series to two colors,
or to black with white, facilitates an exploration of color
in its vast range of expressive potential. For example,
Blue Curve's counterpart, *Red Curve* (in Amsterdam's
Stedelijk Museum), though identical in form, has a
radically different presence.

Major Benefactors   Major Donors

Founding Benefactors

*Donors to
Building Fund*

Howard Ahmanson
The Allen-Heath Memorial
    Foundation
Anonymous
Anna Bing Arnold
Art Museum Council
Allan C. and Janet J. Balch Fund
Mr. and Mrs. David E. Bright
Costume Council
Mr. and Mrs. Theodore E. Cummings
The Fashion Group, Inc.
Mr. and Mrs. Leonard K. Firestone
Dr. and Mrs. Armand Hammer
Mr. and Mrs. H. Leslie Hoffman
Mr. and Mrs. Bob Hope
The James Irvine Foundation
Mrs. Frederick C. Kingston
Samuel H. Kress Foundation
The Los Angeles Clearing House
    Association
Mr. and Mrs. Bart Lytton
Members—Los Angeles County
    Museum of Art
Mr. and Mrs. Samuel Barlow Mosher
Dr. and Mrs. Seeley Greenleaf Mudd
Mr. and Mrs. Edwin W. Pauley
Lucille Ellis Simon
Norton Simon
Caryll M. and Norman F. Sprague
    Foundation
Harry G. Steele Foundation
The Mark Taper Foundation

The Adolph's Foundation
Aerojet-General Corporation
The Honorable and Mrs.
    Walter H. Annenberg
Mr. and Mrs. Roy L. Ash
Atlantic Richfield Company
Mr. and Mrs. Charles H. Babcock
Mr. and Mrs. Sydney R. Barlow
Mr. and Mrs. Leigh McMaster Battson
Welton Becket
Dr. and Mrs. Arnold O. Beckman
Mr. and Mrs. Phil Berg
Mr. and Mrs. Jules Berman
Beverly Hills Federal
    Savings & Loan Association
Mrs. Fred Hathaway Bixby,
    in memoriam
Fred Hathaway Bixby
Mr. and Mrs. Alfred Bloomingdale
The J. R. Bolker Foundation
Mrs. Glenn Winnett Boocock
Mr. and Mrs. Robert Alston Brant
Mr. and Mrs. Sidney F. Brody
Mr. and Mrs. Harold C. Brooks
Mr. and Mrs. Ernest A. Bryant
Mrs. Otis Buckingham
Bullock's, Inc.
Mr. and Mrs. Shirley Carter Burden
CBS Foundation Inc.
California Federal Savings and Loan
    Association
Mr. and Mrs. Asa V. Call
Mrs. Walter W. Candy, Jr.
Carnation Company
Mrs. Barbara Sesnon Cartan
Mr. and Mrs. Edward William Carter
Carter Hawley Hale Stores, Inc.
Mr. and Mrs. Victor M. Carter
Chandis Securities Company
Mr. and Mrs. Ralph J. Chandler
Coldwell, Banker & Company
Mr. and Mrs. Peter Colefax
Community Bank
Michael J. Connell Foundation
Mr. and Mrs. John Brown Cook
Mr. and Mrs. Warren H. Crowell
Dart Industries Inc.
Mr. and Mrs. Justin Dart
Mr. and Mrs. M. Philip Davis
Mr. and Mrs. W. Thomas Davis
Del Amo Foundation
Mr. and Mrs. Armand S. Deutsch
The Elsie de Wolfe Foundation, Inc.
Disney Foundation
Judge and Mrs. Emmett E. Doherty
Douglas Aircraft Co., Inc.
Mr. and Mrs. Charles E. Ducommun
Mrs. Emil Constant Ducommun

Mr. and Mrs. Wesley I. Dumm
Mr. and Mrs. James McAlister Duque
John and Rella Factor Foundation
Mr. and Mrs. Louis Factor
Max Factor Memorial Fund
Finkelstein Foundation
The Fluor Foundation
Mrs. Edward Carnarvon Flynn
Mr. and Mrs. Edward T. Foley
Mr. and Mrs. Theodore A. Fouch
Mr. and Mrs. Patrick J. Frawley
Mr. and Mrs. Louis J. Galen
Mr. and Mrs. John Jewett Garland
The Garrett Corporation
Mr. and Mrs. William Goetz
Mr. and Mrs. Samuel Goldwyn
Mr. and Mrs. Benjamin Graham
Mrs. Dolly Green
Mr. and Mrs. Courtlandt S. Gross
Mr. and Mrs. Robert Ellsworth Gross
Alfred and Viola Hart Foundation
Harvey Foundation
The John Randolph Haynes and
    Dora Haynes Foundation
Mrs. Joseph H. Hazen
William Randolph Hearst Foundation
Mr. and Mrs. Edward Hellman Heller
Mrs. Eugene Hill-Smith
Mrs. Henry Linn Hilty
Mr. and Mrs. Alfred Hitchcock
Hollywood Turf Club
Mr. and Mrs. Herbert Hoover, Jr.
Mrs. Katharine Bixby Hotchkis
Hughes Aircraft Company
The Isaacs Brothers Foundation
Mrs. Elizabeth Bixby Janeway
Mr. and Mrs. Charles Dudley Jennison
Mr. and Mrs. Earle M. Jorgensen
Helen and Felix Juda Foundation
Mr. and Mrs. Willard W. Keith
Mr. and Mrs. Burt Kleiner
Mr. and Mrs. Th. R. Knudsen
Mr. and Mrs. Joseph B. Koepfli
Mr. and Mrs. William Powell Lear, Sr.
Mr. and Mrs. Mervyn LeRoy
Mr. and Mrs. Sol Lesser
Mr. and Mrs. Eric Lidow
Foundation of the Litton Industries
The Ralph B. Lloyd Foundation
Lockheed Aircraft Corporation
Mr. and Mrs. David L. Loew
Los Angeles Herald-Examiner
Mr. and Mrs. Charles Luckman
I. Magnin & Co.
Mrs. Robert Mandel

Donors

The May Department Stores Company
& Mr. and Mrs. Tom May
Mr. and Mrs. John A. McCone
Mr. and Mrs. Shepard Mitchell
Mr. and Mrs. Henry T. Mudd
National Broadcasting Company, Inc.
Dr. and Mrs. Norman Nixon
Andrew Norman Foundation
Mr. and Mrs. Kenneth T. Norris
North American Aviation, Inc.
Northrop Corporation
Occidental Life Insurance Company
of California
Jerome K. Ohrbach
Helen Cannon Ovard
Pacific Mutual Life Insurance Company
The Pacific Telephone and
Telegraph Company
Mr. and Mrs. William L. Pereira
Dr. and Mrs. George Piness
The Spiros G. Ponty Foundation
J. W. Robinson Company
The Roman Catholic Archbishop
of Los Angeles
Mr. and Mrs. Albert Billings Ruddock
The Grace and Henry Salvatori
Foundation
Santa Anita Foundation
Mr. and Mrs. Taft B. Schreiber
Sears, Roebuck & Co.
Mr. and Mrs. Frank Roger Seaver
Porter Sesnon
William Thomas Sesnon, Jr.
Mrs. Evelyn Sharp
Charles P. Skouras Foundation
Lon V. Smith Foundation
Southern California Edison Company
Southern California & Southern
Counties Gas Companies
Standard Oil Company of California
Mr. and Mrs. Elmer Victor Staude
John and Beverly Stauffer Foundation
Dr. and Mrs. Jules Stein
The J. D. Sterling Family Foundation
Mr. and Mrs. James Stewart
Medford W. Stone
Mr. and Mrs. Leonard H. Straus
Mr. and Mrs. Elbridge H. Stuart
Mrs. Reese Hale Taylor
Mr. and Mrs. Charles B. Thornton
The Times Mirror Company
Title Insurance and Trust Company
Foundation
Mr. and Mrs. Holmes Tuttle
Union Oil Company of California
United States Borax & Chemical
Corporation

Mr. and Mrs. Edward Robinson
Valentine
Mrs. William L. Valentine
Mrs. Etta Van Cleef
Mr. and Mrs. Harry J. Volk
Hal Wallis Foundation
Ann B. and Jack L. Warner Foundation
Del E. Webb Corporation
Mr. and Mrs. Frederick R. Weisman
P. G. Winnett
Mladin and Nina Bogdanovich
Zarubica

A & S Air Conditioning
Acme Hardware Co., Inc.
Mr. and Mrs. Edgardo Acosta
The Alcoa Foundation
Alpha Phi Benefit Fund
American Institute of Interior
Designers, So. Calif. Chapter
Anheuser-Busch Charitable Trust Fund
Edw. Apffel Company
Betty M. Asher
Mrs. Russ Avery
Mr. and Mrs. Guilford C. Babcock III
Mrs. Franklin Baldwin
Mr. and Mrs. Hancock Banning, Jr.
Mr. and Mrs. Samuel W. Banowit
Mr. and Mrs. Ingle Barr
Mr. and Mrs. Fred Bartman, Jr.
Dr. and Mrs. Richard Thomas Barton
The Louis D. Beaumont Foundation
Mr. and Mrs. Alphonzo E. Bell, Jr.
Mr. and Mrs. B. E. Bensinger III
The Stanley and Rosabelle Bergerman
Foundation
Mr. and Mrs. Sam Berkman
Sam and Rie Bloomfield Foundation,
Inc.
Mrs. Harriet Blumenthal
The Boyar Foundation
Mr. and Mrs. Philip L. Boyd
G. A. Brakeley & Co. Inc.
Mr. and Mrs. Robert Brandt
Mrs. Thomas J. Brant
Mr. and Mrs. Thomas J. Brant, Jr.
Mr. and Mrs. Walter J. Braunschweiger
Mr. and Mrs. Lester Braunstein
Mr. and Mrs. Walter H. Brewer
The Briskin Foundation
Mrs. Willard Everett Brown
Mr. and Mrs. Willet H. Brown
Georgia Bullock, Inc.
Mrs. J. F. Burkhard
Mr. and Mrs. Homer H. Burnaby
The California Institute of the Arts
Mr. and Mrs. Peter W. Candy
Walter W. Candy, Jr.
Mr. and Mrs. William E. Candy
James H. Cannon Foundation
Mr. and Mrs. William M. Carpenter
Century City
Mr. and Mrs. Otis Chandler
Judge and Mrs. Thurmond Clarke
Mr. and Mrs. William Clayton
Conejo Fund
Mr. and Mrs. John Connell
Continental Air Lines Foundation
Mrs. Glenn Cooper
W. E. Cooper Lumber Company
Dr. and Mrs. Eliot Corday

The Cowles Charitable Trust
Mr. and Mrs. Clarence H. Crawford
Crescent Wharf & Warehouse Company
Mrs. Edward C. Crossett
Olivia De Jane
The Deutsch Foundation
Mr. and Mrs. Kirk Douglas
Mr. and Mrs. Henry Dreyfuss
Mr. and Mrs. Ernest E. Duque
Dwan Gallery
Mr. and Mrs. Ralph Edwards
Mr. and Mrs. Henry Owen Eversole, Jr.
Mr. and Mrs. Majl Ewing
Mr. and Mrs. Albert J. Eyraud, Jr.
Ferus Gallery
Fidelity Bank
Mr. and Mrs. Oliver C. Field
M. Flax, Inc.
Mr. and Mrs. Stanley Freeman
Mr. and Mrs. Thomas A. Freiberg
Dr. and Mrs. Digby Gallas
Gang, Tyre, Rudin & Brown
Charitable Foundation
Mr. and Mrs. Julian Ganz, Jr.
Mr. and Mrs. Freeman Gates
Mr. and Mrs. James M. Gerstley
Mr. and Mrs. Richard Gold
Mr. and Mrs. Marvin I. Golden
Mr. and Mrs. Nat C. Goldstone
Mr. and Mrs. Orville J. Golub
Mr. and Mrs. U. S. Grant IV
Mrs. Margery F. Green
Mr. and Mrs. Tyler G. Gregory
The Francis D. and Irene D. Griffin
Foundation
Mr. and Mrs. Z. Wayne Griffin
Mr. and Mrs. John Stevenson Griffith
Mr. and Mrs. Harry L. Guss
Mr. and Mrs. Mortimer W. Hall
Nathan Hamburger
Mr. and Mrs. Arthur Hanisch
Mrs. Roy P. Harper
Mr. and Mrs. Ed N. Harrison
Mr. and Mrs. Charles Haubiel
Mr. and Mrs. David W. Hearst
Mr. and Mrs. Randolph A. Hearst
Harold M. and
Elizabeth L. Hecht Foundation
Mr. and Mrs. Richard J. Henry
Mrs. Cornelia K. Hepburn
Mr. and Mrs. Carlos E. Herman
Mr. and Mrs. Edmond E. Herrscher
Mr. and Mrs. Melvin J. Hirsh
Dr. and Mrs. Vaino A. Hoover
Mr. and Mrs. John F. Huber
Interstate Restaurant Supply Co.

Mr. and Mrs. George D. Jagels
Jeffries Banknote Company
Mrs. Luther Herman Johnson
Mr. and Mrs. Thomas Victor Jones
Mrs. Luella L. Kasch
Mr. and Mrs. Ira Kaufman
Danny Kaye and Sylvia Fine Kaye
Mrs. Howard B. Keck
Kemper Insurance
Dr. and Mrs. George C. Kennedy
Vice Admiral and Mrs.
    Howard Fithian Kingman
Kotzin Fund
Edward Lee Kozberg and Sons
Mr. and Mrs. Harry Kunin
Mr. and Mrs. Burt Lancaster
The Lantin Foundation
Albert and Mary Lasker Foundation Inc.
Edward and Cynthia Lasker Foundation
Mr. and Mrs. Rowland Vance Lee
Mr. and Mrs. Hoyt B. Leisure
Hoyt M. and Rose B. Leisure
Mr. and Mrs. Albert Levinson
Mr. and Mrs. Frederick Levy, Jr.
Mr. and Mrs. Richard Lewis
Mr. and Mrs. Rudolph Liebig
Mr. and Mrs. Adolph Loewi
Mr. and Mrs. E. Phillip Lyon
M & D Store Fixtures, Inc.
Mr. and Mrs. John R. Mage
B. N. Maltz Foundation
Albert C. Martin and Associates
Mr. and Mrs. Murray Marvin
Mr. and Mrs. Charles O. Matcham
Mr. and Mrs. James H. McCarthy
Edward Meltzer Foundation
Mr. and Mrs. Leo Meyer
The Richard W. and
    Catherine A. Millar Foundation
Minneapolis-Honeywell Regulator Co.
Mirisch Family Foundation
Edward Mittelman Memorial
    Foundation
Modern Bakeries, Inc.
Mr. and Mrs. J. Bell Moran
The Moseley Foundation
Henry T. Mudd, Jr.
John W. Mudd
Dr. and Mrs. Franklin D. Murphy
Mrs. Roy Edgar Naftzger
Mr. and Mrs. Frank Nathan
Mr. and Mrs. Frederick M. Nicholas
O'Melveny & Myers
Mr. and Mrs. Walter Oppenheimer
Oscar of Beverly Hills

Mr. and Mrs. Joseph Osherenko
Mr. and Mrs. James R. Page
Mr. and Mrs. Norman K. Panama
Mrs. Frances M. Parkford
Mr. and Mrs. William James Pattison
C. L. Peck, Jr.
Mr. and Mrs. Gifford Phillips
Mr. and Mrs. James E. Pollak
Dr. and Mrs. A. Borden Polson
Price Waterhouse & Co.
Mr. and Mrs. Vincent Price
Mrs. Anna T. Pryor
Mr. and Mrs. John Rex
Dr. and Mrs. Elmer C. Rigby
Mrs. Harry W. Robinson
Mr. and Mrs. Henry C. Rogers
Mr. and Mrs. Howard H. Rolapp
N. Joseph Ross and
    Jeanette S. Ross Foundation
Mrs. H. Palmer Sabin
Mr. and Mrs. Carl E. Sager
Mrs. Richard Jewett Schweppe
Mr. and Mrs. Milton Segalove
Selectile Company, Inc.
Mrs. Jacqueline Keesling Sesnon
Mr. and Mrs. Kenneth Bell Sharpe
Mr. and Mrs. Richard E. Sherwood
Mr. and Mrs. Robert Shlaudeman
Mr. and Mrs. Charles C. Shoemaker
The Harold E. Shugart Company, Inc.
Mrs. Sherman N. Shumway
Mr. and Mrs. Ben L. Silberstein
Mr. and Mrs. Donald E. Simon
Mr. and Mrs. A. Maxson Smith
Dr. and Mrs. Gordon Knight Smith
Milton Sperling
Mr. and Mrs. Leonard M. Sperry
William R. Staats & Co. Foundation
The Stans Foundation
Dr. Carey Stanton
Mr. and Mrs. Ray Stark
State Plumbing & Heating Co.
Dr. and Mrs. Charles S. Stein, Jr.
Steiner American Corporation
Mrs. Jane Lawler Stern
Mrs. Raymond H. Storm
Sunset International Petroleum Corp.
The Swope Gift Corporation
Mrs. R. Paul Thoman
Time Incorporated
Tissue Foundation
Mr. and Mrs. Maynard J. Toll
Mr. and Mrs. Herbert Towne
Transcon Lines
Mrs. John Treanor
Mr. and Mrs. John Cummings Tyler
United States Steel Foundation, Inc.
Dr. and Mrs. A. James Vance

Mr. and Mrs. Frank Viault, Sr.
Mr. and Mrs. James Vigeveno
Dr. Rufus B. von KleinSmid
Von's Foundation
Mr. and Mrs. Pope Wager
Mr. and Mrs. Irving Miller Walker
Mr. and Mrs. Stuart E. Weaver, Jr.
Dr. and Mrs. Herman Weiner
The Weisman Foundation
Mrs. Marshall J. Wellborn
Mr. and Mrs. John K. West
Whittier Foundation
Mr. and Mrs. Billy Wilder
Mrs. John Cree Wilson, Sr.
William A. Wilson
Miss Marguerite Winston
Women's Architectural League
Mr. and Mrs. Arthur M. Wood
Mr. and Mrs. Robert J. Woods, Jr.
Mr. and Mrs. Frank S. Wyle
Paul Ziffren

Acquisitions Benefactors

Donors of Works of Art or
Acquisitions Funds
as of November 1, 1974

Major Benefactors

Adolph's Food Products
The Ahmanson Foundation
H. F. Ahmanson & Company
Anna Bing Arnold
Mr. and Mrs. R. Stanton Avery
Art Museum Council
Mr. and Mrs. Leigh M. Battson
Mr. and Mrs. Phil Berg
Mr. and Mrs. David E. Bright
Mr. and Mrs. Sidney F. Brody
B. G. Cantor Art Foundation
B. Gerald Cantor
Leona Cantor
The Cantor, Fitzgerald Group, Ltd.
Michael J. Connell Foundation
Contemporary Art Council
George Cukor
Mr. and Mrs. Theodore E. Cummings
Jane and Justin Dart
Charles E. and Palmer G. Ducommun
Mr. and Mrs. Leonard K. Firestone
Graphic Arts Council
Robert E. and Mary B. P. Gross
   Foundation
Frances and Armand Hammer
Nasli and Alice Heeramaneck
Christian Humann
Mr. and Mrs. Arnold S. Kirkeby
Samuel H. Kress Foundation
Mr. and Mrs. William P. Lear
Mr. and Mrs. Harry Lenart
Adele R. Levy Fund and
   Mr. and Mrs. Armand S. Deutsch
Mr. and Mrs. Eric Lidow
Bequest of David L. Loew, in memory
   of his father, Marcus Loew
Paul E. Manheim
Andrew Norman Foundation
Mr. and Mrs. Jerome K. Ohrbach
Joan Palevsky
Mr. and Mrs. Taft B. Schreiber
Times Mirror Foundation
Mr. and Mrs. Hal B. Wallis

Major Donors

The Honorable and Mrs. Walter H.
   Annenberg
Atlantic Richfield Foundation
Mr. and Mrs. Herbert Baker
Mr. and Mrs. Fred A. Bartman, Jr.
The Louis D. Beaumont Foundation
Mr. and Mrs. Michael Blankfort
Mr. and Mrs. Charles Boyer
The Eli and Edythe L. Broad Foundation
Mr. Shirley Carter Burden
Mr. and Mrs. Edward W. Carter
Costume Council
Mr. and Mrs. Robert Engel
Bequest of Charles K. Feldman
Sam Francis
Mrs. Isaac S. Fuller
S. Louis Gaines
Jo Ann and Julian Ganz, Jr.
Mr. and Mrs. John Jewett Garland
Mr. and Mrs. David Gensburg
Phil Gersh Agency, Inc.
Cary Grant
Mr. and Mrs. Felix Guggenheim
Mrs. Lita A. Hazen
Katharine Bixby Hotchkis
Carl Holmes
Isaacs Brothers Company
Elizabeth Bixby Janeway
Bequest of A. T. Jergins
Jasper Johns
Helen and Felix Juda
Mrs. Frederick C. Kingston
The Kleiner Foundation
Mr. and Mrs. J. J. Klejman
Mr. and Mrs. Joseph B. Koepfli
Estate of Miss Loula D. Lasker
Marci Foundation, Inc.
Mrs. Roy C. Markus
The Charles E. Merrill Trust
Mr. and Mrs. Reese Llewellyn Milner
Mr. and Mrs. Kenneth T. Norris
Helen Cannon Ovard
Mr. and Mrs. Will Richeson, Jr.
Paul Rosenberg and Company
Lucille Ellis Simon
Norton Simon
Mrs. Camilla C. Spear
Gerald Stockton
Mr. and Mrs. Paul W. Trousdale
Harold P. and Jane F. Ullman
I. N. and Susanna H. Van Nuys
   Foundation
Paul Walter
Andy Warhol
Mr. and Mrs. Frederick R. Weisman
Doris and Ed Wiener
Mr. and Mrs. Paul Ziffren
Jack Zimmerman

Donors

Mr. and Mrs. Abe Adler
Mrs. Howard Ahmanson
The Allen-Heath Memorial Foundation
Dr. and Mrs. Nathan Alpers
The American Academy of Arts and
   Letters, Childe Hassam Fund
American Art Council
Mr. and Mrs. Luther C. Anderson
Thomas A. Anderson
Mrs. Edit Angold
Betty M. Asher
Avery Products Corporation
Mrs. Charles H. Babcock
Dr. Robert E. Barela
Estate of Rosemary B. Baruch
Dr. and Mrs. Grant Beckstrand
Karl Benjamin
Mrs. James E. Bentley
Edgar Bergen
J. R. Berland Foundation
Herbert A. Bernhard
John C. Best
George Bilson
Edwin Binney, 3rd
Richard Blackwell
Mr. and Mrs. Henry Blanke
Dr. and Mrs. Ralph Bookman
Mr. and Mrs. Robert L. Boorstin
Mr. and Mrs. Murray Braunfeld
Mrs. Margaret Martin Brock
Mr. and Mrs. Stuart Buchalter
Buchalter, Nemer, Fields & Savitch
   Charitable Foundation
Bullock's Downtown
Mrs. Evelyn Burger
Mr. and Mrs. Philip Burton
Dr. and Mrs. Donavan W. Byer
Matilda Calnan
The Leo Castelli Gallery
Father E. M. Catich
Florence and Maurice Chez
Mrs. William Clayton
Mrs. William Coberly, Jr.
Harold Cohen
Richard Cohn
Herbert R. Cole
Jack Cole
Noma Copley
Charles Cowles
John V. and Thomas H. Crawford
Mr. and Mrs. Thomas H. Crawford
Mrs. John H. Cushingham
Dart Industries Inc.
Mrs. S. Prince Davis
Dr. Jean Delacour
Mr. and Mrs. Ross R. DeVean

Robert S. Dickerman
Mr. and Mrs. John E. Dodds
Edward Dominik
Bequest of Muriel P. Donaldson
Mr. and Mrs. Harvey S. Dye
Dr. Harvey Eagleson
Mrs. Nelson Eddy
Dr. and Mrs. Maximilian Edel
Bequest of Cora Eshman
Claire Falkenstein
Far Eastern Art Council
The Fashion Group, Inc.
Mr. and Mrs. Barney Feldman
Major General and Mrs. Robert G.
   Fergusson
Roy Ferren
Ferus Gallery
Herbert Fink
Fischbach Gallery
Harvey L. Flax
William E. Forbes
John Ford
Robert F. Ford Charitable Foundation
Mr. and Mrs. Carl Foreman
Fortuny, Inc.
Mr. and Mrs. John Frankenheimer
Anisia Collas Fruto Fund
Mrs. Howard Fulton
James Galanos
Mrs. Digby Gallas
Miss Gloria Gartz
Mr. and Mrs. Freeman Gates
Gemini, Ltd.
Mr. and Mrs. Philip Gersh
Dr. and Mrs. Joseph Goldyne
Dr. and Mrs. Sanders Goodman
Mr. and Mrs. David Gordon
Mrs. Margery F. Green
Mr. and Mrs. Tyler Gregory
Mrs. John Stevenson Griffith
William Gropper
Mr. and Mrs. Allen Guiberson
Michael Hall, in memory of
   Dr. William R. Valentiner
Hammer Galleries, Inc.
Mrs. Dalzell Hatfield
Dalzell Hatfield Galleries
William Randolph Hearst Foundation
Calvin Helgoe
Frank Heller
Sari Heller Gallery, Ltd.
Friends of Leonard B. Hirsch, Jr.
Mrs. Dorothy H. Hoover
Drs. Aldona and Jorge Hoyos
Mr. and Mrs. Charles G. Huntington
Mr. and Mrs. Thomas E. Inch

Independent Press-Telegram
William Inge
Kango Izumi
Jaffe Agency, Inc.
Edwin Janss, Jr.
Jean-Louis
Mr. and Mrs. Robert E. Jones
Kaiser Steel Corporation
Mrs. Howard B. Keck
Dr. and Mrs. Morton Klein
M. Knoedler & Co., Inc.
Th. R. and Valley M. Knudsen
   Foundation
Dr. and Mrs. Gerald W. Labiner
Elsa Lanchester
Jennings Lang
The Lear Siegler Foundation
Mrs. Rowland V. Lee
Raymond and Ruth Lee Foundation
Dr. Rosemary Lenel
Bequest of Sarah H. LeValley
Mr. and Mrs. Michael C. Levee, Jr.
Mr. and Mrs. Henry Levin
Robert Q. Lewis
Mrs. Rudolph Liebig
Mr. and Mrs. Milton W. Lipper
D. P. Litwin Company
George Longstreet
Jack and Marie Lord
Mr. and Mrs. William S. Lund
Conrad Marca-Relli
Dr. Toni Marcy, in memory of
   Sigbert H. Marcy
Dr. and Mrs. Judd Marmor
Mr. and Mrs. Charles O. Matcham
Mr. and Mrs. John A. McCone
James A. McMahan
McMahan's Furniture Stores
Joseph T. Mendelson
Max Mendelson
Bequest of Beatrice Miestchaninoff
Mr. and Mrs. Ronald W. Miller
Mr. and Mrs. Vincent Miller
Colonel John A. Morgan
Henry T. Mudd
Seeley W. Mudd Foundation
Bequest of Mrs. Lluella M. Murphey
Dan Murphy Foundation
Edward M. Nagel
Netherlands Information Service
Bequest of Norman Norell
Michael Novarese
David Orgell

Dr. and Mrs. Pratapaditya Pal
His Excellency Park Chung Hee
Park View Antique Shop
Frank Perls
Mr. and Mrs. James B. Pick
Mary and Vincent Price
Mrs. Robert L. Pruyn
Mrs. Edith L. Rehnborg
Dale Reis
Mr. and Mrs. Hans A. Ries
Esther and Robert Robles
Anton G. Roland
Mr. and Mrs. Albert Billings Ruddock
Bequest of Helen Crocker Russell
Mrs. Henry Salvatori
Mr. and Mrs. Oscar Salzer
Mr. and Mrs. J. M. Schaaf
Kurt and Werner Scharff
Bequest of Alice F. Schott
M. R. Schweitzer
Daniel Selznick
William T. Sesnon, Jr.
Mr. and Mrs. Arthur Shapiro
Mr. and Mrs. Richard A. Shepherd
Mr. and Mrs. Ira L. Sherman
Mr. and Mrs. Richard E. Sherwood
Shickman Gallery
Chang Shing-t'ze
Mr. and Mrs. Clifford Silsby
Mr. and Mrs. Harold Sonners
Robert L. Spencer
Rose A. Sperry 1972 Revocable Trust
Mrs. Vicci Sperry
Caryll M. and Norman F. Sprague
   Foundation
Dr. and Mrs. Philip E. Stahl
Mr. and Mrs. Ray Stark
Stars for Freedom
Bequest of Guy Robertson Stewart
Mrs. Walter E. Stewart
Mrs. James B. Stoddard
Mr. and Mrs. Irving Stone
Thoss Taylor
Mrs. Florence Lewis Theil
Wallace Thompson
The Times Mirror Company
Universal City Studios, Inc.
Mr. and Mrs. Byron E. Vandegrift
Robert Van Santen
Hyatt Robert von Dehn
Mr. and Mrs. Kurt Wagner
William Walker
Raj Kumar and Kuwarani Wankaner
Dr. George J. Wayne
Mr. and Mrs. Stuart E. Weaver, Jr.
Bequest of Clifton Webb

Benjamin Weiss
David Weisz
Mrs. Marshall J. Wellborn
Keith Wellin
Mrs. Mary P. Wells
Mr. and Mrs. Donald Winston
Howard Wise
Mr. and Mrs. William D. Witherspoon
Diana Zlotnick

Bonnard and His Environment (c)
March 31-May 30, 1965
Museum of Modern Art with the
Los Angeles County Museum of Art
and the Art Institute of Chicago

Drawings by Agostino Mitelli (c)
March 31-May 30, 1965
Los Angeles County Museum of Art

Peter Voulkos (c)
April 14-June 20, 1965
Los Angeles County Museum of Art

New York School:
The First Generation (c)
June 16-August 1, 1965
Los Angeles County Museum of Art

R. B. Kitaj (c)
August 11-September 12, 1965
Los Angeles County Museum of Art

7000 Years of Iranian Art
August 20-September 26, 1965
Smithsonian Institution

Art Treasures from Japan (c)
October 2-November 7, 1965
Los Angeles County Museum of Art
with the Detroit Institute of Arts,
Philadelphia Museum of Art, and
the Royal Ontario Museum, Toronto

Sketches by Constable
October 13-November 14, 1965
Smithsonian Institution

David Smith:
A Memorial Exhibition (c)
November 3, 1965-January 30, 1966
Los Angeles County Museum of Art

Five Younger Los Angeles Artists (c)
November 26-December 26, 1965
Los Angeles County Museum of Art

Knud Merrild (c)
November 26-December 26, 1965
Los Angeles County Museum of Art

John Paul Jones (c)
November 26, 1965-January 9, 1966
Los Angeles County Museum of Art

Alberto Giacometti (c)
January 4-February 20,1966
Museum of Modern Art with the
Los Angeles County Museum of Art,
the Art Institute of Chicago, and
the San Francisco Museum of Art

Craftsmen, USA '66 (c)
February 9-March 13, 1966
Los Angeles County Museum of Art

Ancient Art from Afghanistan
March 25-May 15, 1966
The Asia Society, Inc., New York City

Velvets East and West: From the
14th to 20th Century (c)
March 29-May 22, 1966
Los Angeles County Museum of Art

Edward Kienholz (c)
March 30-May 15, 1966
Los Angeles County Museum of Art

Incised Letters, Designs and Calligraphy
by Father Edward M. Catich
May 24-July 24, 1966
Los Angeles County Museum of Art

American Paintings from
The Metropolitan Museum of Art (c)
June 3-July 31, 1966
The Metropolitan Museum of Art with
the Los Angeles County Museum of Art,
and the M. H. de Young
Memorial Museum

The Ceramic Work of Gertrud and
Otto Natzler (c)
June 15-August 14, 1966
Los Angeles County Museum of Art

Robert Irwin-Kenneth Price (c)
July 7-September 4, 1966
Los Angeles County Museum of Art

Art Treasures of Turkey
August 13-September 25, 1966
Smithsonian Institution

The Sterling Craft
September 28-November 9, 1966
The Worshipful Company of
Goldsmiths, London

Josef Albers: White Line Squares (c)
October 25, 1966-January 1, 1967
Los Angeles County Museum of Art

Picasso:
Sixty Years of Graphic Works (c)
October 25, 1966-January 1, 1967
Los Angeles County Museum of Art

Man Ray (c)
October 25, 1966-January 1, 1967
Los Angeles County Museum of Art

John Mason (c)
November 16, 1966-February 1, 1967
Los Angeles County Museum of Art

The Arts of India and Nepal: The Nasli
and Alice Heeramaneck Collection
February 8-April 2, 1967
Museum of Fine Arts, Boston

Morris Louis (c)
February 8-April 2, 1967
Museum of Fine Arts, Boston, with the
Los Angeles County Museum of Art
and the City Art Museum, St. Louis

Ten Italian Architects (c)
February 8-April 7, 1967
Los Angeles County Museum of Art

American Sculpture of the Sixties (c)
April 28-June 25, 1967
Los Angeles County Museum of Art

Festival Designs of Inigo Jones
June 16-August 27, 1967
International Exhibitions Foundation

Tuscan and Venetian Drawings of the
Quattrocento from the Collection of
Janos Scholz (c)
June 27-August 13, 1967
Los Angeles County Museum of Art
for the Committee to Rescue
Italian Art, Inc.

Fantastics and Eccentrics in
Chinese Painting
July 14-August 27, 1967
The Asia Society, Inc., New York City

Jackson Pollock
July 19-September 3, 1967
Museum of Modern Art

100 European Paintings and Drawings
from the Collection of
Mr. and Mrs. Leigh B. Block
September 21-November 12, 1967
National Gallery of Art with the
Los Angeles County Museum of Art

R. M. Schindler: Architect
September 29-November 19, 1967
The Art Gallery,
University of California, Santa Barbara

The David E. Bright Collection (c)
October 17-December 17, 1967
Los Angeles County Museum of Art

Homage to Rodin:
Collection of B. Gerald Cantor (c)
November 14, 1967-January 7, 1968
Los Angeles County Museum of Art

Rico Lebrun (c)
December 5, 1967-January 14, 1968
Los Angeles County Museum of Art

Aubrey Beardsley
December 12, 1967-February 4, 1968
Victoria and Albert Museum, London

Chaim Soutine (c)
February 20-April 14, 1968
Los Angeles County Museum of Art

Dorothea Lange
February 27-April 14, 1968
Museum of Modern Art

Eight American Masters
of Watercolor (c)
April 23-June 16, 1968
Los Angeles County Museum of Art

Master Bronzes from the
Classical World
May 10-June 30, 1968
Fogg Art Museum with the
Los Angeles County Museum of Art
and the City Art Museum, St. Louis

Dada, Surrealism and Their Heritage
July 16-September 8, 1968
Museum of Modern Art

Sculpture from the Collections of
Norton Simon, Inc., and the
Hunt Industries Museum of Art
August 20, 1968-continuing
Los Angeles County Museum of Art

Image and Imagination:
Oil Sketches of the Baroque,
Collection of Kurt Rossacher (c)
October 1-November 3, 1968
William Rockhill Nelson Gallery with
the Los Angeles County Museum of Art,
Toledo Museum of Art,
Rhode Island School of Design,
and the Minneapolis Institute of Arts

Sculpture of Black Africa:
The Tishman Collection (c)
October 16, 1968-January 5, 1969
Los Angeles County Museum of Art

Billy Al Bengston (c)
November 26, 1968-January 12, 1969
Los Angeles County Museum of Art

H. C. Westerman (c)
November 26, 1968-January 12, 1969
Los Angeles County Museum of Art

Edvard Munch: Lithographs,
Etchings, Woodcuts (c)
January 28-March 9, 1969
Los Angeles County Museum of Art

Mastercraftsmen of Ancient Peru
March 11-June 1, 1969
Guggenheim Museum

American Printmaking:
The First 150 Years
June 17-August 3, 1969
The Museum of Graphic Art,
New York City

Mies van der Rohe
July 22-September 7, 1969
Art Institute of Chicago

Willem de Kooning
July 29-September 14, 1969
Museum of Modern Art

Vincent van Gogh
October 15-December 7, 1969
Vincent van Gogh Foundation,
Amsterdam

The Middle Ages:
Treasures from The Cloisters and
The Metropolitan Museum of Art (c)
January 18-March 29, 1970
The Metropolitan Museum of Art with
the Los Angeles County Museum of Art

Old Master Drawings from Chatsworth
June 20-July 19, 1970
International Exhibitions Foundation

John Marin: 1870-1953 (c)
July 7-August 30, 1970
Los Angeles County Museum of Art

Sculpture of Ancient West Mexico:
The Proctor Stafford Collection (c)
July 7-August 30, 1970
Los Angeles County Museum of Art

The Art of India, Nepal and Tibet:
The Nasli and Alice Heeramaneck
Collection
September 24-November 15, 1970
Los Angeles County Museum of Art

The Cubist Epoch (c)
December 15, 1970-February 21, 1971
Los Angeles County Museum of Art
with The Metropolitan Museum of Art

Man Came This Way:
The Phil Berg Collection (c)
March 9-May 30, 1971
Los Angeles County Museum of Art

Art and Technology (c)
May 11-August 29, 1971
Los Angeles County Museum of Art

Géricault (c)
October 12-December 12, 1971
Los Angeles County Museum of Art

The Armand Hammer Collection (c)
December 21, 1971-February 27, 1972
Los Angeles County Museum of Art

Ancient Indonesian Art
December 22, 1971-February 13, 1972
Asia House Gallery, New York City

The American West (c)
March 21-May 28, 1972
Los Angeles County Museum of Art

The Navajo Blanket (c)
June 27-September 5, 1972
Los Angeles County Museum of Art

Kandinsky
October 3-November 19, 1972
Guggenheim Museum

Bruce Nauman (c)
December 21, 1972-February 18, 1973
Los Angeles County Museum of Art
with the Whitney Museum
of American Art

African Textiles and Decorative Arts
March 22-May 27, 1973
International Council
of the Museum of Modern Art

Ceramic Art of Japan
March 27-May 13, 1973
Seattle Art Museum

Impressionist and Post-Impressionist
Paintings from the USSR
June 15-July 8, 1973
The Soviet Government

Paul Strand
July 3-September 2, 1973
Philadelphia Museum of Art

Winslow Homer
July 17-August 19, 1973
Whitney Museum of American Art

Henry Moore in Southern California (c)
October 4-November 18, 1973
Los Angeles County Museum of Art

Islamic Art (c)
December 18, 1973-March 3, 1974
Los Angeles County Museum of Art

Age of the Pharaohs (c)
April 7-June 16, 1974
Los Angeles County Museum of Art

Gustave Moreau (c)
July 22-September 1, 1974
Los Angeles County Museum of Art

American Narrative Painting (c)
October 1-November 17, 1974
Los Angeles County Museum of Art

Max Bill
December 17, 1974-February 16, 1975
Albright-Knox Art Gallery
Buffalo, New York

A Decade of Acquisitions (c)
April 7-June 29, 1975
Los Angeles County Museum of Art

Special Installations

Los Caprichos by Goya
May 12-September 6, 1967

Adrian Retrospective
June 16-October 8, 1967

Modern Illustrated Books and
Other Prints from the Collection of
Mr. and Mrs. David Gensburg
October 3-December 31, 1967

Costumes from Camelot
October 16-December 3, 1967

A Remembrance of Mariano Fortuny,
1871-1949
December 12, 1967-February 4, 1968

Tamarind Collection, 1966-1967
March 3-June 30, 1968

The Bridal Tradition
March 26-June 30, 1968

The Foroughi Collection of Iranian Art
March 29, 1968-continuing

Wallace Berman
April 26-June 3, 1968

Burgoyne Diller
June 18-July 21, 1968

Children's Clothes from the del Valle,
Schott, and Felix Collections
July 9-August 11, 1968

John Sloan and George Bellows
August 13-October 27, 1968

Brocade: Woven Embellishment
August 27, 1968-February 9, 1969

Recent Prints and
Drawings Acquisitions
September 1, 1968-January 5, 1969

Stravinsky Rehearses Stravinsky:
Photographs by Laelia Goehr
September 6-November 10, 1968

Late Fifties at the Ferus
November 12-December 17, 1968

Eugene I. Holt Memorial Acquisition
January 21-March 9, 1969

Selections from
"Sculpture of Black Africa:
The Tishman Collection"
February 4, 1969-continuing

American Pastels and Watercolors:
Selections from the Mr. and Mrs.
William Preston Harrison Collection
February 4-March 16, 1969

Rembrandt Etchings
from Local Collections
February 18-May 4, 1969

Ballet Costumes from Les Ballets Russes
de Serge de Diaghilev
March 25-May 21, 1969

George Brecht: Sculpture
April 15-May 18, 1969

Jewelry of the Ancient World
May 20-July 13, 1969

New Paintings by Richard Diebenkorn
June 3-July 27, 1969

The Kate Steinitz Collection
August 3-September 21, 1969

The Smart Set—A Development of
Styles: 1910-1930
August 5-October 28, 1969

Summer Selections
from the Children's Workshop
August 5-August 31, 1969

Stephan Von Huene:
The Rosebud Annunciator
August 21-September 21, 1969

Modern Drawings from the
Mr. and Mrs. Edward Lewis Collection
September 2, 1969-January 4, 1970

Chosen Works of American Art,
1850-1924, from the Collection of
Jo Ann and Julian Ganz, Jr.
October 1-November 16, 1969

Recent Prints from Gemini
October 17, 1969-January 4, 1970

Fifty Tantric Mystical Diagrams
October 21-November 23, 1969

From the Bosporus to Samarkand:
Flat-Woven Rugs
November 11, 1969-January 18, 1970

Daumier and Contemporaries
February 3-May 31, 1970

Sam Francis: Recent Paintings
February 10-March 22, 1970

Japanese Textiles
of the Edo Period, 1615-1867
March 3-July 19, 1970

Dimension: An Exhibition of Sculpture
for the Sighted and the Blind
March 10-April 19, 1970

Chinese Paintings from the
Mr. and Mrs. Earl Morse Collection
April 24-May 31, 1970

Mondrian Drawings and the
Salon de Mme. B. à Dresden
July 14-August 30, 1970

Patterns in Fashion
August 4-October 25, 1970

Callot Prints
from a Los Angeles Collection
September 18, 1970-January 3, 1971

Contemporary Art Council
New Talent Award Winners, 1970
November 3-December 27, 1970

Huene and the Fashionable Image
November 24, 1970-February 28, 1971

Scott Grieger
January 12-February 16, 1971

Three Graphic Artists
January 26-March 17, 1971

Tapestry: Tradition and Technique
March 23-September 20, 1971

Marine Photographs by Edwin Janss, Jr.
March 30-September 12, 1971

Contemporary Works
from the Edwin Janss, Jr., Collection
March 30-September 12, 1971

Prints from the Permanent
and Norton Simon Collections
April 30-August 29, 1971

New Works by Los Angeles Artists
May 8-August 29, 1971

C. C. Wang, The Artist, The Collector
May 25-July 25, 1971

Balzac Studies by Rodin
August 1-December 31, 1971

The Art of Black Africa
August 17, 1971-continuing

Blue and White Porcelains
of the Far East
September 1-October 31, 1971

Chuck Close: Recent Work
September 21-November 14, 1971

Picassos in Southern California:
A Tribute to the Artist at 90
October 25-November 21, 1971

Ornamental Costumes of Ancient Peru
November 2, 1971-February 6, 1972

Pre-Hispanic Art of Mexico
December 1, 1971-continuing

The Art of Ancient Iran
December 1, 1971-continuing

Woodner Collection I:
Old Master Drawings Before 1700
December 17, 1971-February 13, 1972

Japanese Paintings of the Edo Period
January 2-January 23, 1972

Harold Cohen: Three Behaviors
for the Partitioning of Space
January 18-February 13, 1972

Los Angeles 1972:
A Panorama of Black Artists
February 8-March 19, 1972

Ceramics of Southeast Asia
February 15-April 30, 1972

Market Street Program
February 22-March 5, 1972

Perception: An Exhibition of Sculpture
for the Sighted and the Blind
February 22-April 2, 1972

Abstract Design in American Quilts
February 23-April 2, 1972

Dürer and His Circle
March 14-June 18, 1972

Two Books
April 11-May 28, 1972

Avigdor Arikha:
39 Ink Drawings, 1965-1972
April 25-September 3, 1972

Body Shells and Shadows
April 25-June 11, 1972

Twenty-four Indian Paintings
June 1, 1972-continuing

Japanese Prints from the Classic Period
June 6-July 2, 1972

Selections from
The Norton Simon Foundation and
The Norton Simon Inc. Museum
July 16, 1972-continuing

The Claude Lorrain Album
June 16-September 3, 1972

Japanese Prints of the 19th Century
July 18-August 13, 1972

Mark Tobey Prints: 1961-1972
July 18-August 27, 1972

Ten Designers of the 20th Century
July 18-October 8, 1972

Youth Expression '72 Winning Entries
August 15-August 27, 1972

Contemporary Japanese Prints
September 1-October 22, 1972

Four Los Angeles Women Artists
September 19-October 29, 1972

Goya and Picasso Confronted
October 31, 1972-continuing

Two Decades
of Art Museum Council Gifts
November 14, 1972-January 7, 1973

Block, Brush and Stencil
November 14, 1972-January 21, 1973

The Golden Age of
Japanese Screen Painting
November 21, 1972-March 4, 1973

Recent Indian Art Acquisitions
December 5, 1972-February 28, 1973

Ten Years of
Contemporary Art Council Acquisitions
December 19, 1972-March 4, 1973

Dimensional Prints
February 6-June 3, 1973

Anatomy in Fabric
February 21-April 15, 1973

Buddhist Art of Japan
April 17-June 17, 1973

California Water Color
Society Collection
May 1-May 27, 1973

Selections from the
Decorative Arts Permanent Collection
May 8-September 2, 1973

Indian Paintings from Staff Collections
May 15-July 1, 1973

William Wegman
May 22-July 1, 1973

Robert Bucknam: Views of the Earth
June 19-July 29, 1973

L.A. Flash
June 19-September 9, 1973

Funerary Art of China
July 24-November 18, 1973

New Loans from
The Norton Simon Foundation and
The Norton Simon Inc. Museum of Art
August 12, 1973-continuing

The Kleiner Gift of Contemporary Art
September 4-November 11, 1973

Paracas and Nazca Ancient Peruvian
Textiles and Ceramics
September 4, 1973-May 31, 1974

The Wells Collection
of English Porcelain
September 18-November 25, 1973

Mother and Child in African Art
September 18, 1973-August 10, 1974

George Luks Watercolors,
Paintings and Drawings
October 10-November 25, 1973

Selections from the Permanent
Collection of Prints and Drawings
October 10-November 25, 1973

Alexander Calder: Painted Planes
October 13-October 30, 1973

If the Crinoline Comes Back
October 16, 1973-January 6, 1974

Circuit: A Video Invitational
October 30-November 25, 1973

Far Eastern Cloisonné
November 6, 1973-February 24, 1974

Steve Reich and Musicians Drumming
November 6, 1973

Chinese Ceramics
from the Heeramaneck Collection
December 18, 1973-March 3, 1974

Old Master Drawings:
Woodner Collection II
December 21, 1973-February 17, 1974

From Within
January 8-February 10, 1974

Still Life: Lemons, Oranges and a Rose
by Francisco de Zurbarán
January 13, 1974-continuing

Monumental Silver:
The Gilbert Collection
January 15-May 12, 1974

American Indian Costumes
January 29-March 3, 1974

Tapestries of Grau-Garriga
February 12-April 14, 1974

Los Four:
Almarez/De La Rocha/Lujan/Romero
February 26-March 24, 1974

Prints as Suites
March 12-August 4, 1974

Chinese Paintings from the Cahill
Collection: Yüan and Ming Dynasties
March 19-April 21, 1974

Picasso Engravings
April 2-May 31, 1974

Chinese Paintings from the Cahill
Collection: Ch'ing Dynasty
April 27-June 2, 1974

The Campbell Museum Collection
April 9-May 26, 1974

Impressionists and the Salon,
1874-1886
April 16-May 19, 1974

The Greek Vase
April 21-December 31, 1974

Holy Family by Fra Bartolommeo
May 7, 1974-continuing

American Paintings
from Los Angeles Collections
May 7-June 30, 1974

Twenty Years of Collecting:
Gifts of the Costume Council
May 14-October 13, 1974

Collectors' Video
May 26-June 30, 1974

The Art of the Japanese Sword
July 2-August 18, 1974

Gold Jewelry of the Ancient World
July 9, 1974-continuing

Art Works from Youth Expression '74
July 15-August 4, 1974

L.A. 6: Summer '74, Part I
July 16-August 11, 1974

Miniature Paintings
and Other Turkish Treasures from the
Collection of Edwin Binney, 3rd
August 13, 1974-January 5, 1975

Bambara Antelope Headdresses
August 16, 1974-continuing

Art of the Pre-Hispanic Americas
August 23, 1974-continuing

L.A. 6: Summer '74, Part II
August 26-September 15, 1974

Robert Rauschenberg's
"Pages" and "Fuses"
October 22, 1974-January 26, 1975

Selections from Cirrus
October 22, 1974-January 26, 1975

Tapestries of Helena Hernmarck
November 12, 1974-January 12, 1975

Matisse/Rouault/Braque
January, 1975-continuing

Austria:
Vienna
Magistrat Der Stadt Wien

Belgium:
Brussels
*Ministere de l' Education Nationale
   et de la Culture*
Musées Royaux des Beaux-Arts

British Crown Colony:
Hong Kong
City Hall Museum and Art Gallery

Canada:
Vancouver, British Columbia
The Vancouver Art Gallery
Ottawa, Ontario
The National Gallery of Canada
Toronto, Ontario
Art Gallery of Ontario
Royal Ontario Museum
Montreal, Quebec
The Montreal Museum of Fine Arts
Museum of Contemporary Art
Regina, Saskatchewan
*Norman MacKenzie Art Gallery,
   University of Saskatchewan*

Czechoslovakia:
Bratislava
Slovenská Národná Galéria

France:
Bordeaux
*Musées de Bordeaux, Galerie des
   Beaux-Arts*
Paris
*Arts et Lettres Réunion des Musées
   Nationaux*
Musée National d'Art Moderne
*Réunion des Musées Nationaux,
   Palais du Louvre*
Strasbourg
*Musées de Ville de Strasbourg,
   Chateau de Rohan*
Toulouse
Musée de Toulouse

Germany:
Berlin
Brucke Museum
Hamburg
Musées des Beaux-Arts de Hamburg
Munich
Haus der Kunst München

Ireland:
Dublin
National Gallery of Ireland

Italy:
Florence
Pitti Palace

Japan:
Fukuoka
The Central Museum of Fukuoka
Prefectural Culture Center Museum
Hakata
The Tokyo Shimbun Newspaper
Kyoto
*The Central Museum of Kyoto
Municipal Museum*
National Museum of Modern Art
Nagoya
The Central Museum of Nagoya
The Tokyo Shimbun Newspaper
Osaka
*Expo Museum of Fine Arts, Japan—
   Association for the 1970 World
   Exposition*
The Tokyo Shimbun Newspaper
Shizuoka
The Tokyo Shimbun Newspaper
Tokyo
The Central Museum of Tokyo
The Japan Art Society
National Museum of Western Art
The Tokyo Shimbun Newspaper

The Netherlands:
Amsterdam
Stedelijk Museum
Eindhoven
Stedelijk van Abbe-Museum
The Hague
Gemeentemuseum
Rotterdam
Museum Boymans-van Beuningen

Romania:
Bucharest
Sala Dalles
Cluj
Galéria de Arta
Timisoara
Museul Banatului

Russia:
Kiev
State Museum of Ukrainian Art
Leningrad
State Hermitage Museum
Minsk
Belorussian State Museum of Fine Arts

Moscow
State Pushkin Museum of Fine Arts
Odessa
State Picture Gallery

Riga
*State Museum of Latvian and
   Russian Art*

Scotland:
Edinburgh
Royal Scottish Academy

Spain:
Barcelona
*Productores Nacionales de Fibras
   Artificiales y Sinteticas*

Sweden:
Stockholm
Moderna Museet

Switzerland:
Basel
The Kunsthalle
Bern
The Kunsthalle
Zürich
Kunsthaus

United Kingdom:
London
The Arts Council of Great Britain
Institute of Contemporary Art
Royal Academy of Arts
The Tate Gallery

West Germany:
Baden-Baden
Staatliche Kunsthalle
Berlin
Akademie der Künste
Düsseldorf
Stadtische Kunsthalle
Frankfurt am Main
Frankfurter Kunstverein
Stuttgart
Staatsgalerie

Alabama:
Montgomery
Montgomery Museum of Art

Arizona:
Phoenix
Phoenix Art Museum
Tempe
*Matthew Center, Arizona State
    University*
Tucson
Tucson Art Center
University of Arizona Museum of Art

Arkansas:
Little Rock
Arkansas Art Center

California:
Bakersfield
Cunningham Memorial Art Museum
Barstow
Visual Arts Project
Berkeley
*University Art Museum, University
    of California*
Beverly Hills
B.G. Cantor Art Foundation
*Beverly Hills Library, City of
    Beverly Hills*
Bishop
Visual Arts Project
Chico
Chico State College
Claremont
Art Department, Pomona College
Art Gallery, Harvey Mudd College
*Gladys K. Montgomery Art Center,
    Pomona College*
Lang Art Gallery, Scripps College
Commerce
Department of Public Social Services
Davis
*Memorial Union Art Gallery, University
    of California*
Dominguez Hills
California State College
El Monte
Department of Public Social Services
Fresno
Fresno Arts Center
Fullerton
Art Gallery, California State College
Irvine
*University Art Gallery, University
    of California*

La Jolla
La Jolla Museum of Contemporary Art
Long Beach
Art Gallery, California State College
Long Beach Museum of Art
Los Angeles
Armenian Allied Arts Association
*The Art Galleries, University of
    California*
Black Arts Council
Blind Children's Center
*California Museum of Science
    and Industry*
*Chouinard Art School, California
    Institute of the Arts*
City of Los Angeles
*Constitutional Rights Foundation,
    Municipal Arts Department*
*County of Los Angeles, various
    departments*
Cultural Heritage Board
*Fisher Gallery, University of Southern
    California*
French Consul General
*Grunwald Graphic Arts Foundation,
    UCLA*
*Hawkins Family Foundation and
    Patrons of The Black Arts Museum*
Hollywood Museum
*Junior Art Center, Municipal Arts
    Department*
*Los Angeles County Museum of
    Natural History*
Los Angeles Valley College
Loyola University
*Martin Luther King, Jr. General
    Hospital*
Municipal Art Gallery
Museum of Cultural History, UCLA
*Museum and Laboratories of Ethnic
    Arts and Technology, UCLA*
The Music Center
Otis Art Institute
*Skirball Museum, Hebrew Union
    College*
*Vincent and Mary Price Gallery,
    East Los Angeles College*
Westside Jewish Community Center
Malibu
The J. Paul Getty Museum
Mill Valley
Mill Valley Quilt Authority
Newport Beach
Newport Harbor Art Museum
Northridge
California State College
Norwalk
Cerritos College

Oakland
The Oakland Museum
Orange
Chapman College
Palm Springs
Palm Springs Civic Art Association
Palm Springs Desert Museum
Palo Alto
*Arts Department Cultural Center,
    City of Palo Alto*
Palos Verdes
*Palos Verdes Community Art
    Association*
Pasadena
Pacificulture Foundation
Pasadena Art Museum
Pasadena College Library
Redlands
*Peppers Art Center, University
    of Redlands*
Riverside
Art Gallery, University of California
Sacramento
California Arts Commission
E.B. Crocker Art Gallery
San Bernardino
Fine Arts Gallery, Visual Arts Project
San Clemente
California White House
San Diego
Art Gallery, University of California
Fine Arts Gallery of San Diego
San Francisco
*Achenbach Foundation for
    Graphic Arts*
*California Palace of the Legion
    of Honor*
M.H. de Young Memorial Museum
San Francisco Museum of Art
San Luis Obispo
San Luis Obispo Art Center
San Marino
*Henry E. Huntington Library
    and Art Gallery*
San Mateo
*San Mateo County Historical Association
    and County Historical Museum*
Santa Barbara
*The Art Galleries, University
    of California*
Santa Barbara Museum of Art
Santa Clara
*de Saisset Art Gallery, University
    of Santa Clara*
Triton Museum of Art

Santa Cruz
*Cowell College Library, University
of California*
*Mary Porter Sesnon Gallery, University
of California*
Stanford
*Hoover Institution of War, Peace and
Revolution, Stanford University*
*The Leland Stanford, Jr. Museum
Stanford University*
Torrance
El Camino College
*Recreation Department, City
of Torrance*
Whittier
Whittier College

Colorado:
Colorado Springs
Colorado Springs Fine Arts Center
Denver
Denver Art Museum

Connecticut:
Kent
Kent School
New Haven
New Haven Colony Historical Society
Storrs
*Museum of Art, University of
Connecticut*

District of Columbia:
Washington
American Association of Museums
Corcoran Gallery of Art
*Museum of African Art, Frederick
Douglass Institute of Negro Arts
and History*
*Museum of Natural History,
Smithsonian Institution*
*National Collection of Fine Arts,
Smithsonian Institution*
*National Gallery of Art,
Smithsonian Institution*
The Phillips Collection
The Textile Museum
Washington Gallery of Modern Art
The White House

Florida:
Fort Lauderdale
Fort Lauderdale Museum of the Arts
Gainesville
*University Gallery, University
of Florida*

Jacksonville
Cummer Gallery of Art
St. Petersburg
Museum of Fine Arts
Sarasota
*John and Mable Ringling Museum
of Art*
Tampa
*Tampa Bay Art Center, University
of Tampa*

Georgia:
Athens
*Georgia Museum of Art, University
of Georgia*
Atlanta
*John D. Rockefeller, Jr. Galleries,
Spelman College*
Macon
Mercer University

Hawaii:
Honolulu
Honolulu Academy of Arts

Illinois:
Chicago
The Art Institute of Chicago
Museum of Contemporary Art
Peoria
*Lakeview Center for the Arts
and Sciences*

Indiana:
Bloomington
Fine Arts Museum, Indiana University
Indianapolis
Indianapolis Museum of Art
Notre Dame
Art Gallery, Notre Dame University

Iowa:
Cedar Rapids
Cedar Rapids Art Center
Des Moines
Des Moines Art Center
Iowa City
Museum of Art, University of Iowa

Kansas:
Lawrence
Museum of Art, University of Kansas
Wichita
Wichita Art Museum

Kentucky:
Louisville
J. B. Speed Art Museum

Louisiana:
New Orleans
New Orleans Museum of Art

Shreveport
The R. W. Norton Art Gallery
Maine:
Brunswick
Bowdoin College Museum of Art

Maryland:
Baltimore
Baltimore Museum of Art
College Park
Art Gallery, University of Maryland
Towson
Goucher College

Massachusetts:
Boston
Art Gallery, Boston University
Boston Institute of Contemporary Art
Museum of Fine Arts
Cambridge
Fogg Art Museum, Harvard University
Massachusetts Institute of Technology
Northampton
Museum of Art, Smith College
Waltham
Rose Art Museum, Brandeis University
Worcester
Worcester Art Museum

Michigan:
Ann Arbor
Museum of Art, University of Michigan
Detroit
Detroit Institute of Arts
Flint
Flint Institute of Arts

Minnesota:
Minneapolis
Minneapolis Institute of Arts
Walker Art Center

Missouri:
Kansas City
*William Rockhill Nelson Gallery,
Atkins Museum of Fine Arts*
St. Louis
City Art Museum of St. Louis
Gallery of Art, Washington University

Nebraska:
Omaha
Joslyn Art Museum

New Jersey:
Montclair
Montclair Art Museum

New Mexico:
Albuquerque
*University Art Museum, University
of New Mexico*

New York:
Albany
Albany Institute of History and Art
Binghamton
*Roberson Center for the Arts
and Sciences*
*University Art Gallery, State University
of New York at Binghamton*
Brooklyn
The Brooklyn Museum
Buffalo
Albright-Knox Art Gallery
Huntington
Heckscher Museum
Ithaca
*Andrew Dickson White Museum
of Art, Cornell University*
China Institute in America, Inc.
New York City
American Federation of Arts
*Asia House Gallery, The Asia
Society, Inc.*
Columbia University
*Department of Art History and
Archaeology, Columbia University*
*Educational Foundation for Fashion
Industries*
Finch College Museum of Art
The Jewish Museum
M. Knoedler & Co., Inc.
The Metropolitan Museum of Art
Museum of Modern Art
New York Cultural Center
Parsons School of Design
Public Education Association
Ruder & Finn, Fine Arts Department
The Solomon R. Guggenheim Museum
Whitney Museum of American Art
Wildenstein & Co., Inc.
Oswego
State University College
Poughkeepsie
Art Department, Vassar College
Rochester
*Memorial Art Gallery of the University
of Rochester*
Utica
*Museum of Art, Munson-Williams-
Proctor Art Institute*

Ohio:
Cincinnati
Cincinnati Art Museum

246

Cleveland
Cleveland Museum of Art
Dayton
Dayton Art Institute
Oberlin
The Dudley Peter Allen Memorial Art Museum, Oberlin College
Toledo
Toledo Museum of Art

Oklahoma:
Norman
Museum of Art, University of Oklahoma
Oklahoma City
Oklahoma Art Center
Tulsa
Philbrook Art Center

Oregon:
Portland
Oregon Historical Society
Portland Art Museum

Pennsylvania:
Philadelphia
Free Library of Philadelphia
Institute of Contemporary Art, University of Pennsylvania
Museum of the Philadelphia Civic Center
Philadelphia Museum of Art
University Museum, University of Pennsylvania
Pittsburgh
Museum of Art, Carnegie Institute

Rhode Island:
Providence
Museum of Art, Rhode Island School of Design

South Carolina:
Columbia
Columbia Museum of Art

Tennessee:
Knoxville
Dulin Gallery of Art
Memphis
Brooks Memorial Art Gallery

Texas:
Austin
University of Texas
Dallas
Dallas Museum of Fine Arts

Fort Worth
Amon Carter Museum of Western Art
Fort Worth Art Center Museum
Houston
Art Department, University of St. Thomas
Museum of Fine Arts
San Antonio
Marion Koogler McNay Art Institute

Utah:
Salt Lake City
Utah Museum of Fine Arts, University of Utah

Washington:
Seattle
Charles and Emma Frye Art Museum
The Henry Gallery, University of Washington
Seattle Art Museum
Spokane
Cheney Cowles Memorial Museum
Eastern Washington State Historical Society
Spokane World Exposition
Tacoma
Tacoma Art Museum

Wisconsin:
Madison
Madison Art Center

The catalog was designed and
produced in Los Angeles, California.

Design and format are by Ken Parkhurst.

The text was set in Linotype
Garamond under the supervision of
Vernon Simpson.

Color preparation and lithography
on Warren's Lustro Dull book paper
were by Graphic Press.